Jan-Christoph Heilinger
Cosmopolitan Responsibility

Jan-Christoph Heilinger

Cosmopolitan Responsibility

Global Injustice, Relational Equality,
and Individual Agency

DE GRUYTER

An electronic version of this book is freely available, thanks to the support of libraries working with Knowledge Unlatched. KU is a collaborative initiative designed to make high quality books Open Access. More information about the initiative and links to the Open Access version can be found at www.knowledgeunlatched.org

 Knowledge Unlatched

The Open Access book is available at www.degruyter.com

ISBN 978-3-11-076300-3
e-ISBN (PDF) 978-3-11-061227-1
e-ISBN (EPUB) 978-3-11-061128-1

This work is licensed under the Creative Commons Attribution-Non Commercial-No Derivatives 4.0 Licence. For details go to http://creativecommons.org/licenses/by-nc-nd/4.0/.

Library of Congress Control Number: 2019952790

Bibliographic information published by the Deutsche Nationalbibliothek
The Deutsche Nationalbibliothek lists this publication in the Deutsche Nationalbibliografie; detailed bibliographic data are available on the Internet at http://dnb.dnb.de.

© 2021 Jan-Christoph Heilinger, published by Walter de Gruyter GmbH, Berlin/Boston
This volume is text- and page-identical with the hardback published in 2020.
Cover: Greater Antilles Islands in the Caribbean Sea, AKG Images
Printing & binding: CPI books GmbH, Leck

www.degruyter.com

Für Rasmus und Felix
und für Nina

The idea that some lives matter less is the root of all that's wrong with the world. —*Paul Farmer*

La majorité du monde habite là où nous ne regardons pas ; là où nous ne voulons plus voir, les Suds, les Suds dans le Nord. —*Yanick Lahens*

Someone should be doing something about it. —*Iris M. Young*

Acknowledgements

The act of writing is a solitary business, but doing philosophy is a collective undertaking. The arguments I defend in this book draw on the work of many others. To highlight a few: Iris M. Young's work inspired, as will become obvious throughout the book, my entire project on *cosmopolitan responsibility*. My account of *global relational egalitarianism* builds heavily on Elizabeth Anderson's theory of democratic equality. Volker Gerhardt has directed my philosophical attention to the role of the *individual person* and Philip Kitcher has strengthened my belief in the *possibility of progress*; both have been invaluable teachers and supporters.

Furthermore, I am extremely grateful for the philosophical inspiration, advice, support and feedback I received in one form or another from many people over the years of working on this text. Among them are Verina Wild, Deborah Zion, James Wilson, Heather Widdows, Eva Weber-Guskar, Friedhelm von Blanckenburg, Rodrigue Thomas, Aron Telegdi-Csetri, Uwe Steinhoff, Marco Solinas, Jan Slaby, Christos Simis, Alexander Schulan, Samuel Scheffler, Veronika Sager, Mehran Rezaei, Martin Rechenauer, Philippe Quesne, Alison Phipps, Konrad Petrovszky, Eva Maria Parisi, Liav Orgad, Julian Nida-Rümelin, Fabian Newger, Thomas Nagel, Nikil Mukerji, Oliver Müller, Srinjoy Mitra, Christopher McDougall, Georg Marckmann, Ansgar Lyssy, Tanja Krones, Isabel Kranz, Colin King, S. Karly Kehoe, Elizabeth Kahn, Matthias Jung, Markus Huppenbauer, Christoph Henning, Nora Heinzelmann, André Grahle, Anna Goppel, Anca Gheaus, Sebastiaan Garvelink, Agomoni Ganguli-Mitra, Orsolya Friedrich, Carina Fourie, Rainer Forst, Richard Fonseca, Alan Fishbone, Karsten Fischer, Gerhard Ernst, Jake Ephros, Lisa Eckenwiler, Lorenzo Del Savio, Angus Dawson, Housamedden Darwish, Katja Crone, Fausto Corvino, Molly Cochran, Ryoa Chung, Francis Cheneval, Gillian Brock, Christine Bratu, Jason Branford, Suzanne Bouclin, Eike Bohlken, Monika Betzler, Holger Baumann, Sarah-Aylin Akgül, Eva Alisic, Darline Alexis, Maike Albertzart, and Zed Adams. I am also grateful for the helpful comments and suggestions of two anonymous reviewers for de Gruyter.

I also want to express my gratitude for the possibility to present my work and for the feedback I received at the Universities of Auckland, Bamberg, Birmingham, Cologne, Delhi, Dortmund, Frankfurt, Kiel, Melbourne, Munich, Passau, Regensburg, Saint Andrews, St. Gallen, Sydney, Tübingen, Zurich, as well as at Ecole Normale Supérieure Paris, Ecole Normale Supérieure Port-au-Prince, New York University, Scuola Superiore Sant'Anna Pisa, the Universidad de Chile and the University of Ghana.

Financial and institutional support for my research was not only provided by my home institutions during the time of working on the manuscript, the Universities of Zurich and Munich, but also by Fritz Thyssen Foundation, German Academic Exchange Service (DAAD), German Research Foundation (DFG), Global Young Academy, and the Swiss National Science Foundation (SNSF).

Earlier this year, Scuola Superiore Sant'Anna in Pisa hosted a workshop dedicated to this manuscript prior to its publication. My special thanks for valuable criticism go to all the participants.

My encounters and discussions with students and colleagues at Ecole Normale Supérieure de l'Université d'Etat d'Haiti, where I regularly teach, also had an important impact on my thinking about the topics of this book. I am very grateful for this.

It was again a great pleasure to work with de Gruyter publishers, Berlin. My sincere thanks go to Christoph Schirmer, Tim Vogel and Florian Ruppenstein.

I am immensely thankful for my friends and my family, for their unwavering love, support and encouragement. I dedicate this book to Nina—the best partner I can imagine for sunshine and storms in life; and inspiring critical reader of my many drafts—and our perfectly wonderful children, Felix and Rasmus, with all my love and gratitude.

Cologne, October 2019

JCH

Contents

Introduction: The challenge. Global injustice and the individual agent —— 1
1 The 'circumstances of cosmopolitanism' —— 5
2 The idea of cosmopolitanism —— 8
3 Towards a global political ethics —— 9
4 The pragmatic impulse —— 11
5 Overview —— 12

Part I
The cosmopolitan ethos

Chapter 1: Cosmopolitanism. The ideal of global justice, past and present —— 21
1 Global citizenship —— 21
2 Moral cosmopolitanism as egalitarian universalism —— 23
3 The evolution of cosmopolitanism —— 28
4 The current debate on global justice. A brief overview —— 43
5 Global justice and global ethics —— 57

Chapter 2: Equality. Towards global relational egalitarianism —— 65
1 Domestic luck vs. relational egalitarianism —— 68
2 What is the point of global equality? —— 92
3 Global luck egalitarianism—a critique —— 93
4 Towards global relational equality —— 97
5 Global relational egalitarianism—for and against —— 109
6 The priority of relations, the relevance of distributions —— 115

Chapter 3: Pragmatism. Practice and the possibility of progress —— 119
1 Cosmopolitanism as a personal way of life —— 119
2 From criterial monism to pragmatic pluralism —— 123
3 Elements of a pragmatic ethics —— 125
4 The role of philosophy —— 131

Part II
Challenges

Chapter 4: Impact. Do my acts matter? —— 137
1 Competing problems —— 137
2 Making no difference? Imperceptible harm and threshold effects —— 142
3 The most good you can do? —— 147
4 Making a difference in social structures —— 151
5 The responsibility to make a difference —— 159

Chapter 5: Impartiality. The fragmentation of morality —— 161
1 The puzzle of partiality —— 161
2 Preference for oneself —— 164
3 Relationships and integrity —— 168
4 Parental partiality —— 172
5 Preference for compatriots —— 183
6 Two standpoints and the fragmentation of morality —— 190

Chapter 6: Imperfection. Overdemandingness and the inevitability of moral failure —— 193
1 Cosmopolitan demands and the danger of moral failure —— 193
2 Demanding too much vs. demanding enough —— 195
3 Can cosmopolitan moral requirements be met? —— 207
4 Necessarily non-effective moral requirements —— 212
5 Cosmopolitan sincerity —— 220

Conclusion: The ethos of cosmopolitan responsibility —— 221
1 Responding to global injustice —— 221
2 Four features of global individual responsibility —— 222
3 The cosmopolitan ethos —— 226
4 Citizens of the world —— 234

Bibliography —— 236

Index —— 251

Introduction: The challenge.
Global injustice and the individual agent

The world we live in is unjust. A just world would not feature a distribution of resources wherein a few of the richest people control massive, even increasing amounts of wealth—while large numbers of people live in dire poverty. Nor would a just world feature thousands of people dying every day from unsanitary living conditions, or easily preventable diseases. Nor would so many people suffer oppression, exploitation, and exclusion from the decision making processes that have a significant impact on their lives. A just world would not be one in which nearly all of the women who die as a result of childbirth are from low- and middle-income countries; nor one in which excessive consumption of natural resources in the Global North has led to negative environmental outcomes such as a changing climate severely affecting those living elsewhere, not to mention future generations; nor one in which people seeking to flee war, persecution, deprivation or disaster are often denied access to security, are sent back, or knowingly kept in places where their basic rights are violated. And a just world would clearly not be one in which many of these forms of inequality and injustice, despite of some significant improvement and progress, appear to be on the increase due to such diverse reasons as ongoing unfair trade regulations, rising nationalism and supremacism, ongoing environmental pollution, and so on. This list of injustices reigning in today's globalised world—with its unprecedented international connections and interactions, and movements of people, knowledge, capacities, goods and capital across national borders—could, alas, be further extended.

Obviously, existing political and institutional structures on the national and international level have, so far, failed to address these injustices in an adequate way. The persistence and severity of such inequities in the face of institutional shortcomings thus raise the vexing yet unavoidable question of whether other agents, such as individual people, must step in and do something about them. From the combined perspective of political and moral philosophy, one would then have to ask, *what is demanded of individual moral agents given the current unjust conditions of our globalised world?* With a narrower focus on a specific group of individuals, the question would be: *What should the rather well-off, conscientious citizens of the prosperous countries do about current injustices?*

Given the urgency of the challenge and the insufficient responses of institutional agents this question may appear obvious: of course, someone, including individual people, has to do something about these massive injustices. Yet, this answer suggests a perplexing connection between extremely large and complex global challenges on the one hand, and the smallest unit of agency, single individuals, on the other. It will be the task of this book to explore the complicated and problematic link between the possibilities of individual agency and urgent need to address global, structural injustices. In it, I reconsider and reassess pertinent normative values, rules and principles that can be deployed to determine the content of individual responsibility in the global context. And I contend that the moral demands for advantaged and privileged individuals like ordinary citizens living in relative security and affluence in the countries of the Global North are more stringent than the prevailing, rather lenient views suggest.

This exploration thus has both practical and theoretical facets. Practically, the question is: What should advantaged individual agents *do* in the face of massively unjust global structures that clearly favour their material interests and secure their privilege? This practical question, however, turns on a prior, more theoretical one: how should one *reason* about individual moral responsibility for globally unjust circumstances? The focus of this book on *cosmopolitan responsibility* will be primarily on the theoretical side and explore and defend from the perspective of moral and political philosophy a possible theory of *cosmopolitan responsibility* and discuss several challenges for such a theory. Yet, this is done with the conviction that a better understanding can also inform and inspire adequate action and reform.

The distinctive focal point of this book is thus the individual person, seen simultaneously as a needy human being and a bearer of rights on the one hand, and as an active moral agent who is subject to moral demands on the other. As agents, humans are capable of acting with reference to normative concepts, concepts that can also be employed to evaluate the moral quality of a person's actions. Making progress in addressing injustices and promoting justice will, on the side of individual agents, inevitably also require self-scrutiny and a critical examination of one's own life in the social and global context.

The idea of *moral cosmopolitanism*—i.e. the egalitarian and universalist assumption that each human being is equally morally relevant and that all human beings form a morally relevant community—provides the normative starting point for my exploration of the role and responsibilities of individual agents in the contemporary global context. I will pay particular attention to the *attitudes* moral agents should develop in response to global injustices if they accept the basic assumption that all human lives are of equal moral importance. This is a normative and pragmatic inquiry into a cosmopolitan, egalitarian *ethos*, understood as a set of values, norms and concepts that shapes how individuals feel, think, talk and act about global issues in an interconnected world. Such an analysis of the moral and political roles and responsibilities of *individual* agents in an unjust world contributes to an account of global political *ethics*, understood as a 'bottom up' complement to the 'top down' accounts of global *institutional justice*. Offering the analysis of individual responsibility as a *complement*, not a replacement, thus does not curtail the importance of institutional responsibility. Often, only structural, top-down reform—through laws, regulations, financial incentives and penalties and so forth—can bring lasting change. Nevertheless, structural change will not occur unless a sufficient number of committed individuals credibly demand such reform.

Three central ideas that I will explore and defend in this book inform and guide my thinking. *First*, the extensive degree of interconnection, interaction and interdependency among countries, institutions, and people around the world make it impossible to focus only on the *immediate* environment of any individual moral agent when assessing the moral quality of any act. While it is uncontroversial to state that the reality of globalisation and the factual 'circumstances of cosmopolitanism' fundamentally shape the contemporary global order, I will argue that cosmopolitanism should feature in our normative understanding of how we as moral agents ought to conduct ourselves within that order, as well. This is particularly important since the advantage of some is frequently connected with the disadvantage of others through the dynamics of structural injustice. Acknowledging not only the *reality* of the circumstances of cosmopolitanism but also the *ideal* of moral cosmopolitanism precludes focussing on narrow frames; instead it entails expanding the circle of moral concern to all members of the global order, connected in one way or another—a move that may carry with it dramatic implications for the sphere and content of our responsibilities.

The *second* idea is that discomfort, indignation, and outrage are appropriate responses towards what appears to count as the "normal," "inevitable," even "acceptable" background conditions of the lives of the well-off citizens in the industrialised, democratic, high-income countries of the Global North. Often enough, the privileged turn a blind eye to unjustified inequalities and structural injustices, consider them to be remote or perhaps regrettable facts of our world, but essentially unconnected to their lives.[1] Instead of indifference and complacency, a significant, uncomfortable but "healthy dissatisfaction with the familiar" (Nagel 1991, 8) is urgently needed. The presumably normal but dramatically unjust "background conditions" (Young 2006b, 120) of the radically unequal world we inhabit provide a morally repugnant context for all of our actions.

---

[1] While thoughts and actions often positively indicate one's moral values, it is important to consider also what one does *not* think or do. One's moral convictions are often reflected most accurately by the wrongs and injustices one is willing to overlook.

This background must be acknowledged to have a bearing on any moral assessment of what we do, as well as of what we fail or refuse to do.[2]

Third, I am persuaded that individual agents and their actions do matter on a global scale, even if global problems and challenges appear overwhelmingly large, complex and numerous. But—as I will argue—individuals have more options than engaging in isolated single acts: they can also become politically active, inform and coordinate with others; they can inspire, call for, and work to bring about collective and institutional change, reform and action that are consistent with cosmopolitan values. This is done best, I argue, by fostering and developing an egalitarian and cosmopolitan ethos to guide one's thought, action and commitment to others in one's potentially global social environment. Ultimately, I do not call for selected transactional contributions to addressing injustice, but for transformational change in how agents think, feel, and respond to it. Indeed, a crucial weakness of the current debate about global justice may well be its failure to sufficiently address the role of individual agents necessary to counterbalance and complement institution-based accounts. After all, the commitments and actions of numerous individuals—ordinary citizens, political activists and official leaders alike—inform and shape existing institutions and the creation of new ones; and, under conditions of institutional shortcomings, ineffectivity or even outright failure, individuals are called upon and become primary subjects of moral demands. These considerations raise rather than diminish the importance and fundamental role of individual agents. Thus, besides political philosophy, *moral* philosophy has to play a central role in the global context as well. In combining these two dimensions of practical philosophy, my proposed theory of *cosmopolitan responsibility*[3] should be read as a contribution to a *global political ethics*.

Three main theoretical influences shape my proposal: an analysis of *structural injustice* and its implications for determining the role and responsibilities

---

[2] Injustice is, unluckily, the baseline from which thinking about justice will have to start. Cf. also Shklar (1990, 17).

[3] The concept of 'responsibility' itself is rich and notoriously difficult to pin down. Miller has rightly called it "one of the most slippery and confusing terms in the lexicon of moral and political philosophy" (Miller 2007, 82). I agree and only propose a lean understanding of 'responsibility' as the way how individual agents morally ought to *respond*—cognitively, emotionally and, of course, practically—to a given global issue of moral salience. Responsibility thus importantly includes, but is not limited to, the 'moral ought,' the 'obligation,' the 'duty,' or the 'requirement' that applies to a particular agent in a given situation. For more conceptual work on the notion of responsibility, cf. Hart (2008) and Miller (2007, ch. 4); or the recent fine-grained analysis by Beck (2016, 40). As will become obvious throughout the book, my own views about responsibility are deeply indebted to the work of Young (2006b, 2011).

of individuals in this context in the tradition of Young (2011); *relational theories of equality* (Scheffler 1993, Anderson 1999, Scheffler 2015), deployed in a modified form to explore the nature of moral obligations that extend beyond the domestic frame to the global scale; and *pragmatic accounts of ethics* and their assumptions about normative pluralism, the importance of habits and social dynamics, and the possibility of moral and social progress (Dewey and Tufts 1932, Dewey 1939, Kitcher 2011).

1 The 'circumstances of cosmopolitanism'

In the past, most human beings lived without detailed *knowledge* about (or even an awareness of) different cultures in far away regions. Today, by contrast, only few human beings remain detached from the forces of global communication, trade and politics. Indeed, the contemporary world, more than ever before, is characterised by a dense set of intensive *connections* and *interactions* among individuals and institutions very nearly everywhere (Widdows 2011; 5, 271). Moreover, even those very few with little or no direct exposure to the modern technological world are now nonetheless affected by it, notably through diffuse phenomena such as environmental pollution and *climate change*. Even isolated, non-industrial societies living deep in uncharted areas of the Brazilian rainforest, for example, cannot escape the consequences of changing weather patterns. The consequences of global *trade*, furthermore, affect local markets even in the most remote areas of the world, as the aggregate effect of global consumerism leaves virtually no producer or consumer untouched; global trade and ruthless economic competition have resulted in the creation of "special export zones," in which workers manufacture often trivial consumer products under inhumane conditions; intellectual property regimes prevent access to essential medicines; famines are aggravated by financial sector speculation on staple foods; illicit financial flows and off-shore business encourages tax evasion which prevents poorer and richer countries alike from providing essential services to their citizens. There are also *global events* like the soccer world cup that do not only bring people together by providing sports-centered entertainment to a truly global audience. They also create a sphere of global publicity that triggers political discussions ranging from the management of the tournament by its organising institutions, over the diversity of the teams mirroring the history of the country, to the political situation in host countries and the often fraught political relationships between countries.

Global interconnectedness and interdependence has reached historically unprecedented levels; it has brought about institutionalised forms of interaction of states and international bodies that cover communication and media, the rules and practices of both local and global business, and people's leisure activities, travelling, consumer preferences and choices. Such connections, relations and interactions have such a massive and *pervasive impact* on the lives of people—both positive (advantageous) and negative (limiting)—that they have effectively become *unavoidable,* as it is neither possible to escape them, nor to be unaffected by them. They are also in an important sense *non-voluntary,* since no one was asked or able to give prior consent to being subject to such global dynamics. The extensive connections between states, institutions and individuals are thus an inescapable fact, which I call the *de facto circumstances of cosmopolitanism* or the existing global order (even though I do not mean to insinuate that it is particularly well-ordered). The circumstances of cosmopolitanism are constituted by the multiple, inevitable and highly significant connections between people around the globe.

However, the last decades have also brought about many remarkably successful interventions and enlightened developments—even though no achievement is immune to challenges and potential failure. Supranational structures like the United Nations and the European Union continue to evolve to better defend universal rights and basic standards for the treatment of all people (albeit not without an abundance of conflict and new challenges) via the proclamation and progressive realisation of the goals of various instruments such as the Universal Declaration of Human Rights and the Sustainable Development Goals. As a result of such developments, for example, a smaller percentage of the world's population lives under conditions of severe poverty today than at any time before.[4] Strides are also being made in cooperation to combat climate change, with the results of the COP21 meeting in Paris in late 2015 being something of a breakthrough for being at least partially legally binding—even though the current global political climate at the time of writing these lines poses significant new threats to the achieved agreements.

In fact, despite some progress, existing institutions and patterns of interaction have yet to achieve substantial and enduring improvements for the billions of people who continue to live in extreme deprivation and/or continue to be unjustly dominated by others. This type of injustice, as Iris M. Young characterises it, and the morally alarming persistence of the unequal distribution of new benefits and costs, qualifies as an instance of *structural* injustice (Young 2011). It takes a very particular form:

---

4 Cf. e.g. https://ourworldindata.org [last accessed: 1 July 2019] or Pinker (2011) and Deaton (2013).

> Structural injustice exists when social processes put large categories of persons under a systematic threat of domination or deprivation of the means to develop and exercise their capacities, at the same time as these processes enable others to dominate or have a wide range of opportunities for developing and exercising their capacities. Structural injustice is a kind of moral wrong distinct from the wrongful action of an individual agent or the willfully repressive policies of a state. Structural injustice occurs as a consequence of many individuals and institutions acting in pursuit of their particular goals and interests, within given institutional rules and accepted norms. (Young 2006b, 114)

It is important to emphasise that this disadvantaging of a sizeable proportion of humanity is the collateral result of many agents acting in ways that have been and continue to be widely considered "normal," "legal," and even morally unproblematic, such as the powerful pursuit of national interests by political leaders and the pursuit of personal interests by already advantaged individuals.[5] Alas, this does not alter the fact that repeated patterns of presumably unproblematic and permissible behaviour within established structures not only secure privilege and advantage but ultimately lead to and perpetuate negative outcomes for vast swathes of humanity. A massive proportion of human disadvantage is not the result of unavoidable causes (like natural disasters), but is anthropogenic, in the sense that it is socially and politically constituted, or could—through coordinated effort—be avoided. Hence, human beings and the social structures they bring about are at the origin of the ongoing disaster of structural injustice in the world.

Acknowledging these 'circumstances of cosmopolitanism'—including the disastrous global outcomes of structural injustice, created and maintained by normal practices widely regarded as acceptable—is not easy for those enjoying the advantages of security, political stability, and economic prosperity.[6] Such acknowledgement would compare and link—partly through a factual, causal connection through interactions; partly through a conceptual connection through the ideal of the equal moral standing of all—the advantages of some with the disadvantages of others. But then, as Nagel has formulated pointedly: "The magnitude of the world's problems and the inequality in access to its resources produce a weight of potential guilt that may, depending on one's temperament, require considerable ingenuity to keep roped down" (Nagel 1986, 190). Yet,

---

[5] Of course, there are also malevolent and ruthless disruptive interventions by political and public figures, institutions, and individuals, that aggravate existing or trigger new injustices.
[6] Dewey also acknowledges this: "It is difficult for a person in a place of authoritative power to avoid supposing that what he wants is right as long as he has power to enforce his demand. And even with the best will in the world, he is likely to be isolated from the real needs of others, and the perils of ignorance are added to those of selfishness." (Dewey and Tufts 1932, 226).

most of the rather well-off citizens of affluent countries seem to muster that ingenuity with ease, so that they live their comfortable lives more or less unaffected by feelings of complicity with or responsibility for the unjust structures that enable or perpetuate their privilege. The core challenge put forward in this book is to make some progress in understanding the role and responsibilities of individuals in light of the disastrous background conditions just described.

2 The idea of cosmopolitanism

A guiding normative idea of this book is to understand human beings as "cosmopolitans", as citizens of the world. The fact that all human beings today live in a highly interconnected world makes them, *nolens volens*, members of a jointly shared system of interaction: everyone is a member of the global order (even if, once again, its dysfunctions and inherent structural injustices make the use of the term "order" here rather less than a literal one). First developed in early Greek philosophy, the idea of "world citizenship" designated the very idea that all human beings are bound together as equals in spite of the differences between groups and individuals and jointly form a morally relevant community. Initially largely idealistic, the increasing interconnections across the globe today have made it more obvious than ever before that there is indeed some form of a factual global sphere of mutual influence and community of which all human beings are members. A moral account of cosmopolitanism is hence based on two assumptions: that each human being is of equal moral standing; and that the morally relevant community includes all humans. This ideal can be used to assess states of affairs from a normative perspective, and to morally demand particular acts and institutional arrangements: It first states the interconnected global reality (circumstances of cosmopolitanism); it then diagnoses several moral flaws in the current global order, based on the moral view that, even in the absence of an actual world-state, every member of the human community is entitled to being respected and treated as a moral equal; and it then assigns *cosmopolitan responsibilities* to individual and institutional agents.

Unlike other contributions based on the cosmopolitan commitment to equality and universality, my focus here is not so much on giving detailed advice about concrete practices and actions of individuals (e.g. Singer 2009), nor on an analysis of the political dimension of cosmopolitanism (e.g. Hahn 2017) or specific recommendations for institutional reform (e.g. Wenar 2016, Neuhäuser 2018, Cabrera 2018). Instead, I will take a step back and approach cosmopolitanism as a distinctive big-picture moral outlook with implications for the morally demanded underlying *ethos* that should inform an individual agent's feelings, thoughts, and actions. This approach is based on the idea that it is possible to promote and implement the cosmopolitan ideal not only from top down but also from the bottom up: cosmopolitanism can then start being realised 'within borders,' such as in an agent's direct, local sphere of influence or in one country or a federation of countries that are willing to take a lead.[7] Individual agents can *integrate global thinking into their local action*; and institutional agents can already *respect their global responsibility in their confined sphere of influence.*

3 Towards a global political ethics

The ongoing scholarly debates about global justice are rich and manifold. They include normative discussions about the existing global institutional order, about the establishment and regulation of fair trade relationships between nations, about corporate social responsibility of multinational companies, about what constitutes a just distribution of benefits and burdens between different global players, about the conditions for just war, and about possible limits of state sovereignty, particularly with regard to the control of borders, but also with regard to the right or duty of states to intervene to assist citizens in other countries, regardless of sovereign prerogative or cost to the intervening countries (cf. e.g. Brock and Moellendorf 2005, Brock 2013). These are very important debates. Most of the participants in these debates, however, adopt Rawls's lead[8] in largely ignoring the role of the *individual* when it comes to matters of justice, which he initially proposed could only be an emergent feature of the political and social *institutions* of a liberal society. According to Rawls, justice is "the first virtue of institutions" (Rawls 1999b, 3), and the individual is, as a result, accorded only a minor role in his theory of justice. A similar marginalisation of the role and responsibility of the individual has dominated the debates about global justice.

It is not that I object to a focus on institutions or states in the debate about (global) justice. It is clearly appropriate and necessary to elaborate on institutions, interstate interaction and global structures, especially when these are causally implicated in the generation and maintenance of structural injustice and

---

7 Cf. e.g. Wild and Heilinger (2013).
8 While they follow Rawls in this regard, the extension of the scope of justice from the domestic to the international realm is a modification of the Rawlsian doctrine, which limited talk of justice to the sphere of the nation state (Rawls 1999). My own view thus differs from Rawls's theory of justice in two ways: First, I dedicate more attention to individuals as agents of justice; second, I assume the scope of justice is global.

where institutional reform constitutes the most effective, maybe even the only way to eventually overcome structural injustices. But Rawls notwithstanding, it must not be ignored that, ultimately, institutions are not "natural kinds" existing independently of human beings. Instead, they are created by people, frequently with the intention to better fulfill what they deem to be important tasks. Ultimately, *individuals shape institutions and social structures*, and continue to fill them with life and spirit—for better or for worse. This, in turn, implies that the *ethos* of people—i.e. their normative commitments and ambitions that shape their dispositions and habits of feeling and thinking, talking and acting—has a significant impact on the existence and functioning of institutions. Individuals also exercise influence on the social norms that govern behaviour and on the (politically and morally relevant) ideas that exist in a group.

Thus, I suggest to direct, in questions about global justice, particular attention to the potential role of individual moral agents, and both the direct and the indirect effects of their behaviour.[9] This will, I contend, open potentially fruitful avenues for analysing their responsibilities and guiding their attitudes and actions. My inquiry into the role and responsibilities of individual moral agents in an interconnected, unjust world is not meant to replace, but to *complement* debates over global institutional *justice*. It brings into consideration this neglected level of global political *ethics*, the level of individual agency. It requires individuals to accept responsibility, acknowledges and discusses challenges, but concludes with empowering arguments for the importance of individual engagement under current conditions of injustice.

Even though the focus of this work is clearly on the individual's role in the face of global injustice, I do not mean to imply that comprehensive solutions to global injustice are likely to flow from isolated instances of individual action alone. Cooperative and collective action, and a smart division of the moral labour, ultimately involving institutional agency in the right way, are still necessary. However, all agents are also *individually* subject to moral demands, and bear *personal* responsibility to promote the changes necessary to fight existing injustice and advance egalitarian justice globally. In the absence of adequate institutions *and* in the absence of an ethos of *cosmopolitan responsibility*, the chances for genuine egalitarian progress appear limited, even grim. But individuals can start and continue making a credible case for change and reform to promote justice; they can, through their acts, also inform and influence others, and this is the best possible way forward for individuals to contribute to addressing and possibly eventually overcoming the massive wrongs that dominate our world.

---

9 Cf. also Young (2011, 73), Cohen (2008) and the concluding chapter below.

Such individual dispositions matter particularly in time of crisis where suddenly the established order and patterns of conduct are questioned and become fragile. The ideas that are in the air at a time of crisis can then be taken into account, guide action, inspire and inform reforms and thus shape the future. It is the important task of individuals to keep the right ideas alive and available, especially under adverse conditions, so that they are at hand when the opportunity arises to deploy and implement them on a larger scale.

4 The pragmatic impulse

The ideas expressed in this book take up several impulses from the tradition of US-American pragmatism, found notably in the writings of Dewey. Most importantly, a pragmatist perspective on ethics emphasises a moral outlook characterised by three elements that I take to be central to my task: an emphasis on the individual agent (and his or her habits) in social contexts as the core concern of morality; preference for a pluralist method of moral inquiry over the defense of any narrow set of criteria, principles or conclusions; and a resolute optimism that moral and social progress is possible.

Many current global issues—such as inequality and world poverty, climate change and the unjust dynamics in the global economy—are also distinctively moral challenges resulting from and influencing the actions and experiences of persons. It is the habitual actions of individual agents, the things we do day after day (including seemingly trivial consumer decisions or travel preferences), that are at the root of many global problems related to structural injustice.[10] Morality, in the pragmatist tradition, stresses the importance of constantly evaluating, re-evaluating, and intentionally shaping our habits, based on moral insight drawn from the full spectrum of sources, rather than from any single normative theory, which, for Dewey at least, would be too limited to be of much practical service. Moral decision-making is complex and multi-faceted, both for individual agents considering their obligations, and for answering the questions of what better political and institutional arrangements would look like, and which actions are likely to help bring about such arrangements. My approach is focussed on the careful cultivation of appropriate habits as a method for ongoing

---

[10] At another level, of course, the repeated and unquestioned preference by politicians and decision-makers to prioritise the gains of themselves and their communities with no regard to the costs imposed on others, plays a particularly influential role.

practical reasoning, moral decision making, and action about the current global challenges.

Following Kitcher (2011), I regard reflections about all forms of individual ethical conduct to be inherently embedded in the larger "ethical project" of living together in an ever larger, now truly global community of human beings on this planet. I contend that the ideals of *cosmopolitan responsibility* must ultimately translate into "a personal way of individual life" in light of the reality and nature of globalised human relations. Such a "personalisation" includes:

> the possession and continual use of certain attitudes, forming personal character and determining desire and purpose in all the relations of life. Instead of thinking of our own dispositions and habits as accommodated to certain institutions we have to learn to think of the latter as expressions, projections and extensions of habitually dominant personal attitudes. (Dewey 1939, 226)

Such an account invites a politisation and "ethicisation" of daily life, a change from the assumed innocence and amorality of ordinary behaviour. While it does not require us to be always and exclusively concerned with moral considerations, it charges all our actions with an ethically relevant dimension. Yet, pragmatic ethics does not stop with such a focus on individual agency: it points to the need to structure the political and social environment in a way that it both reflects the considered normative commitments of people and facilitates individual behavior that aligns with these commitments. Individual behaviour thus has a public and political dimension; and democratic structures inform and shape individual behaviour. Making intelligent use of these dynamics thus can facilitate moral and social progress in the form of structural change.

5 Overview

This book confronts the pressing question about the role and responsibility of individual agents in an unjust world. I consider this to be among the defining moral, political and philosophical challenges of our time. It would be folly to suggest that a single book, let alone this one, could once and for all settle such an issue. Instead, I only hope to offer some routes for morally reflective individuals to consider as they attempt to navigate the difficult terrain surrounding the question of how to act in the face of global structural injustice.

With this aim, the book proposes a *theory* of *cosmopolitan responsibility* to analyse and determine the role and the responsibility of individual agents in the context of global structural injustice. This theory lies at the intersection of moral and political philosophy and can be called a *global political ethics*. Concretely, it consists of an account of a *cosmopolitan ethos*, i.e. a set of ideas, values and commitments that can shape how individuals feel, think, talk and act about global issues in the local context they find themselves in. This cosmopolitan ethos, with its three central elements—the idea of world citizenship; a commitment to global relational egalitarianism; and a pragmatic understanding of ethics, action and habit—is presented in part I. The ethos is elaborated further in part II with the help of three important challenges that can appear once one starts weighing options for action out of the cosmopolitan ethos: the problem that individual acts may be too small to generate any relevant impact on global issues; the tension between universal obligations towards all and special obligations towards some particularly near and dear to us; and the danger of inevitable failure because cosmopolitan obligations exceed what is humanely possible.

Chapter one offers a historical and conceptual overview about the idea of cosmopolitanism in its different diagnostic and normative forms in Western philosophy from antiquity to the 20th century. While the first half of chapter one is more historical, the second half introduces important contemporary concepts and discussions, such as about the scope of justice, the universalist and particularist poles of the debate, different metrics and patterns of justice, and the notion of structural injustice. It concludes with an outlook on global political ethics with reflections on the relationship of individuals and institutions, the division of labour in society, and the possibility of fostering an egalitarian ethos.

Chapter two considers the basic notion of *equality* that lies at the heart of the present analysis. I compare and contrast distributive and relational accounts of egalitarianism, both on the domestic and the global level. Ultimately, I argue for *global relational egalitarianism* as the best account to capture the fundamental commitments of *cosmopolitan responsibility*. This view understands equality as a lived practice, something we *do*, not as a static state of affairs or pattern of distribution. It demands, negatively, that oppression, domination, exploitation, marginalisation, exclusion, etc. have to end; and it demands, positively, that equality must reign in all possible and actual interactions and relationships. This understanding of the ideal of equality also has normative implications for individual behaviour and will thus inform my further arguments about the way how individual agents should respond to issues of global inequality and injustice.

Chapter three brings into relief some impulses from the philosophical tradition of American pragmatism which underlie and inspire my account of *cosmopolitan responsibility*, such as the possibility to integrate normative values into the individual and collective "way of life", the importance of habits over single acts, and an optimistic belief in the possibility of social and moral progress. Pragmatism also assigns philosophy a modest but constructive role in addressing problems and identifying solutions to facilitate and improve the living together of all.

In advancing the moral ideal of cosmopolitanism, the theory of global relational egalitarianism and the pragmatic perspective, part I will provide the normative groundwork for my theory of *cosmopolitan responsibility* that can be integrated in the personal ethos of individual agents.

Part II moves on to weighing action. Its three chapters discuss three pressing challenges that arise once agents endorse and attempt to act out of the cosmopolitan ethos, presented in part I. How does individual action matter? Does cosmopolitan responsibility leave room for any preferential treatment of those particularly near and dear to us? And: Can we ever hope to live up to the apparently excessive demands of cosmopolitan responsibility?

Chapter four addresses the tension between the large size of problems of global injustice and the inevitably very small impact of individual agency: Given this discrepancy, any agent weighing different reasons for action will wonder whether her actions will matter at all; and whether they will be able to generate any meaningful impact. The chapter discusses several ways in which even single acts of individual agents matter morally: as small contributions to large harm; as small triggers that can set of a cascade of events; or as contributions that (even if they make only a negligible difference to addressing a complex global problem) make a very big difference for some who are affected by a complex global problem. To conclude, the chapter introduces Young's social connection model to explain how not only single acts, but particularly repeated patterns of individual action matter in contexts of structural injustice. It identifies several criteria that can help determine the content of individual responsibility. The results reached in this chapter will be taken up and expanded further in the concluding chapter of the book.

In *chapter five*, I address the puzzle of partiality, an important and practically relevant objection against an account of *cosmopolitan responsibility*. This puzzle is based on the tension between universal, impartial demands on the one hand, and partial, more immediate demands on the other. This challenging tension becomes palpable once individuals consider *everyone* as a being of equal moral standing, while still feeling a special commitment or obligation towards *some* that are particularly near and dear. This tension is difficult to solve: even if impartiality *always matters morally*, it clearly is *not all that matters morally*. The chapter discusses the grounds for special obligations and preferential treatment for oneself, for one's intimates, and also for one's compatriots. I argue that relationship-dependent reasons for preferential treatment, as they result from personal connections, have some genuine moral weight that can render some degree of preferential treatment morally permissible. Membership-dependent reasons for preferential treatment, however, as they result for example from shared nationality, cannot claim to have similar moral force: if not all have equal access to the relevant communities, that are not shaped by close interpersonal relations, preferential treatment of the in-groups comes at the morally unjustifiable expense of those who are excluded.

However, even in the case of well-justified and permissible forms of preferential treatment within special relations, the universal and impartial reasons can never be fully eliminated. Thus, a tension between the two incommensurable standpoints of partiality and impartiality will inevitably persist, at least under conditions of massive inequality. Consequently, morality as such does not appear as an integrated and comprehensive whole but as a fragmented set of competing perspectives and values, that renders the possibility of successfully navigating through mutually exclusive demands dubious.

Chapter six pursues this insight further by addressing the moral overdemandingness objection: *cosmopolitan responsibility* might generate *impossible moral requirements* if, under current conditions, weighty and non-negotiable moral requirements (that are able to pass an interpersonal justification test) bind agents, no matter whether they are actually capable of acting upon them. The chapter critically reviews different possible strategies to ease the moral burden that results from a cosmopolitan extension of moral concern. But arguments for reducing the moral burden of individual agents to what they consider not excessively demanding and/or feasible is not the only option. Alternatively, one could accept that it is impossible, under current conditions of extreme inequality and injustice, to live a fully moral live. In the second half of the chapter I explore and defend this second option, however much more controversial and much less appealing it may be. Yet, *taking the needs and unmet basic rights of the disadvantaged seriously deserves priority over worrying about the moral innocence of the advantaged.* Thus, I propose a qualified account of impossible moral imperfection, even failure, that distinguishes its objective, diagnostic dimension from its subjective and intersubjective dimensions. Generally, it should not count as a flaw of any (sufficiently demanding) moral theory if it places apparently excessive moral burdens on those who could, in principle, act. Instead, such overdemandingness rather indicates a flaw of the world that needs to be corrected.

The critical reflections of part II—on the limits of individual agency in a global context, on the puzzle of partiality and on moral overdemandingness—elaborate my understanding of the role and responsibility of individual agents in the face of global structural injustice: As morally equal citizens of the world, agents aspire to contribute to realising global relational equality. Committed, from a pragmatic perespective, to normative pluralism, and equipped with a firm belief in the possibility of progress, they understand that their direct impact will inevitably be limited. But even apparently tiny contributions might matter, particularly if they are repeated over long periods of time and if they start to spread, influence behaviour of others, shape ideas and consolidate themselves in institutions. Clearly, the social and epistemic networks that today connect people across the globe will not only impose limits to unconstrained preferential treatment for oneself and for those particularly near and dear; it will also make moral perfection unavailable under current conditions. But acknowledging these unpleasant realities can motivate responsible cosmopolitan agents to take pride in contributing—through concrete and often local action out of global thinking—to realising a world in which the circumstances are such that global structural injustice ceases to exist; in which everyone's basic needs and interests are fully met; and in which, consequently, preferential treatment for some becomes less problematic and moral failure, in the sense analysed, can be avoided.

In this spirit, the book concludes with a chapter on the *ethos of cosmopolitan responsibility*. The adequate response of individual agents to global injustice consists in developing an egalitarian, cosmopolitan ethos that informs and influences one's way of feeling, thinking, talking and acting about injustice. Given the pervasive nature of global structural injustice, promoting an egalitarian ethos—in individuals and groups—would be, I contend, a suitable contribution to addressing the distinctive wrong of pervasive structural injustice from the side of individuals. An ethos links the cognitive-rational, the socio-emotional and the dispositional-behavioural dimensions of a person and thus does not only trigger small direct ('vertical') action to address injustice; it also generates indirect ('horizontal') effects by communicating one's moral and political commitments to other agents in one's community. No individual in isolation can have a meaningful impact upon the massive and complex challenge of global injustice; but joint normative commitments, shared aims, and coordinated political and systemic action, of which individuals can be part, can generate impact and bring reform.

As I argue throughout the book, a major shift in perceiving the wrong of injustice is necessary: global problems have to be moved from the periphery of our attention more to the centre; and they have to be conceptualised as challenges that must not be left to ineffective or inexistent institutions: they require responses from individual moral agents, too. Fostering an ethos of *cosmopolitan responsibility* with its pervasive impact on how agents feel, think, talk and act does just this.

Of course, for those seeking specific guidance about what to do, my account of *cosmopolitan responsibility* will most likely appear insufficiently concrete. And obviously, a great number of questions remain unaddressed and unanswered in the following pages. But the goal of my philosophical analysis is—in spite of its ambitious scope and its firm conviction that promoting a cosmopolitan ethos is urgently needed—quite modest: to engage in a conceptual inquiry into the values, norms and principles that can determine and help guide individual responsible action in the global context. Thinking through the issues presented in this book will hopefully provide readers with some thought provoking material to form their own judgements about *what to do* and then to take responsible action, once that the importance of individual contributions to respecting the equal moral importance of all and to addressing global wrongs has been firmly established.

Part I **The cosmopolitan ethos**

The chapters of part I introduce the three central elements of my theory of *cosmopolitan responsibility:* the idea of world citizenship; an account of global relational equality; and a pragmatic understanding of ethics, action and habit. The moral ideas and concepts developed in these chapters form the normative core of the cosmopolitan ethos that can shape how individuals feel, think, talk and act in response to global issues in an interconnected world.

Chapter 1
Cosmopolitanism. The ideal of global justice, past and present

The idea that all humans form a morally relevant global community has a long history that continues to inspire and shape debates until today. This chapter introduces and explicates the notion of cosmopolitanism and will establish it as the first core element of a cosmopolitan ethos. It does so by discussing the idea of global citizenship and its normative content; and the major phases of its historical development to the present—with a particular focus on the Cynics, Stoics and the Enlightenment philosophy of Immanuel Kant. It provides a brief overview of the contemporary debate about global justice, some basic distinctions with regard to metrics and patterns of justice, and explains the relationship between thinking about global *justice* and about global *ethics*.

With this, the idea of world citizenship is introduced as the first and foundational normative element of my theory of *cosmopolitan responsibility*. Agents who understand themselves and others as citizens of the world will acknowledge the numerous morally relevant connections that link people across the globe. The scope of justice and the scope of one's moral concern will then no longer be limited by national borders; and global structural injustice—that links the advantages enjoyed by some with the disadvantages suffered by others—becomes a matter of urgent moral concern also for the privileged who, initially often unknowingly, benefit from it.

1 Global citizenship

The word "cosmopolitan" is of Greek origin and means "citizen of the world". It is a compound noun combining the words "cosmos" (world, order) and "polites" (citizen). The tension between these two components generates something akin to an oxymoron: after all, the notion of a citizen *of the world* seems to contradict itself. Citizenship is generally understood to be individual legal membership with a defined national, social and political community. The term as currently and conventionally used specifies a particular subgroup of humans who form a distinct—and by definition not an all-inclusive—community. In the classical Greek context, citizenship was linked to a specific polis, a city-state like Athens or Sparta. Later on, the nation-state became the primary unit specifying citizenship. Today, supranational institutions like the European Union have emerged that provide citizens of member states with an emerging, new form of supra-citizenship, although this is still dependent upon their prior national citizenship. What such developments demonstrate is that, whatever the current organising unit, the size, constitution and complexity of citizenship-conferring communities has varied over time and space, and continues to do so.

Citizenship refers to a special status that individuals possessing it enjoy, including a specific range of expected, required and permitted actions. Citizens are normally expected to participate in their community, to express their voice through, for example, voting on issues of communal importance. Furthermore, citizens, in exchange for following the laws governing their community, are entitled to certain advantages, such as the use of common goods or the privilege of traveling with a passport of the respective community. Such special status, defined by a specific set of expectations, obligations and entitlements, can only be conferred by a community that is institutionally organised in specific ways (Carens 2000). Due to this legal (or political) understanding of citizenship, citizenship in the cosmopolitan sense of being *of the world* may appear nonsensical.

However, a closer analysis of the word "cosmos" reveals an innovative and provocative idea that dispels the oxymoron. Unlike our contemporary understanding of "cosmos" as outer space (all that lies beyond our planet world as such), "cosmos" in the classical Greek sense had a very different connotation: it referred to the world as *an already structured and organised harmonious whole*. Cosmos signified for the Greeks the universal order governed by logos, and was the opposite of "chaos," the unstructured, formless and lawless void —in other words, the term had a meaning quite opposite to the one we currently attach to it. The assumption of such a meaningful and harmonious cosmic order, which is governed by natural (or divine) eternal laws, moderates the oxymoron in the word "cosmopolitan". It points to the possibility of perceiving individuals as members in a structure that expands beyond the polis or nation. Here, citizenship is understood as an anthropological or a psychological[11] phenomenon that is largely independent of actual political or legal arrangements. The presumed contradiction fades away under this assumption and makes room for an admittedly optimistic ideal of coherence, and for allegiance to a community that transcends local groups. In this sense, humans as humans can be understood to

---

[11] My distinction between a legal and a psychological understanding of citizenship is based upon the distinction between different dimensions of citizenship made by Carens. He suggests that there is a *legal* dimension of citizenship, referring to the legal status of an individual, a *political* dimension, regarding the individual's participation in collective decision making processes, but also a *psychological* dimension, that is constituted through psychological attachment (Carens 2000, 161–176).

form a community for which all contingent discriminatory characteristics like nationality, religion, culture, class, ethnicity, sex, gender or sexual preference, etc. are irrelevant for community membership purposes.

The cosmopolitan claim of a single, normatively relevant community of all humans endorses the normative anthropological claim that, in spite of all factual and circumstantial differences between individuals, all living human beings are equally entitled to membership in this overarching human community, which includes certain rights and entitlements, but also brings with it certain duties and obligations.

2 Moral cosmopolitanism as egalitarian universalism

Cosmopolitanism, the idea of "world-citizenship," is grounded in the fundamental idea that all human beings are jointly members of one global order, which is based on the widely shared normative assumption of the equal moral worth of all. Cosmopolitanism thus expresses a normative stance that gives rise to a moral project in several domains, most notably the political, cultural and moral. In its different forms, it (1) addresses a set of *questions* about living together, (2) shares a *diagnosis*, and (3) tends to agree on a set of central *claims* and *commitments*.

(1) The assumption of the existence of a single overarching human community that justifies regarding all individuals as "citizens" (at least metaphorically) suggests that there are certain expectations, requirements and entitlements connected to this status. Indeed, cosmopolitanism's central question is *how should human beings coexist? How should we live together?*[12] More concretely, this question can be split into several sub-questions: Which normative rules should govern human action in order to coexist well on planet Earth?[13] Which rights and entitlements do human individuals have as citizens of the world? And which obligations and duties do they have to meet, towards one another and also towards non-human animals and the environment?

(2) Asking these questions follows from the particular *diagnosis* of what I have called in the introduction the de facto "circumstances of cosmopolitanism". They consist of three elements. *First*, all humans, whatever the differences be-

---

[12] The adequate way of living together will also have implications for dealing with non-human animals and the environment. In any case, Nagel correctly and pointedly states that "we really do not know how to live together" (Nagel 1991, 5).

[13] "The ethical life belongs to human beings, living together in ever larger groups, and working out their shared lives with one another." (Kitcher 2012, 2) For this, see also below, chapter two.

tween individuals, are strikingly similar with regard to trans-temporally, transculturally, and inter-individually stable features. Human beings generally all have a roughly similar body, basic needs and interests, they also have standardly a capacity to have experiences, feel emotions and to reason, even if the concrete ways in which these capacities are used and experienced may differ to some degree between individuals, groups and cultures. Humans are able to interact and to communicate with one another, establishing relations that can bridge existing differences, including differences of language and culture. The obvious differences in, say, languages, fashion, parenting styles or burial rites thus must not obscure the striking similarities between humans accross time and regions: all are needy creatures, all relate to and depend from others (at least during some periods of their lives), all can standardly govern their behaviour through employing reasoning and deliberation, and all have an interest in being well.[14] These features ground the idea of a community of humans.

Second, we live in an increasingly *interconnected world* in which actions have both direct and indirect impact on the lives of many others. I would argue that this was already true at the very beginning of human history: rare in the historical record are individuals or communities that were permanently self-sufficient. New human groupings and settlements originated from the interactions and movements of older ones, and even when groups seek to define themselves as self-sufficient (or even hostile to other groups), those others are by definition the counterpart of such self-understandings. Once population levels increase in any area, meeting and interacting between groups becomes inevitable: it is and remains nearly impossible to abstain permanently from interaction with others. Nor is it possible not to have an impact on the lives of others, or not to be influenced by their actions (Appiah 2007). Such interaction and mutual impact is not impeded by the demarcation of groups, nor, in more recent times, by national boundaries. Today, global trade and climate change are but two particularly striking examples of the far-reaching entanglement of all human lives. The products we buy have often been produced in far away places, and so a long causal chain of interactions connects individual consumer decisions with the working conditions of manufacturers, sometimes very far away. Individual actions that generate CO_2-emissions directly contribute to processes like global warming: flying anywhere in the world, from Albania to Zambia, materially adds to the amount of greenhouse gases in the atmosphere that influence weather phenomena elsewhere. And even those living in remote areas of the planet, e.g. the Maldives, are not merely heavily affected by the activities of others in

---

[14] Cf. Appiah (2007), Ganten et al. (2008), Heilinger (2010, part IV), Nussbaum (2011a).

far away places that contribute to changing weather patterns and rising sea levels; entire islands are at risk of disappearing completely and forever as a result.

The significance of these two elements of the diagnosis of the de facto circumstances of cosmopolitanism—the possibility and inevitable reality of human interconnectedness—is heightened by a *third* observation: the striking contrast between the living conditions of humans in different places on the planet, which are defined by an almost unimaginable scale of *inequality* with many people not even having *sufficient* means to live a minimally decent life, due to poverty, exploitation, environmental degradation, etc.[15] The existing inequalities indicate a problem that can appear in an absolute and a relative form: Absolute deprivation is always morally problematic, because the basic needs of people are not met. Relative inequality might turn out to be less worrisome from a moral perspective, if those worse off are still reasonably well off and are able to live a decent life. Relative inequality, however, becomes particularly problematic, if the worse off are denied the opportunity to live a decent life all the while the relatively better off not only have access to the conditions of a decent life, but enjoy massive amounts of privileges and advantages, that are generated and upheld, at least partly, even at the expense of the worse off. This is the morally outrageous situation of our current world, constituting the third element of the descriptive diagnosis of the circumstances of cosmopolitanism.

(3) On these grounds a distinctively cosmopolitan position will take a *normative* stance. The particular normative commitment of cosmopolitans is that of egalitarian universalism taken seriously, with real world outcomes as the yardstick. The cosmopolitan perspective can be used in two senses: it can normatively evaluate and assess a given state of affairs, and it can be guide and demand particular forms of action and reform[16]—always based on the grounds of the equal moral standing of all.

The fundamental claim about equal moral status of each individual does not —in my view—stand in need for a specific justification beyond the widely shared description of circumstances of cosmopolitanism.[17] The onus of proof lies, rath-

---

[15] Extreme inequalities also occur within nations, raising problems similar to the ones discussed here. Cf. Milanovic (2011).

[16] Beitz has distinguished cosmopolitanism as a "perspective" or "point of view" seeking to "encompass the whole world" on the one hand, and cosmopolitanism as a "substantive moral and political doctrine" on the other (Beitz 2005, 15).

[17] However, such justifications of equal moral standing of humans are possible and standardly opt for one of three possibilities: *shared needs, interests, or capacities*, like reason, are seen as constitutive of equal value, *external fixation* of equal value by a divine entity or a natural law, or *collective self-attribution* of equal value through the community of communicating agents. Gen-

er, on the side of those denying the fundamentally equal moral standing of all humans: those who might claim that some persons (women, people of colour, children, homosexuals or atheists, for example) do *not* have the same basic moral weight as others do, must provide arguments to defend the *moral* relevance of distinctions made on the grounds of gender, sexual preference, skin colour, age or religion. In the last few generations, many such distinctions have come rightfully under attack, some have already fallen. While the political realities in many parts of the world currently indicate challenges to such progress, even attack past achievements and institute regressive change, I assume that, based on the fundamentally self-evident insight into the moral equality of all, genuine progress will remain possible.[18]

Cosmopolitanism in any case argues that the fundamental claim about the moral equality of all has to be taken seriously. And because cosmopolitanism *stresses* this prima facie uncontroversial assumption, it becomes controversial, thus calling for further reflection. Three central normative elements can be identified within the cosmopolitan commitment to the equal moral standing of all: *normative individualism, egalitarianism/impartiality*, and *universal scope*.[19]

First, each and every human *individual, as such*, is a basic unit of moral concern (Pogge 1992, 48). No additional conditions beyond humanness are necessary to qualify a human individual as fully morally relevant.[20] Notably, it is impermissible to make any exceptions and to exclude some from the moral concern because of their ethnicity, religion, nationality, family membership, sex, gender,

---

erally, the equal moral worth of all has become a foundational conviction in contemporary moral philosophy, cf. e.g. Dworkin (1977, 180–183) or Nagel (1991, 14). Note, however, that equal moral standing and the demand to treat all as moral equals does not imply that everyone has to be treated equally. Treating different people differently—e.g., by locking up the bank robber, while being friendly to one's cousin—may even be morally required in order to fully respect the fundamentally equal moral standing of everyone.

18 For a critical discussion of the claim that all persons have equal moral worth, cf. the papers collected in Steinhoff (2015) and Steinhoff (2013).

19 Cf. Pogge (2007, 316), Brown and Held (2010, 1–2), Pogge (1992, 48–49). The principles of normative individualism and egalitarian universalism can be found in many modern moral theories. Implicitly or explicitly, they are fundamental for Hobbes, Locke, Kant, and for utilitarian and contractarian theories.

20 The question whether the exclusive focus on *human* beings—and the corresponding neglect of animals and other rational or sentient beings—is problematic because in itself arbitrary (the objection of "speciesism") will not be discussed here. Equally, I will not address the challenge that some human beings like newborn children or severely mentally impaired people are not in a full sense *persons*, if personhood is based on the condition of rationality. I will simply talk about human beings and interactions between human beings, while being aware of some unanswered questions in the background.

sexual preference, culture, etc. Furthermore, *only* human individuals are such units of concern. 'Races,' religious groups, nations, families, etc., have no independent moral standing, as normative collectivists might argue. For normative individualists, collectives matter morally only insofar as the individuals that are constitutive of the group matter.

Second, each of the individuals is to be seen as an *equally important* basic unit of moral concern. Not only are all human beings relevant, but they are equally relevant. Kings and beggars, criminals and saints, friends and strangers are indistinguishable in their fundamental moral relevance. They all have equal moral weight. Correspondingly, everyone's interests, needs, claims, well-being etc., are fundamentally of equal moral importance. The default weighing of the interests, etc., of different people is hence one that can be characterised as impartial. All deviations from such impartial consideration stand in need of particular justification.[21]

Third, the scope of cosmopolitanism is unrestricted and maximally inclusive. It is *universal* in two senses: no matter when and where an individual lives or who she or he is, she or he matters equally; and he or she also matters equally for everyone. The first sense stresses what Pogge has called the "all-inclusiveness" of moral cosmopolitanism, the second its "generality" (Pogge 2007): cosmopolitanism fundamentally asks *every* individual to expand his or her concern to *every other* individual.

It is clear that a cosmopolitan theory and practice will face many challenges, both theoretical and practical. If it is to become a defensible, widely accepted and policy-relevant view, one will have to spell out how exactly the cosmopolitan community distributes entitlements, permissions and obligations, and what would be the appropriate institutional arrangements to secure the core demands of cosmopolitanism. With the intention of making progress in this regard, the chapters in this book will take up important challenges and seek to advance the understanding of the complex notions of equality, responsibility, impartiality, rights and their practical implications. But first I want to focus further on the development of the cosmopolitan ideal in the history of ideas, since knowing the history of a concept may also help to understand its current use more accurately.

---

21 Unlike Pogge (1992), Pogge (2007) avoids the notion of "equality" when determining the central normative commitments of cosmopolitanism. To prevent the impression that cosmopolitanism endorses an egalitarian view about *distributive* justice, he talks of "impartiality" which better captures the idea that all individuals *matter equally*. I discuss both notions separately in chapters two and five below.

3 The evolution of cosmopolitanism

The following section presents some important phases in the evolution of the idea that humans as citizens of the world form a morally relevant community.[22] I will look at the origins and at the cosmopolitan "agenda setting" in ancient Greece and will present the unfolding of this ideal during the Enlightenment period, notably in Kant's seminal writings, before concluding with some brief thoughts about cosmopolitanism in the 19th and 20th century. It should become clear that the contemporary discussion of the content and form of cosmopolitan thinking owes much to its historical predecessors. What has mostly changed over time is that cosmopolitan ideals have become more and more applicable to an increasingly globalised—and thus factually cosmopolitan—reality.

3.1 Cosmopolitanism in ancient Greek philosophy

The explicit discussion of the notion of cosmopolitanism starts in the Greek Cynic and Stoic tradition at around 350 BCE. Yet, the idea that all human beings constitute a joint community is most probably even older and not restricted to the Western tradition of thought. The Egyptian pharaoh Akhenaten (around 1300 BCE) may already be seen as an early proponent of universalistic monotheism. He accepted that he had the same duties towards all human beings, regardless of their 'race' or nationality (Harris 1927). The Chinese philosopher Mozi (around 400 BCE) also endorsed an idea of impartiality on the basis of a principle of "universal love" (cf. Caney 2005b, 4). A similar idea of universal obligation towards all appears in the Hebrew bible, and both Homer and Herodotus endorsed claims that call for an overcoming of narrow conceptions of (polis-) patriotism (Harris 1927). However, the origin of an elaborated idea of world-citizenship can be found "in the earlier classical period of Greek thought" (Harris 1927, 2; Nussbaum 1997b).

Explicit discussion of cosmopolitanism appears to have begun with the controversial Diogenes of Sinope (400/390 – 328/323), one of the prominent figures of Cynicism. A skeptic of the culture of the Greek polis, he has been pointedly described as "a cross between a satirical comedian and a homeless performance artist" (Warburton 2013). He rejected all possessions and lived as a pauper in order to express his disdain for material wealth. Seneca and others report that

---

[22] This section is particularly indebted to work by Nussbaum (1997b). It also contains revised material published earlier (Heilinger 2015).

Diogenes had lived in a tub (Seneca, Ep., 90.14). Because of his "dog-like" lifestyle as a beggar without possessions, expressing without shame the different needs and impulses of his body in public, following like a dog the steps of Antisthenes whom he deeply admired (Diogenes Laërtius, VI.6, 18, 21), and because of his praise for the virtues of dogs, people called Diogenes himself a dog (Greek: *kyon*). Diogenes accepted this label as a title of honour and his teachings became known as *Cynicism* (Müller 1976, Ottmann 2001, 260, 276–288).[23] It is reported that Diogenes disagreed with Plato about the adequate interpretation of Socrates' teachings: Plato was in Diogenes' eye too theoretical a philosopher, in contrast to Socrates, who had the right attitude towards the priority of practice. However, Diogenes agreed with both Socrates and Plato in certain respects: like both of them, he questioned the widely accepted ethical exclusivism which privileged the in-group of one's polis over all other humans.

The core elements of the emerging cynical philosophical school were the self-sufficiency of the wantless individual (autarchy), the need for open expression of thoughts (parrhesia or shameless speech) and—here one finds the first reported actual use of the word "cosmopolitan"—a universal conception of human community transcending city or state boundaries. Once, when asked where he came from, Diogenes is said to have answered: "I am a citizen of the world."[24] This claim to be a member of a universal community was perceived as a serious provocation of the established views because Diogenes implicitly rejected with this statement a definition of his own status and ancestry within the narrower terms of state or city affiliation that mattered so much to his fellow citizens. His self-description as cosmo-polites situates him in a larger community of all human beings—and in doing so places him outside of the narrowly confined borders of the Greek polis. Contradicting the standard self-perception of a citizen in a Greek polis in a way that must have appeared insulting to many, Diogenes drew a parallel between shared citizenship in a polis in the conventional understanding of his contemporaries on the one hand, and the mutual relationship of all human beings as cosmopolitans on the other. Such an expanded idea of shared citizenship implied that hospitality and fraternal affection were owed to all human beings, and not only to one's fellow citizens in a particular polis.

---

23 Diogenes Laërtius and Plutarch report further anecdotes about Diogenes, among them Diogenes going at plain daylight with a lamp to the Athenian marketplace and searching for an (honest) human being (an image later taken up by Nietzsche when presenting his Zarathustra). Diogenes is further said to have mocked Alexander the Great when the king promised to grant him a favour, whatever it may be: "Stand out of my sunlight!"

24 Cf. Diogenes Laërtius (VI.63); a saying, however, that Cicero also attributed to Socrates in *Tusculanae Disputationes* (Cicero, Tusc. Disp., V.37, 108).

This early understanding of cosmopolitanism has two features that greatly influenced later uses of the concept. First, it seeks to empower the *individual*, insofar as one is freed from parochial allegiances to any narrower community such as the Greek polis-state. This was of particular importance to Diogenes since, in his time, the social structures of the polis had begun to decay and become increasingly fragile. Such individual self-assurance, expressed as independence from narrow-mindedness and crumbling communities, highlights the autarchy of each individual in a meaningful universal order. Second, this self-understanding of an empowered individual is embedded in the specific social concept of a universal *community* that is constituted by the relations between all individuals. It is this larger community within which humans stand in a relation of equality to one another, and in which mutual allegiances are owed.

The story continues with Diogenes teaching his Cynic thoughts to Crates of Thebes who influenced, together with Diogenes, Zeno of Citium, the founder of the school of *Stoicism*, which prevailed into Roman times. Zeno argued prominently for a universal "city under one law"[25] which specifies the claim of Diogenes to be a citizen of the world: the single law that all have to follow is conceived of as a *natural law*, existing independently of all agreements in particular cities or states. Here is how Plutarch presents Zeno's view:

> The much admired Republic of Zeno is aimed at this one main point, that our household arrangements should not be based on cities or parishes, each one marked out by its own legal system, but we should regard all men as our fellow-citizens and local residents, and there should be one way of life and order, like that of a herd grazing together and nurtured by a common law. Zeno wrote this, picturing as it were a dream or image of a philosopher's well-regulated society. (Long and Sedley 1987, 429)[26]

Zeno's utopia hence went beyond the fraternal relations[27] argued for by Diogenes. The universal natural law ultimately demands a universal political order to which all human beings submit.

Another Stoic, Hierocles, addressed a challenge implicit in any demand for a universal law and universal allegiances among all human beings as human be-

---

[25] Even if the word "city" designates obviously not the entire world, the direction of Zeno's argument is clear. The notion of "law" is not to be understood in a modern sense. What Zeno refers to is again a meaningful structure governed by the "logos".

[26] More philosophical sources about Stoic political philosophy can be found in Long and Sedley (1987, 429–437).

[27] And, of course, one must not oversee that several groups of people—among them women and slaves—were not always fully acknowledged as equals even in accounts defending a universal and egalitarian expansion of concern.

ings, which will also be discussed later in this book: How to deal with the particular and special relationships towards those nearer and dearer to us? If all human beings are equally important morally, then special treatment of my fellow citizens in local communities becomes problematic: Do we truly have to treat all human beings alike? How about the special concern I may foster for my parents and children, my friends, etc., as opposed to a general benevolence towards all human beings? Hierocles, living in the first and second century BCE, employed a metaphor—also later used by Cicero in his *De Officiis* (I.50 sqq.)—to make his point: we should understand our allegiances to other human beings as a series of "concentric circles," with ourselves being at the centre and the other human beings grouped around us in ever larger circles. The first circle around oneself would be the immediate family, then the extended family, next friends, neighbours, fellow polis-inhabitants until ultimately the largest circle would comprise all human beings. The challenge and the task of human beings as moral agents would then be to "draw the circles somehow toward the centre," so that the larger circle collapses with the next smaller circle.

Here is a long quote from Stobaeus, the compiler of extracts from Greek authors who worked in the early 5th century, illustrating in detail how Hierocles understood these concentric circles:

> Each one of us is as it were entirely encompassed by many circles, some smaller, others larger, the latter enclosing the former on the basis of their different and unequal dispositions relative to each other. The first and closest circle is the one which a person has drawn as though around a centre, his own mind. [...] Next, the second one further removed from the centre but enclosing the first circle [...]. The third one has in it uncles and aunts, grandparents, nephews, nieces, and cousins. The next circle includes the other relatives, and this is followed by the circle of local residents, then the circle of fellow-tribesmen, next that of fellow-citizens, and then in the same way the circle of people from neighbouring towns, and the circle of fellow-countrymen. The outermost and largest circle, which encompasses all the rest, is that of the whole human race. Once these have all been surveyed, it is the task of a well-tempered man, in his proper treatment of each group, to draw the circles together somehow towards the centre, and to keep zealously transferring those from the enclosing circles into the enclosed ones [...]. The right point will be reached if, through our own initiative, we reduce the distance of the relationship with each person [...]. But we should do more, in the terms of address we use, calling cousins brothers, and uncles and aunts, fathers and mothers [...]. For this mode of address would be no slight mark of our affection for them all, and it would also stimulate and intensify the indicated contraction of the circles. (Long 1987, 349–350)

These cosmopolitan ideas about expanding the circles of concern and contracting the circles of proximity were taken up and refined more and more by the rich and diverse Roman Stoic tradition with proponents like Cicero, Seneca and Marcus Aurelius (Nussbaum 1994, ch. 9–12).[28] In general, *three main elements of Stoic cosmopolitan thinking* appear to have evolved out of Diogenes' original claim.[29] *First*, the foundational starting point is the assumed similar *human capacity for reason* that is constitutive for the assumed universal community of all human beings. Reason is conceived of as the divine faculty that allows us to make moral choices, and this faculty is shared by all human beings as human beings. Nussbaum explains: "Male or female, slave or free, king or peasant, all are alike of boundless moral value, and the dignity of reason is worthy of respect wherever it is found. This reason, the Stoics held, makes us fellow citizens" (Nussbaum 1997b, 7).

A *second* important Stoic claim is the *dual belonging* of human beings to both a local and a global community both of which entail different kinds of moral obligations and rights. Starting from the assumption that it is purely by chance, by brute luck, that we are born into a given nation or particular community, it becomes necessary not to overrate this accidental and morally arbitrary fact. The Stoics do not deny our particular obligations in concrete surroundings; they do, however, deny that these obligations provide an excuse for not taking into account the appropriate concern owed to any other individual who happens not to be a compatriot or family member. As Nussbaum has it, again referring to the underlying shared capacity of reason, "We should recognize humanity wherever it occurs, and give its fundamental ingredients, reason and moral capacity, our first allegiance and respect" (Nussbaum 1997b, 7).

The *third* central claim is the Stoic stipulation of elements of a *fundamental natural law* that, if followed, would allow human beings to live in a universal harmony with one another and the world. Here, Stoic thought relies on metaphysical assumptions about divine entities to provide a justification for their claims about the existence of such a universal natural law. Yet, the assumption of a natural law—even on specifically religious grounds—does not lead Stoic thought to claim a single, true religion. Neither does Stoicism call for a single world state. As Nussbaum writes, the Stoics argue "that a style of political life that recognises the moral/rational community as fundamental promises a more reasonable style of political deliberation and problem solving, *even when our institutions are still based on national divisions*" (Nussbaum 1997b, 8, my italics). The Stoic claim hence allows for stepwise improvements or gradual developments towards more realisation of and compliance with the natural law, with-

---

28 This metaphor has a lasting impact until today (cf. e.g. Singer 1981, 120, Kitcher 2011, 215).
29 Here I follow a reading of these authors along the lines of Kantian ideas, similar to Brown and Held (2010, 4–5) and on the basis of Nussbaum (1997b). Kant's stance on cosmopolitanism will be explained below.

out any totalitarian impulse to enforce these laws immediately. The Stoics' suggestions are certainly pertinent when thinking about how to organise the co-existence of all humans in the world.[30]

Based on these early ideas about cosmopolitanism, it is possible to identify *three important challenges* that are also much discussed in the contemporary debate about cosmopolitanism. *First*, we need an understanding of the anthropological underpinnings of any universalistic moral account: focussing predominantly or exclusively on reason (as done frequently in the Stoic and the Enlightenment tradition) might be too narrow and fail to capture the many relevant dimensions of human lives. The anthropological basis of cosmopolitan thinking has to be extended beyond reason, given that there is a bewildering plurality of possible properties that justify the special normative status of all human beings.[31] *Second*, the double membership of human beings in both a local and a global community, diagnosed already by the Stoics, calls either for some kind of moderation of strong universal obligations or for some kind of holistic unification of universal and particular obligations, in order to avoid obvious contradictions between the differing claims from the two realms. It will be necessary to "embed" universalism: the challenge then consists in defining precisely how to deal with this factual plural membership in more than one community. *Third*, the Stoics started from the metaphysically demanding assumption of a fixed, eternal natural law that has currently lost much of its appeal. At best, we can—through anthropological considerations—identify certain core elements of human lives or conditions of human flourishing that justify legitimate moral claims or claims of justice, but these will be insufficient for stipulating or justifying any specific and determinate "natural law".[32] The third challenge then consists in overcoming and replacing the idea of a natural law (and the assumption

---

30 It is interesting to see the central role Stoicism assigns to *individual* agency under cosmopolitan "law" in contrast to *institutional* arrangements. Choosing between an individual and an institutional understanding of cosmopolitanism will become an important challenge in contemporary cosmopolitan thinking.
31 Beside reason, it could be, e.g., the status of personhood, sentience, certain preferences or interests, will, needs, desires, an idea of human well-being, or capacities like the possibility to agree, to communicate, etc. I do not engage in a detailed discussion of how to justify the moral status of all humans in this book, but only stipulate that human beings should be understood as having both a needy, physical side that makes persons stand in need of other persons on the one hand, and an active side of—possibly rational, reasoned, moral, autonomous—agency on the other, where both sides are closely engaged with one another. Cf. e.g. Nussbaum (2011a), Anderson (1999, 317), and the contributions in Mackenzie and Stoljar (2000).
32 However, the "new natural law theorists" assume it is possible to justify at least a fundamental natural law (Finnis 1980).

of a possible universal harmony) with another approach that allows one to make justified normative claims about obligations in the global domain.

Cosmopolitan thinking evolved further during late Antiquity and the Middle Ages, and Stoic cosmopolitanism continued influencing Christian thinkers like Paul, Augustine, Thomas Aquinas and Martin Luther.[33] Particularly striking and consequently influential is the statement of universalism and a single human community by Paul: "There is neither Jew nor Gentile, neither slave nor free, nor is there male and female, for you are all one in Christ Jesus" (Gal 3, 28). Religious differences are—on this account—as irrelevant to this community, as are social or gender differences.

Particularly influential for the development of cosmopolitan thought were, according to Brown and Held, "the works associated with the School of Salamanca and the cosmopolitan theories generated by the Neo-Thomist thinkers of Bartolome de las Casas, Francisco de Vitoria, and Francisco Suarez" (Brown and Held 2010, 10). These thinkers developed the theory of a natural right and a natural law further—yet on ever stronger religious foundations. Its particular religious grounding, however, makes this tradition dubious to many today. The most forceful expression of cosmopolitanism in the history of philosophy appeared when the assumption of universal law was liberated from its specific religious underpinnings due to the religious scepticism of the Enlightenment period, notably in the work of Immanuel Kant.

3.2 The Enlightenment expansion of cosmopolitan thought

The Enlightenment period, with its optimistic belief in the possibilities for improving the human lot, developed the cosmopolitan idea into an elaborate and forceful normative view that had direct and indirect practical implications. As such, it has continued to inspire thinkers and practitioners to this day. Numerous Enlightenment philosophers embraced the idea of a morally significant joint membership of all humans in a single community—among them, most prominently, Hugo Grotius, John Locke, Voltaire, Thomas Paine, Adam Smith, Marquis de Condorcet and Thomas Jefferson (Forman-Barzilei 2009; Schlereth 1977). Cosmopolitanism was an integral element in the broader set of Enlightenment ideas that were in the air by that time, as it provided an ideal and a direction to guide the generally optimistic belief in progress and step-by-step change

---

[33] Obviously, my account is limited in its focus on the tradition of Western philosophy; cf. Delanty (2014).

in human lives towards perfection. Ultimately, the American Declaration of Independence, the French Revolution and the *Declaration des Droits de l'Homme et du Citoyen*, as well as the Haitian revolution and independence[34] were born out of this cosmopolitan Enlightenment spirit, which insited upon the freedom of the individual, the equality of all and an overarching relationship between human beings. However, to some degree and in spite of their universal ambition, these all expressed a "cosmopolitanism within borders" (Wild and Heilinger 2013) in which the fundamentally egalitarian universalism was taken seriously only at the level of an individual country. An important pioneer of the extension of cosmopolitan reasoning *beyond* the state was Kant.[35]

Kant is the paradigmatic philosophical representative of the entire Enlightenment period. It was he who inspired ever more cosmopolitan thinking and, as Brown and Held rightly claim, "all [...] cosmopolitan themes are influenced, directly or indirectly, by Kant's moral and political philosophy" (Brown and Held 2010, 9).

Kant obviously wrote in a very different context than the Stoics. By the 18th century, people had become able to travel around the entire globe (although, perhaps interestingly, Kant himself did not), the actual economic interactions between peoples had increased significantly, and colonialism—with people forcefully entering countries and oppressing and exploiting others—had begun to be subjected to moral scrutiny. During the Enlightenment period, political thinking took into account these changed circumstances. Kant was sensitive to these developments and, in his influential work *Perpetual Peace*, he described an emerging global community in the following way:

> The peoples of the earth have thus entered in varying degrees into a universal community, and it has developed to the point where a violation of laws in *one* part of the world is felt *everywhere*. The idea of a cosmopolitan law is therefore not fantastic and overstrained; it is

---

34 Although often neglected in listing the important progressive and egalitarian historic events in the spirit of Enlightenment, the Haitian revolution and subsequent declaration of independence from colonial France in 1804 merit special attention when studying egalitarian and cosmopolitan thinking. After all, the successful insurrection of self-liberated slaves was the only one that ultimately led to the founding of a state, firmly committed to the revolutionary ideals of egalitarianism, in which both former rulers and ruled, white and non-white people, ruled together. Only the Haitian revolution realised the universalism of human rights fully by overthrowing slavery, thus radicalising the notion of natural human rights by exposing the unsolved and persisting tensions and contradictions in American independence and the French declaration. Cf. the seminal James (2001 (1938)) and, more recently, Fick (2007), Knight (2000) and Bhambra (2015).
35 Kant's contribution and its historical context is analysed in Cheneval (2002).

a necessary complement to the unwritten code of political and international law, transforming it into a universal law of humanity. (Kant AA 8: 360; ed. Reiss 107)[36]

In *Perpetual Peace,* Kant developed nothing less than a "theory of politics" (Gerhardt 1995) that takes into account the need for lawful interaction beyond the spheres of influence of the individual nation states.

The stipulation of a "cosmopolitan law," which would be added to the already existing forms of public law—constitutional and international—is the major theoretical innovation suggested by Kant in his treatise on *Perpetual Peace*. It is true that Kant is mostly known for his contribution to international law. His writings about a "league of nations" had a tangible impact which ultimately inspired and influenced the shaping of institutions like the actual League of Nations (1920) and the United Nations (1945). While such global political bodies do, of course, give rise to issues that will also be discussed under the label of political or legal cosmopolitanism (and hence figure as integral parts of the contemporary debate about cosmopolitanism), Kant used the term "cosmopolitan law" distinctively to designate a particular form of interaction, which is different from what is regulated by the other forms of law.

In cosmopolitan law, Kant stipulates, "individuals and states, coexisting in an external relationship of mutual influences, may be regarded as citizens of a universal state of mankind (*ius cosmopoliticum*)" (AA 8: 349; ed. Reiss 98–99). This universal state of mankind is the larger framework within which cosmopolitan law determines the dealings of individuals and states. It is based on understanding individuals as "citizens of the world" and not as citizens of a particular state with a particular nationality. The focus of *ius cosmopoliticum* is neither on the relationships between states (international law), nor on the relationship of citizens to "their own" states (constitutional law) but on the "status of individuals in their dealings with states of which they are not citizens" (Kleingeld 1998, 72).

In the scholarly literature about Kant's *ius cosmopoliticum* this somewhat unusual addition of a third sphere of law has been widely accepted (cf. Kleingeld 1998, Williams 2007). For instance, Kleingeld argues that "despite problems with how he works it out, Kant's idea of reserving theoretical space for a third level of public law in addition to constitutional and international law is sound" and "can be developed into a position that is relevant to contemporary issues" (Kleingeld 1998, 73).

---

[36] I quote from Kant's *Perpetual Peace* in indicating the volume and pages from the German Akademieausgabe, but also the page of the English edition by Reiss (1991).

To do full justice both to the depths of Kant's argument, and to recent scholarly debate about it, is not possible here for reasons of space. Such a discussion would also require extensive expertise in the field of law that I do not possess. Given the scope of this historical sketch, I will instead focus on the core of his cosmopolitan law as an important element in the history of cosmopolitan thinking.

In the third "Definitivartikel" of *Perpetual Peace*—preceded by the six "Präliminarartikel" describing immediate measures to be undertaken in order to progress towards perpetual peace, and by two more "definitive articles" stipulating what would be necessary for a lasting foundation of perpetual peace—Kant spells out the core of cosmopolitan law: the *right to hospitality*. Kant writes: "Cosmopolitan right shall be limited to conditions of universal hospitality" (8: 357; ed. Reiss 105). Now, this claim of hospitality seems rather modest, since it comprises only "the right of a stranger not to be treated with hostility when he arrives on someone else's territory" (8: 358; ed. Reiss 105). The right to hospitality does not even include, then, a right to be treated with friendliness nor as a welcome guest or visitor on someone else's territory. Rather, it only includes a right to come to the borders of another state and to contact other people and states in other parts of the world (cf. Gerhardt 1995, 105, Kleingeld 1998, 75).

However, this right, Kant explains, may only be denied "if this can be done without causing his death" (8: 358; ed. Reiss 105–106). The German word "Untergang," employed by Kant, is open to interpretation. "Death" is but one of its possible translations. Literally the terms is closest to "sinking" in English, but it is arguably employed more commonly to mean "ruin," "doom" or "demise" of a person. This may also consist of a person being tortured, oppressed etc.—and does not necessarily have to involve one's certain death. On this wider understanding of "Untergang," it is possible to appreciate the wider implications of the right to hospitality. It implies a right to political asylum, as well as a right to be admitted into a foreign country if the chances of decent survival in the country of origin are low because of political insecurity, food shortages or natural disasters.

One may wonder why Kant did not explicitly mention these important and rather obvious implications of cosmopolitan law. But his quite modest demand for a right to hospitality can be explained from the specific circumstances Kant had in mind when formulating the cosmopolitan law. He was less concerned with the particular challenges of *our* time—e.g., refugees fleeing wars, natural disasters or extremely dire economic conditions. Instead, he focused more on the devastatingly intrusive and brutal practices of European colonialism. Here, the cosmopolitan law as stipulated by Kant develops its full impact: colonialism stands in clear violation of cosmopolitan law.[37]

Kleingeld convincingly sums up Kant's understanding of "universal hospitality". To him, it means "that states and individuals have the right to attempt to establish relations with other states and their citizens, but not a right to enter foreign territory. States have the right to refuse visitors, but not violently, and not if it leads to their destruction. This implies an obligation to refrain from imperialist intrusions and to provide safe haven for refugees" (Kleingeld 1998, 72).

To fully appreciate Kant's contribution to cosmopolitan thinking, it is important to be aware of the specific justification Kant offers for his cosmopolitan law. One might think that Kant employed here the basic assumptions of his moral reasoning, which sees every human being as a member of a kingdom of free rational beings and an end in her- or himself. This is the prominent foundation underlying Kant's *Critique of Practical Reason* and the *Metaphysics of Morals*. Yet, the justification he gives in the political context of *Perpetual Peace* is a different one.

Following again Kleingeld's concise reconstruction of the argument (Kleingeld 1998, 77–79, Kleingeld 2012), Kant's justification for cosmopolitan law is based on a right to communal possession of the earth's surface (cf. 8: 358; ed. Reiss 106),[38] i.e., the idea that land is originally possessed by all before any initial acquisition of property, which would consequently prevent others from taking what now belongs to specific individuals. This understanding of the acquisition of individual property is similar to the acquisition of land by a nation, whose territory consequently cannot be claimed rightfully by foreigners arriving later. "But all parts of the earth […] continue to be thought of as parts of the whole to which everyone had an original right. This […] implies that all nations stand in a community of possible physical interaction" (Kleingeld 1998, 78). The possible physical interaction on the earth's surface, to which originally all humans have a right, seems to be the justification of cosmopolitan law that Kant offers in his political writings. Yet, this remains an incomplete and somewhat unsatisfactory argument, for it is not fully clear how the assumption of the original community of the land, which has been changed into rightfully ac-

---

37 Generally, Kant's relationship to colonialism was complex and shifted over time (cf. Ypi and Flikschuh 2014).

38 Recently, Risse, standing in a long tradition ranging from Grotius to Kant, has suggested such "common ownership of the earth" as a basis for claims and obligations in the context of global justice (Risse 2012).

quired land, can lead, together with the sheer possibility of interaction, to the cosmopolitan right to hospitality.

The difficulties with Kant's justification probably explain why several scholars have suggested an alternative justification, which would have been available to Kant based on his general moral philosophy. In his contribution on the occasion of the 200th anniversary of the publication of *Perpetual Peace*, Habermas briefly points towards an argument for cosmopolitan law based on the fundamental theory of human autonomy and dignity (Habermas 1995, 303–304). Similarly, Nussbaum endorses such a reading of Kant's argument for cosmopolitan law (Nussbaum 1997b, 12) and Kleingeld follows Habermas when she writes that "the innate human right to freedom is all one needs to back up the principle of hospitality. For this right implies precisely the two aspects central to Kant's understanding of the hospitality principle: that prospective visitors have no right to intrude into the sphere of freedom of others against their will, and that neither states nor individuals have the right to refuse visitors when this would lead to the annihilation of their freedom (their destruction)" (Kleingeld 1998, 79).

On both grounds—the actual one offered in *Perpetual Peace* and the hypothesised one that later emerged from readings of his normative understanding of humans as rational beings—Kant's idea to augment constitutional and international law with cosmopolitan law is an important step in the evolution of cosmopolitan thinking. It may actually be best understood as the beginning of the transition from accounts based on natural rights, domestic law and international law, to historically novel modern accounts of individual rights in the context of institutions, such as nations, of which the respective individuals are not a part. While earlier forms of cosmopolitan thinking were spelled out in the form of equal moral standing within a given community (even if it was a global moral community), Kant's innovative suggestion paves the way for institutionalised rights that individuals have as moral subjects vis-à-vis institutional agents like states. He refines cosmopolitan thinking significantly by taking into account the realities of actual states as well as their interests in sovereignty. This formulation has also had a lasting impact on contemporary debates on human rights and international justice.

To conclude this brief discussion of Kant's idea of cosmopolitan law within his *Perpetual Peace*, I want to point to an ambiguity in Kant's writings that has influenced cosmopolitan reasoning ever since, which is his refusal to endorse the idea of a single international state. Kant's argument that a global governmental body with coercive powers would not be desirable for the implicit danger that it may turn into despotism was most notably expanded upon by Rawls. He writes: "I follow Kant's lead in *Perpetual Peace* (1795) in thinking that a world government [...] would either be a global despotism or else would rule over a fragile empire torn by frequent civil strife as various regions and peoples tried to gain their political freedom and autonomy" (Rawls 1999a, 36). Yet, Kant's take on this matter is—in spite of this reference—more ambiguous. This becomes particularly obvious in the paragraph immediately preceding the third definitive article, which spells out the cosmopolitan law. Kant writes:

> There is only one rational way in which states coexisting with other states can emerge from the lawless condition of pure warfare. Just like individual men, they must renounce their savage and lawless freedom, adapt themselves to public coercive laws, and thus form an international state (*civitas gentium*), which would necessarily continue to grow until it embraced all the peoples of the earth. But since this is not the will of the nations, according to their present conception of international right (so that they reject in hypothesi what is true in thesi), the positive idea of a world republic cannot be realised. If all is not to be lost, this can at best find a negative substitute in the shape of an enduring and gradually expanding federation likely to prevent war. (8: 357; ed. Reiss 105)

It is hence the empirical assumption that states will be unwilling to give up their interpretation of state sovereignty and international law, an interpretation that speaks, in Kant's view, against the idea of an international state (*civitas gentium*). Things have changed over the past 200 years, and the development of the League of Nations and the United Nations, as imperfect as they were and remain, have altered the international political landscape significantly. Many states are now actually willing to give up some degree of their sovereignty in order to gain a greater good, as is particularly obvious with the current European Union experiment (as beleaguered as it may be presently). One could also follow Kant's cosmopolitan reasoning with regard to the demand for an international, institutionalised body with at least some, although not unconditional, power.[39]

Kant's arguments have hence further developed the idea of cosmopolitanism and made it available and relevant even today. His distinctive focus on the cosmopolitan law provides a lasting inspiration for and influence upon contemporary cosmopolitans, even though, after Kant, the debates about cosmopolitanism have evolved further and gained more complexity.

---

[39] Others have suggested that Kant may be a "false friend" in his rejecting a world government. After all, Kant favours a world republic over a league of nations and his argument for a league of sovereign states seems strategic, cf. Gerhardt (1995, 103–104), Kleingeld (1998, 83, fn. 19).

3.3 Economic and political cosmopolitanism

During the 19th and 20th century, the moral and political forms of cosmopolitanism were further developed. Given the rapid developments in industrialisation, production and economic exchange, the dominating strain of cosmopolitanism during the time centred on economic relations and challenges.[40] Communist thinkers Karl Marx and Friedrich Engels prominently endorsed cosmopolitanism in their writings, yet with a dual valence (Renton 2002, Henning 2006). On the one hand, they were sharply critical of cosmopolitanism, which they saw as an integral part of the ideology of capitalism. As a capitalist doctrine, cosmopolitanism was understood by such thinkers to have an inherent tendency to expand beyond borders in order to generate more capital and to access ever new markets. Free trade beyond borders can be labelled an economic version of cosmopolitanism since it claims the existence of a single, global market community of all human beings (cf. Nida-Rümelin 2006). According to Marx and Engels, however, such free trade allows the bourgeois class to exploit the whole world, while benefitting only that class and pauperising all others. On the other hand, Marx and Engels themselves suggest a transnational (in other words cosmopolitan) union of the proletariat of all countries to counter the capitalist version of economic cosmopolitanism. The exploitation suffered by the proletarians everywhere inspires a common interest to overcome the class-divided society. The call "Workers of the world, unite!" is meant to establish a cosmopolitan union of proletarians simply on grounds of their shared misery. Ultimately, revolution will follow from such a union, or so Marx and Engels argue. The result of this revolution, in turn, is supposed to be a class-less society which can be understood as "a form of cosmopolitanism of its own" (Kleingeld 2013, 9), because its scope will be truly global and not end at any national border.[41]

The effects of Enlightenment enthusiasm about cosmopolitanism also extended beyond the economic sphere. As already mentioned above, in the *political* domain, many of the ideas endorsed by Kant in his *Perpetual Peace* inspired political reasoning and action. The establishment of the League of Nations in 1920 and, following World War II, of the United Nations in 1945, stand firmly in the Enlightenment tradition. More recent developments like the installation of the International Criminal Court in 2002, also can be understood as steps

---

[40] This section builds on Kleingeld (2013).
[41] Smith, von Hayek and Friedman also defend economic cosmopolitanism as free global trade and open markets; cf. e.g. Forman-Barzilei (2009).

that were already imagined much earlier as necessary contributions to securing peace among the nations.

Furthermore, the codification, refinement and implementation of Human Rights Law in the 20th century are serious attempts to determine precisely the fundamental rights and entitlements that individuals have "simply in virtue of their humanity" (Tasioulas 2012). Important steps after the Universal Declaration from 1948 were the two Covenants from 1976 (the International Covenant on Civil and Political Rights, ICCPR, and the International Covenant on Economic, Social and Cultural Rights, ICESCR) and later steps undertaken to transform the claims of the declaration into actually binding international law.

Cosmopolitan ideas about the limited importance and moral irrelevance of nationality have been practically realised by international aid agencies like *The International Red Cross and Red Crescent Movement*, *Oxfam*, *Partners in Health*, *Médicins du Monde*, *Médicins sans Frontières*, and many others. These organisations aim to help people in need, such as victims of wars, famines, and natural catastrophes, wherever possible. In so doing, they do not restrict the scope of their attention to any specific region or group of individuals (cf. Forsythe and Rieffer-Flanagan 2007).

So far, a sequence of three main steps in the history of cosmopolitan thinking and practice have been identified.[42] Each of them has influenced how the core commitments of cosmopolitanism are understood today. The first focussed on developing the idea of a shared community of all human beings in the poleis of ancient Greece. Here, the idea of global citizenship was already fully developed and central objections as well as important challenges to this idea were spelled out. The second phase enthusiastically developed this ideal further into specific aspects, some of which were even partly realised in some nations. The institutional arrangements within a nation that endorsed cosmopolitan Enlightenment ideas aimed to respect the equal moral standing of each individual citizen. Interestingly, it was the territorially defined nation-state that emerged as the prominent structure of political organisation during the Enlightenment period, and, as with the prior locus in ancient Greece, cosmopolitan ideals were sought largely "within borders". This did, however, explicitly include treating the citizens of *other nations* on one's own territory according to certain cosmopolitan standards. In a third phase, the implementation and realisation of cosmopolitan values began at a global scale, through an extension of economic

---

[42] Of course, there are alternative narratives available, stressing different influences and phases, cf. e.g. Fine and Cohen (2002); for alternatives that stress non-Western traditions, cf. Giri (2006) or Appiah (2007).

trade, and the installation of the first global institutions with specific legal arrangements. This is where we stand today. Progress has been made, albeit slowly. The diverse flaws of generally weak global institutions have even suggested to some that the cosmopolitan idea is without force, hopelessly utopian. It hence remains an open question: Will the refinement and realisation of cosmopolitan values in global institutions continue, and if so, how?

4 The current debate on global justice. A brief overview

Given global inequality levels, the degree of preventable deprivation, and the dynamics of global interaction, it is obvious that our world is unjust. The current debate about *global justice* in political philosophy and related disciplines aims to explain whether—and, if so, which—claims of justice hold at the global level. The point of departure in the debate is this question: To what extent can basic principles of social justice, which are widely shared at least within democratic nation states, be transferred to the global level? And if such a transfer is impossible, which other principles hold at the global level?

In this brief overview, I will introduce some basic distinctions and concepts that shape the current debate about global justice. This debate provides the background for the complementary debate about global political ethics dealt with in this book.

4.1 The scope of justice

Rawls's seminal book *A Theory of Justice* stipulates two principles of justice that ought to hold in a liberal society, and justifies them with the help of a contractarian procedure (Rawls 1971).[43] In a hypothetical situation, which Rawls calls the "original position," the contract partners agree upon two basic principles of justice. They provide the reference to which different possible basic structures of societies can be compared, and through which the best possible, just, and fair order of society can be identified. This original position is characterised by the idea that all parties involved are under a "veil of ignorance". This means that they are free and equal persons ignorant of their own or any other contracting parties' personal characteristics, including sex, gender, 'race', religion, or social

---

[43] Sections 4.1. and 4.2. of the present chapter draw on my contribution to a co-authored article (Heilinger and Pogge 2015).

status in society, all of which Rawls, like cosmopolitans, regards as morally irrelevant. This way, the contracting parties make decisions about principles of justice independently of such morally arbitrary information about themselves, and any of their concomitant special preferences or interests. The principles of justice that, according to Rawls, result from such an ideal deliberation are the following:

> (a) Each person has the same indefeasible claim to a fully adequate scheme of equal basic liberties, which scheme is compatible with the same scheme of liberties for all; and
>
> (b) Social and economic inequalities are to satisfy two conditions: first, they are to be attached to offices and positions open to all under conditions of fair equality of opportunity; and second, they are to be to the greatest benefit of the least-advantaged members of society (the difference principle). (Rawls 2001, 42–43)

Rawls thus demands equality for all members of a society with regard to their basic freedoms. These include, among others, political freedoms (freedom of speech and assembly or active and passive voting rights), as well as freedom of conscience. Under ideal circumstances, inequalities with regard to these basic freedoms are, as a matter of principle, illegitimate.[44] Furthermore, Rawls demands that all have fair, i.e. fundamentally equal, opportunities for holding attractive offices and positions. Fair equality of opportunity means that access to such privileges actually depends on a person's talents and effort and not on, say, her parents' socioeconomic position. If these two conditions are met, thus if all have equal amounts of basic freedoms and compete for offices under conditions of fair equality of opportunity, certain socio-economic inequalities—for example in property or income—may be acceptable. However, for this to be the case, another condition has to be met, namely that special concern is directed towards the worse off: unequal distributions are acceptable only under the condition that these inequalities make the worst off be as well off as possible.

The justification offered by Rawls for his focus on institutions largely depends on the profound influence such institutions have on the life prospects of people living in a society.[45] Consequently, the principles of justice should

---

[44] Under the conditions of non-ideal reality, however, Rawls allows for several exceptions; cf. Rawls (1971, ch. 4).

[45] Rawls argues that "taken together as one scheme, the major institutions define men's rights and duties and influence their life prospects, what they can expect to be and how well they can hope to do. The basic structure is the primary subject of justice because its effects are so profound and present from the start. The intuitive notion here is that this structure contains various

apply to these institutions as "justice is the first virtue of social institutions" (Rawls 1971, 3).

The publication of *A Theory of Justice* initiated an intense debate on social justice in liberal societies which has yet to abate. Rawls's theory still figures prominently in these debates as an original version of "ideal theory" or, as he has it, as a "realistic utopia". Even if the principles are not fully enacted in any society on earth, it is imaginable and desirable from the point of view of a theory of justice that they be so; or so argues Rawls, who himself explicitly restricted the scope of his *Theory of Justice* to nation state-societies; in the international realm, different rules supporting peaceful cooperation among peoples and international assistance in cases of emergency apply (Rawls 199a).

Soon after the first publication of *A Theory of Justice*, several scholars attempted to extend Rawls's liberal theory, and his contractarian approach, beyond the nation state to the international setting. Why should the principles of justice be only applicable *within* the borders of a state, they asked, but not on a global scale? Furthermore, it became more and more obvious that Rawls's understanding of nations as generally self-sufficient and isolated entities, no longer matched emerging political realities (cf. Buchanan 2000). This is why Beitz (1979) and Pogge (1989) considered in depth the possibility of a global extension of Rawls's contractarian model, and became influential thinkers in their own right. Their aim was to strive for social justice on a global scale (or cosmopolitan Rawlsianism). Contrary to Rawls's focus on the nation state, Beitz and Pogge endorse, in their respective accounts of global justice, a distinctively cosmopolitan perspective.

With this, the two poles between which the complex and diverse current debate on global justice unfolds can be distinguished. On the one hand are advocates of cosmopolitanism, who claim that substantial principles of justice exist on an international level and apply globally, similar to those at the domestic scale (cf. Gosepath 2001). These principles impose duties of justice upon both citizens and governments—e.g., with regard to the design and enforcement of supranational social institutions. On the other hand, there are defenders of *particularism*—or *statism* or *nationalism*, cf. Valentini (2011, 2)—whose aim is to restrict the duties of justice to the near range of a commonly shared institutional order. According to such views, a state's responsibility for just structures within its own territory has priority over any other possible moral or political responsibilities in

---

social positions and that men born into different positions have different expectations of life determined, in part, by the political system as well as by economic and social circumstances" (Rawls 1999b, 6–7).

global relations. Both positions, cosmopolitanism and particularism, are not only important to political philosophy but also have implications for the field of ethics, for example with regard to the determination of individual agents' moral duties. In the following, I will explore the assumptions basic to both positions.

4.2 Cosmopolitanism vs. particularism

Above, I mentioned three normative properties defining cosmopolitanism: *normative individualism* (every single human being—and not, say, groups or states—is of ultimate moral importance); *egalitarianism* or *impartiality* (every single human being is of equal moral importance, all have the same moral status and, accordingly, the claims of all need to count equally); and *universalism* (all human beings stand in relations of justice to one another, which are comparable to the relations between citizens of a state). On the basis of the assumption of moral equality, cosmopolitanism demands of moral agents, at least prima facie, that they grant unknown people from other countries the same moral importance as their compatriots and people in their near range. What practically follows from cosmopolitanism is, on the one hand, an obligation that every *single moral agent* consider (and act to prevent or limit) the harm of faraway people and, on the other hand, the requirement that, in an *institutional way*, it be guaranteed that the interests of all human beings are given the same weight.

These considerations point toward the possibility of several variants of cosmopolitanism: first, there is *moral* cosmopolitanism, which focusses on the moral rights and duties of individuals in the international context. This must be distinguished from *political* or *institutional* cosmopolitanism, which focusses primarily on the rights and duties of political institutions. A third form of cosmopolitanism shall at least briefly be mentioned, namely *cultural* cosmopolitanism. Here, rights and duties of individuals or institutions are of lesser importance than the development of cultures in the age of globalisation. Cultural cosmopolitanism opposes assumptions of static cultural "purity" and emphasises that cultures necessarily develop through dealings with other communities and changing environments. Such cultural changes, and the emergence of hybrids of different cultures are, according to cultural cosmopolitanism, the adequate response to a globalised world (cf. Waldron 2000).

Moral and political cosmopolitanism also come in different shades according to how strong the normative demands are formulated. One can distinguish a "moderate" version from a "strict" version of cosmopolitanism. "Moderate" cosmopolitanism only holds that all human beings are of equal moral importance and have fundamentally equal claims of justice to conditions of a minimally decent life, without, however, placing any particularly demanding obligations upon those who are capable of realising these conditions. As so little is gained from such a position, it has been criticised as only minimally insightful (Miller 2002). "Strict" cosmopolitanism, on the other hand, demands of all agents that other human beings be treated equally for their equal moral status. This, in turn, may lead to extreme demands upon moral agents, which are practically impossible to discharge and therefore implausible (Miller 2002, Pogge 2007, 328).

In contrast to cosmopolitan views, *particularist* positions stipulate a restricted scope for the application of principles of justice, usually to the nation state. Moreover, particularism attaches special moral importance to group membership. Accordingly, it is at least morally permissible, and sometimes even demanded, that greater moral weight be assigned to the interests of people in the near range. The moral rights and duties in the near range thus differ from those on the global level. Examples are the special moral weight of family members and friends for an individual agent, or the preferential treatment of a state's citizen by its institutions, both of which imply a particular responsibility for certain (groups of) people and, at the same time, a lower responsibility for those who are not family members, friends, or compatriots. According to particularists, cosmopolitanism fails to capture this commonly held and rarely questioned intuition about the fundamental and important moral difference between all human beings and those nearer and dearer to an agent (Miller 2002).

Particularism hence contains three normative features:
- *Egalitarianism/Universalism:* Just like cosmopolitanism, particularist positions also hold that all human beings have the same fundamental moral status, and they oppose discrimination by sex, skin colour, nationality, etc. There is, in short, no difference between particularist and cosmopolitan views on this matter, and barring extreme views—racist, sexist and otherwise (with which I do not engage)—egalitarianism is now very broadly accepted and endorsed. The substantial differences between cosmopolitan and particularist views do not lie in the basic conviction that all human beings are equally important moral subjects, but rather in the question of what exactly follows from this assumption. In particular, there is disagreement on what instances of unequal treatment and unequal distribution can be justified in light of the equal moral standing of all.
- *The particular importance of groups:* Instead of endorsing normative individualism, particularists hold that groups of people may have moral value and can give rise to genuinely particular duties of justice. A family, a club, or an entire country, have genuine intrinsic value, independent of the instrumental value of the advantages that membership confers on those in the

group. The actions that enact this value must be morally acceptable. In this vein, Miller has argued that certain forms of preference and partiality for compatriots are legitimate—which implies that diminished obligations exist towards non-compatriots (Miller 2005).
- *Restricted scope of justice:* Particularists hence argue for more constrained principles and duties within certain groups. A normative argument for restricting the scope of justice to the state level is that justice in the narrower sense is understood as a property of institutions (Rawls 1971, 3). The realm of individual action between individuals, or the realm of international interaction beyond national borders, where there is no superordinate institutional order, is consequently excluded from the evaluation via established principles of justice (Nagel 2005). A consequence of this position is that—at least as long as there is no global institutional order—there will be no relations of justice (in the narrow sense) on a global level. The rights, for example, of people suffering from hardship within a poor country engage only that state's institutions (however weak they may be), and only in certain exceptional cases (such as historic tort) can there be claims upon other, richer states or their citizens. If wealthier countries choose to help the poor in other countries, this certainly is, according to particularists, a morally praiseworthy act of assistance, but would not constitute the discharging of a duty of justice.

Particularism presents a position that closely matches the status quo reality of our current world of nation states. Cosmopolitanism, on the other hand, appears more idealistic and utopian. Because of this, particularism can be seen to provide a moral justification of the existing state of global affairs.

In their extreme and purest forms, neither strict cosmopolitanism nor strict particularism are particularly convincing. Both neglect important insights that figure prominently in the other. That I should treat a person I do not know from a country I have never heard of in the same way as I treat my own child is just as implausible as the assumption that Japan's public health insurance ought to cover the medical costs of Mexican patients in Mexico. On the other hand, it is also implausible to think that special concern for the already well-off people in my in-group should be able to trump the most basic needs of people who happen not to be members of my group; it is also implausible that norms of justice must generally remain confined to contingent entities like states.

Applied to concrete cases, for example of world poverty or inequality in access to health care, the extreme positions often contribute very little in the way of helpful and practically relevant guidance. Extreme cosmopolitanism is quickly dismissed as utopian and unrealistic, and strict particularism often is not even capable of acknowledging why a *duty* of justice beyond mere voluntary generosity should exist towards distant strangers and states in the first place. The most interesting debates today are thus found in between these two poles, and have to do with approaches to accommodating both cosmopolitan and particularist intuitions.

4.3 Metrics and patterns of just distributions

According to the (Rawlsian inspired) understanding of justice as a virtue of institutions, a prominent question is how these institutions distribute the advantages or goods people need in order to live a good life. This question is pertinent on both the domestic and the global level. A central element of the debate on global justice is hence the distributive question: *Who* should get *how much* of *what*? Rawls has suggested a distinctive distributive theory of justice in which basic social goods are distributed equally, while economic inequalities are acceptable if and only if the unequal distribution occurs under conditions of fair equality of opportunity, and if and only if the unequal distribution is altogether maximally beneficial to the worst-off in society. Rawls's theory of justice hence answers the question of *what* should be distributed (social primary goods, opportunities and economic resources) and *how* it should be distributed (equally and with special priority to the worst off). His answer indicates that there are several options with regard to the two question about the "currency" or "metric" of justice on the one hand and about the "patterns" of distribution on the other.

Let us focus on the "currency" or "metric" of justice first. Is the advantage to be distributed a resource (like fundamental rights), or an all-purpose economic good (like money), or is it actual well-being, or opportunities to achieve certain goods, or is it still something else? I will mention the main answers to this question of what should be distributed, since they play a particularly important role in the current debates about global justice.[46]

To provide an admittedly simplified reconstruction of the ongoing complex debates, one can distinguish three main views when it comes to answering the question what should be the currency or metric of justice, or what should be distributed in a certain way in a just society: resources, welfare or capabilities/functionings. Resources and capabilities can be called "objective" metrics of justice

---

[46] For this brief overview over a very fine grained and complex debate I rely on Anderson (2010c), Arneson (1989), Dworkin (2000), and Brock (2011).

because they determine justice by referring to objectively measurable states of individuals or their possessions; well-being, on the other hand, is a subjective metric since it relies upon the subjective evaluative states of individuals with regard to their happiness or preferences (Anderson 2010c, 85). I will only briefly review these metrics and, for introductory purposes, will assume that we aspire to achieve such an equal distribution. I will then complicate matters, towards the end of this section, by briefly mentioning alternatives to this pattern of distribution: besides equality one could consider priority, sufficiency and adequacy as patterns.

As an obvious candidate for determining what should be distributed in a certain way in a just society, *resources* come first to mind. Resources are an objective metric of justice since they can be externally assessed and measured (Dworkin 2000). In Rawls's theory, which is fundamentally resourcist, the social primary goods are a way of spelling out the basic needs of individuals. Accordingly, the distribution of social primary goods is what matters for a just society. The basic goods Rawls lists are diverse and include rights (both civil and political rights), liberties, income and wealth, the social bases of self-respect, and others. Often, the distribution of money is taken as a valid proxy for assessing the distribution of resources generally, since money, as an all-purpose good, can be easily transformed into several different goods according to the preferences of the agent.

Yet, there are problems with distributing resources that have led some to claim that it would be preferable to be concerned about a just distribution of actual well-being. A first obvious problem is that equal amounts of, say, money, do not secure that people are equally well off. Let us assume that two people, A and B, have equal preferences and generally equal abilities, but that B suffers from a physical handicap that makes it necessary for him to rely on costly medical aid to move. An equal distribution of resources to both will disadvantage B significantly since he would have to spend much of his available resources to establish his mobility which A gets "for free," such that A has more resources available to promote his interests.

Dworkin, a defender of resourcism, discussed this objection and suggested, as a way forward, that personal endowments and talents be included among the resources that are to be distributed equally (Dworkin 2000, ch. 2).[47] Focussing on actual external resources like money fails to take into account such personal resources. But Dworkin's suggestion faces a problem, as he acknowledged himself:

---

47 Rawls had excluded these goods, which he called natural primary goods (intelligence, imagination, health, etc.), from being taken into account for an equal distribution.

the "slavery of the talented" objection (Dworkin 2000, 90). If personal inborn differences are to be counted among the resources to be distributed, those with better endowments might be compelled to give away their resources indefinitely in order to compensate those with lesser endowments. This, however, would result in a relative disadvantage, and even some kind of punishment for those who are born with talents. But punishing people for something which is completely beyond their control, is morally objectionable. So, measuring distribution in terms of resources faces significant challenges and might generate counter-intuitive, even unjust requirements.

Against resourcism, others have claimed that measuring the actual *welfare* of people provides the appropriate metric of justice.[48] Welfare could be understood as the actual well-being or degree of happiness of a person, but in the debates about utilitarian standards, the satisfaction of ideally considered preferences has proven to be superior to the rather blunt standard of happiness ("preference utilitarianism"). Again, space constraints here rule out an extensive discussion of the many difficulties raised by establishing such standards, but it is clear that, as the metric of justice, comparing the welfare of people has some important advantages over comparing the resources available to them, since this places the focus on what matters most, which is on how people are actually doing. But here yet another problem appears, since people can end up with very different states of well-being simply by virtue of their reasonable choices. Would it then be appropriate to distribute the necessary means to achieve certain levels of well-being in such a way that also "expensive" preferences of people are met? What if I have an acquired taste such that only eating caviar makes me happy? What if my decision to be politically active and to improve the situation of the poor in my country counts more for me than my personal motivation to achieve levels of welfare? Should people be forced to reach certain levels of well-being if this is the metric of justice? Such questions indicate that actual levels of welfare might also be quite far from being a suitable metric of justice.

These challenges have led some to defend *opportunities* for achieving welfare (Arneson 1989) or *capabilities* to achieve functioning (Sen 1992) as the metric of justice, which indeed offer a particularly fruitful way of measuring justice. Arneson writes: "An opportunity is a chance of getting a good if one seeks it" (Arneson 1989, 85). He explains further that equal opportunity for welfare among a number of persons demands that each person encounters equivalent sets of op-

---

[48] This view presupposes that it is possible to make sound interpersonal comparisons of subjective mental states, which will, of course, be more difficult than to compare objective resources, but let us assume that this is possible.

tions to achieve satisfaction of his or her rational preferences. They do not have to be the same options, but overall they have to add up to the same prospect of achieving well-being. People do not have to end up achieving the same levels of well-being, but they are to have equal opportunities to do so. It will be still up to the individuals themselves to decide and to act freely. The development of personal preferences and decisions (for example to trade well-being against other goods, such as the pursuit of political activism) are still available to individuals.

The capabilities approach, developed by Sen and Nussbaum, offers a structurally analogous way of determining the goods that are to be distributed in a just setting. Here again, the advantage in question is not the actual fulfillment or the actual exercise of certain actions, but the capability, i.e., the real opportunity to do or be what is valued.[49] This freedom to achieve functioning is of primary moral importance, because it not only captures well-being and advantage but also the "well-being freedom" that itself contributes directly to well-being.

Among capability theorists there is a great deal of dispute about whether it is necessary to provide a comprehensive list of capabilities in order to be able to assess and compare individual well-being, and the various forms of social arrangements under which individuals do (or conceivably could) live. Sen has denied this need of the capability approach, and has defended its "incompleteness" (Sen 1992, 46), while Nussbaum has repeatedly suggested a list of basic capabilities, among them life, bodily health and integrity, practical reason, affiliation, play, and control over one's environment (e.g. Nussbaum 2006, 76–78).

The notion of "well-being freedom" (Sen 1992, 40), central to the capabilities approach, captures well the advantages of this view[50]: it is not narrowly focussed on the distribution of resources but concerned with people's actually accessible options, while still leaving room for the individual preferences and decisions of people who may often be willing to exchange higher levels of personal well-being in order to achieve other goals.[51]

---

[49] Terminologically there is an important difference for capability theorists between the "functionings," i.e., the "beings and doings" of a person, his or her states and activities on the one hand, and the "capabilities," i.e., a person's (set of) real freedoms or opportunities to achieve certain functionings. Capabilities are hence the effectively possible valuable opportunities available to a person.

[50] This holds true for both its "incomplete" and its "determined" variant, and also for the opportunities for achieving welfare approach.

[51] Already here, I want to hint towards a critique of the largely resourcist accounts of luck egalitarianism that will figure prominently in chapter two below. According to criticism by Anderson (1999), the focus in theories of justice about matters of distribution misses the fundamental point of the idea of egalitarian justice. It is not of prior importance to determine who should get how much of what, but it is important that people interact with one another as equals,

Of these three different attempts to define (non-relational) goods that must be distributed in a certain way in order to be just, the capabilities approach is the one which is most closely related to relational theories of justice, since it aims to secure the possibility for each to develop his or her human capacities undominated by others. But, in order to fully cover the current debate about justice, let us turn to the different *patterns* according to which certain types of advantage (which we now know can be expressed in different metrics or currencies of justice) can or should be distributed.

Assuming that a decision in favour of any one of the different goods has been made, what exactly would we want the distribution of that good to look like? Which "pattern of distribution" should be aimed for? Generally, there are three main options available. First, it could be claimed that each individual should have equal shares of the respective good.[52] Such an *egalitarian* intuition comes to mind quickly, but is subject to the notorious "levelling down objection," which points out that equality can also be reached by diminishing everyone's level of advantage to the level of the worst off. Alternatively, it could be claimed that inequality is not problematic *per se*, but only when it is so severe that the worst off are very badly off indeed, and thus deserve special concern and attention. All distributions thus should assign priority to those worse off than others. Such a *prioritarian* pattern of distribution has been defended, among others, by Parfit, and also by Rawls.[53] Third, it can be argued that inequality is not always problematic and that giving priority to the worst off is also at least sometimes not the point (e.g., if the least advantaged are already extremely well off), so that the prior concern of justice should be in promoting that all have *enough* (for living a minimally decent life). Such a *sufficientarian* view stipulates a threshold to be reached by all, above which certain degrees

---

which would lead them to resolving questions about distribution in cooperative ways. From this perspective, generally known as a relational view, matters of distribution are less important for theories of justice than are matters of how people interact with one another (whether people interact with one another as equals or within hierarchies where some are oppressed, dominated, silenced, etc.). Distributive inequalities are often symptomatic of underlying inequalities in social standing and, of course, massive inequalities that place some below a reasonable threshold of sufficiency are of particular concern for relational theorists. The relational view has significant distributive implications of course, but the core concern for relational theorists of justice is not the distribution of advantage but the quality and the structures of interaction.
52 Prominent egalitarian views can be found in Rawls's first principle of justice (Rawls 1971), in Arneson's defence of equal opportunity for welfare (Arneson 1989) and in Dworkin's theory of equal resources (Dworkin 2000).
53 Rawls's difference principle claims priority for the worst off (Rawls 1971); cf. also Parfit (1997).

of inequality are acceptable.[54] Among sufficientarian approaches, there is ongoing debate about the formulation of more ambitious "adequacy" thresholds (cf. e.g. Satz 2007). These would not just call for a minimally decent threshold but set more ambitious demands that would allow people to live a more than minimally decent life, to be functioning well as full citizens in a democratic society (Anderson 1999), or maybe even as global citizens in the world (see below, chapter two, section four).

4.4 Global structural injustice

The introduction already briefly mentioned structural injustice as a particular moral wrong which systematically disadvantages large groups of people while others are enjoying privileges that are generated at the expense of the disadvantaged people (Young 2011).[55] Global structural injustice is characterised by three particular features. First, the distinctive metric of structural injustice is the quality of the relations and connections between people that is shaped by inequality, hierarchy, systematic exploitation and domination. However, unequal distributions of resources and welfare can also be indicative of relational inequalities. The second feature is, that this form of injustice is deeply embedded in social structures. A structure can be understood as "a set of rules and resources recursively implicated in the reproduction of social systems in a way that both presupposes and creates certain patterned constraints on agents' positions and on the degree of social and political power that they control" (Ypi 2017, 9). The place of structural injustice hence consists of the acts and interactions of persons in a shared social framework, encouraging or disencouraging certain patterns of individual or collective behaviour through mechanisms like social expectations or economic, political or legal regulations. Such structures exist not only within the domestic sphere but they extend, in an interconnected world, around the globe. A third distinctive feature of structural injustice is that such injustice can occur without malevolent intent and without causally decisive and identifiably culpable behaviour. Instead, such injustice is deeply embedded in the *accepted social background conditions* of peoples's lives and may result from apparently innoc-

---

[54] Cf. Anderson (1999), Frankfurt (1987), and Nussbaum (2011a). For an overview, cf. Fourie (2017).
[55] A much discussed example are global economic interactions linking workers producing apparell under exploitative conditions with consumers elsewhere. Cf. below, chapter four, section four.

uous actions and decisions, when people or groups of people follow their seemingly unproblematic and fully legal preferences. The injustice in question is hence often a problematic result of the behaviour of persons who do nothing which they would consider particularly wrong.[56]

Three main strategies can be distinguished to justify that the privileged individuals bear moral responsibility in the face of global structural injustice: individuals can be said to have contributed to causing or upholding the problem; they can enjoy unjustified advantages; and they can be in a position to contribute to ending a severe moral problem. The underlying idea for each strategy is that a morally relevant connection or relation exists between the disadvantaged and the advantaged people generating responsibility for members of the advantaged group, i.e. the rather affluent, morally sensible, well-informed and capable citizens in the industrialised countries of the Global North. These connections, however, are of very different kinds.

Many of the large scale problems, particularly the consequences of climate change and the injustices in the global market, are influenced by aggregated individual behaviour. While probably no-one intended to cause global warming by greenhouse gas emissions, all those who contributed to the increase of greenhouse gases in the atmosphere are – albeit only in a minuscule way—part of the group that collectively caused the problem at hand. It has been subject to debate whether such minuscule contributions that in themselves do not cause any measurable or perceptible harm generate some kind of moral responsibility. But a strong argument from tort law can be put forward to justify responsibility also in these cases: as a member of the group whose collective behaviour caused a problem, one is a "necessary element of a sufficient set" and hence also personally, causally responsible for its existence (Wright 1985). Being part of the problem (even if the problem would not be solved had one acted differently) assigns a share of causal responsibility to all persons involved, and as such those who have caused the problem should also bear a responsibility to deal with it and to provide solutions (Barry and Macdonald 2016). This holds true even if individual agents cannot be said to have been contributing to bringing the problem into existence in the first place: Even if their actions contribute only to upholding the problem, they are entangled in it and bear moral responsibility both for its persistence and for addressing it (Pogge 2008).

---

[56] This, of course, does not exclude the possibility that global structural injustice may in some cases result from or be increased by careless or straightforward malevolent actions; cf. the discussion in Young (2011).

Such connections—and the resulting relations of responsibility—become clearer and weightier, if the problematic structures are seen as conveying unjustified advantages to some—at the cost of corresponding, unjustified disadvantages suffered by others. The opportunities of citizens in high-income countries (e. g. to drive in polluting, private cars or to purchase cheap clothing or to vacation in low-income countries) are a flip-side of limited opportunities of others elsewhere (who have, e. g., to deal with rising sea-levels, have to work in factories under sweat shop conditions, or whose economies are disadvantaged by international trade regulations). On this account, it is simply inadequate to limit the normative assessment of the quality of citizen's actions to the immediate outcomes in the near range: the complex global background-conditions need to be considered as well; if they appear as morally dubious, even massively unjust, then the seemingly innocent activities of well-intended citizens in Western societies become morally questionable. The enjoyment of unjustified advantage thus indicates specific connections and responsibilities (Butt 2007, Calder 2010). Iris M. Young's seminal argument from "social connections" is the paradigmatic version of this argument: The ongoing social connections that constitute the shared framework of structurally unjust interaction establish a link of responsibility between the beneficiaries of these structures and those suffering the generated disadvantages (Young 2011).

Another type of arguments for individual responsibility—more controversial than the preceding ones because it assumes only a loose connection between the advantaged and the disadvantaged—is not based on any claims about actual social or causal connectedness or the enjoyment of advantages. Rather, it stipulates the sheer ability to help someone in distress to be sufficient to generate some degree of personal responsibility to do so.[57] Given the urgency of the need of a disadvantaged person or group, being capable of addressing it constitutes already a morally relevant relationship and connection: the fact that someone's fate existentially depends on what an agent does establishes a relation, even though an asymmetric one in which only one side has the privilege to act about the disadvantage or need in question. Such a relation, shaped by unilateral vulnerability, persists even if it is not developed further; i. e. when those who could initiate an actual interaction remain passive. Yet, refusing to take action does not eliminate the channel of connection. In such cases, omissions to act should be understood as passive contributions to global structural injustice.

---

[57] In the context of human rights, for example, Sen argues convincingly: "Human rights generate reasons for action for agents who are in a position to help in the promoting or safeguarding of the underlying freedoms" that go "beyond volunteered charity or elective virtues" (Sen 2004, 319). Cf. also Griffin (2008, 102) and Ashford (2007).

These different connections or relations, often hidden or unacknowledged, link those suffering from the structural injustice in question with those who are better off and, in consequence, justify individual, forward-looking responsibility.

In sum, the notion of global structural injustice provides a concept pointing to the often hidden *connections* between the advantages enjoyed by some and the disadvantages suffered by others. As such the diagnosis of global structural injustice helps one to see through the surface of morally problematic states of affairs to the fundamental structures generating them within a shared system of interaction. The relevant form of injustice in the case of global structural injustice is primarily *relational*, not distributive: it is about relationships of domination, of privilege, power and exploitation, which, as part of social patterns and structures, do not have to follow from malevolent intent. Subsequent distributive inequalities—with regard to income, wealth, access to resources and opportunities for example—are indicative of these fundamentally relational inequalities. Given the complexity of global structural injustice and its deep rootedness in widely shared standard patterns of interaction and behaviour, remedying them will certainly be difficult. Significant political and social reforms leading to institutional and individual changes in interaction and behaviour seem to be necessary. However, the massive and obvious institutional shortcomings in effectively addressing global structural injustice point to the question of whether nothing else can be done or whether there are no other bearers of responsibility. Or, to put it more concretely: What is the role and the responsibility of individual persons in fighting the distinctive wrong of global structural injustice?

5 Global justice and global ethics

Now more than ever, it is necessary to address the signature challenges of our globalised world—global poverty, global inequality, global warming and climate change, global trade etc.—from an institutional perspective with a focus on the role of institutional agents, international agreements and structures of interaction. Nevertheless, it is not my ambition to contribute to this side of the debate. Rather, the catastrophic global state of affairs provides the relevant normative background for my project. While we see that the current institutional system does not prevent massive inequalities nor secures sufficient well-being for all, and while the important debate continues about how feasible and effective institutional arrangements would look like, more focus is needed on the role and responsibility of individual agents right now. While it is clear that many (institutional and individual, collective and national) agents *fail* to do what is necessary in order to solve the problems we face globally, this must not serve as an excuse for individual inaction which can be understood as "passive injustice".[58] Rather, the question is: How should—capable and willing—moral agents think about their roles and responsibilities in a world which is shaped by ongoing injustice? How should we determine the moral demands we are subject to in the absence of a just world order?

In other words, the challenge is to develop a *global ethics* to guide individual actions in a world in which global justice is (as yet) out of reach. This individual ethical dimension is under-explored in current debates about global justice, which continue to suffer from Rawls's decision to focus on institutional arrangements at the cost of neglecting the role of individual agents. I want to stress again that my interest lies in complementing such ongoing debates with an analysis of the role of the individual, without denying the importance of institutional concerns. It is not a shortcoming of these debates that they have such a focus, but in a time when meaningful success on the global institutional level appears distant, it is important to dedicate attention to individuals, their actions and their inaction, as a possible additional avenue for seeking such progress. In this section, I will first explain my view on the relationship between *institutions and individuals*, before discussing the possibility and the limits of a meaningful *division of moral labour* in the present context.

---

[58] The claim that inaction under conditions of structural injustice is morally problematic is also supported by Judith Shklar's concept of "passive injustice" which can be found among those who could and should be doing something about it. Passive injustice is a distinctively civic failure if citizens "fail to stop private and public acts of injustice" (Shklar 1990, 6). Such passive injustice goes beyond the basic general indifference one might have towards the suffering and misery of others, because it presupposes the existence of relationships in a shared framework. Shklar explains: "As citizens, we are passively unjust [...] when we do not report crimes, when we look the other way when we see cheating and minor thefts, when we tolerate political corruption, and when we silently accept laws that we regard us unjust, unwise, or cruel." (ibd.) While Shklar discusses the concept of passive injustice in a domestic, I contend that it is also applicable to the global domain, when "citizens of the world" tacitly tolerate and accept structures, laws, and patterns of international interaction that are shaped by domination, exploitation and thus systematically disadvantage large groups of people. Those enjoying the corresponding advantages, if they fail to acknowledge these processes and do not speak up against them, even deny the existence of such problematic relations, are in their passivity integral and constitutive elements of the injustice, they become silently complicit.

5.1 Individuals and institutions

The relationship between individuals and institutions is complex and I cannot here do justice to the intricate debates in sociology and social ontology. But I contend that individuals are ontologically and morally prior to institutions, where the latter are understood as complex social forms that emerged over time in social life, with an ability to reproduce themselves and to endure (cf. Miller 2014). This claim is meant to support the importance of directing attention to the role and responsibilities of individuals to promote justice even though one would, under more ideal circumstances, wish that institutions deliver it. The notion "institution" itself is ambiguous and refers to diverse phenomena, such as governments, the family, universities, hospitals, business corporations, and the legal system, all of them shaping social practices, i.e. the ways individuals behave and interact. Institutions, however, have been brought into existence over time by humans, sometimes more and sometimes less intentionally, most often in order to serve specific purposes. Frequently, those purposes have to do with some sort of individual or collective human need. Here is an example: the need to get mail carried from a to b is the point of the institution of a postal service. In order to secure a task effectively without obliging everybody to do it her- or himself, work can be organised, divided and distributed to some, with the help of an institution. This implies conversely that without a need of persons to have their mail taken from a to b, there would be no point for the institution of postal service. Frequently, institutions mirror existing (problematic) power structures, examples would be the institutions of monarchy or the caste system. And the absence of institutions can indicate a lack of interest or commitment to a certain cause. So, existing institutions require scrutiny, and identifying unmet needs and social problems invites considering the creation of institutions.

One upshot of this understanding of institutions is that they do not have an independent "life" of their own, detached from individual persons. Ontologically, institutions depend on persons for at least two reasons: because individuals's needs and acts led to the creation of institutions in the first place and because individuals uphold institutions.[59] I find this priority of individuals also expressed in the writings of Dewey who claims: "Instead of thinking of our own dispositions and habits as accommodated to certain institutions we have to learn to think of the latter as expressions, projections and extensions of habitually dom-

---

[59] In cases where institutions develop a "life" on their own, like a hyper-bureaucracy as described in Franz Kafka's writings, individuals feel alienated and objectified. Yet, this is rather a perversion of the original function and point of institutions, and this possibility of things going awry does not speak against my claims.

inant personal attitudes" (Dewey 1939, 226). Also in the context of debating moral questions, individuals can be understood as remaining the primary bearers of responsibility. Nussbaum has made a similar argument in the context of her capabilities approach. She writes: "Institutions are made by people, and it is ultimately people who should be seen as having moral duties to promote human capabilities." (Nussbaum 2006, 307).

The lasting importance of individuals in the functioning and shaping of institutions backs my claim about the ontological and moral priority of individuals. Institutions, as *patterns* of human behaviour or interaction, need actual humans to fill them with life. This, however, provides individuals with the constant possibility of transferring their individual spirit or ethos to the institutions which they comprise. Of course, the bigger and the more established institutions become, the bigger becomes their inertia and the smaller becomes the potential impact of any single individual attempting to influence an institution's functioning. But individuals remain responsible not only for bringing the right institutions into existence. In the case of already existing institutions, they remain responsible for influencing their functioning in the right way.

The basic distinction between individuals, individual agency and the realm of *ethics* on the one side, and institutions, institutional agency and the realm of *justice* on the other, serves as a helpful starting point for structuring an immensely complex debate about different agents of and responsibility for (global) justice. Yet, as we will see, there is significant overlap between both sides: institutions and social backgrounds influence individual behaviour; and individual acts shape social and institutional arrangements. The influence between individuals and institutions is mutual.[60] Thus, when institutional action is absent or inadequate to reach some sufficiently important goal, individuals themselves are ultimately called upon to secure what, under ideal conditions, could fall under the responsibility of an effective institution (e. g. realising justice or securing basic needs of other persons). A global ethics, outlining the responsibilities of individuals, hence is—at least for the time being under non-ideal conditions—an important complement to theories of global justice.

---

[60] More on the individual ethos of a person, understood as an intra-personal 'institution,' in the concluding chapter below.

5.2 The division of moral labour

The analysis of the role and responsibilities of individual agents is pertinent also in the debate about a possible "division of (moral) labour" with regard to realising (global) justice. Maybe some tasks can be taken over by institutions, others by individuals, so that in some cases some agents are *not* called upon? Rawls gave an important impulse to this debate for the domestic context. He defended the need for a division of moral labour—for separating principles for just institutions from rules for individual conduct—as a consequence of moral pluralism.[61] "The principles of justice for institutions must not be confused with the principles which apply to individuals and their actions in particular circumstances. These two kinds of principles apply to different subjects and must be discussed separately" (Rawls 1971, 54–55). Once there are adequate institutions within a just 'basic structure of society,' individuals are allowed to "lead their lives in such a way as to honour the [different] values appropriate to small-scale interpersonal relationships" (Scheffler 2005, 236).[62] And indeed, institutions and individuals are distinct entities and types of agents, and thus it seems implausible to demand that both act exactly in the same way guided by exactly the same rules and principles. On the other hand, however, one could ask why the same basic aims, values, and principles of justice, if they are sufficiently important, should not apply to both types of agents, individual and institutional, even if their respective obligations will be different in kind. Specifically, one should ask: Should individuals be morally *permitted* to *neglect* their individual roles and their possible contributions, however minimal, to addressing massive social and global problems of justice? Are they allowed instead to confine their moral concern to the values and challenges of their own personal, individual lives and immediate surroundings? In other words, what should a possible division of moral labour look like if adequate institutions to secure justice are absent?

---

[61] See Scheffler's reconstruction of Rawls's original argument (Scheffler 2005, 237–240).
[62] Elsewhere, Rawls argued that the "principles of justice, and in particular the difference principle, apply to the main public principles and policies that regulate social and economic inequalities. They are used to adjust the system of entitlement and earnings and to balance the familiar everyday standards and precepts which this system employs. [...] It applies to the announced system of public law and statutes and *not to the particular transactions and distributions, nor to the decisions of individuals and associations, but rather to the institutional background against which these transactions and decisions take place*" (Rawls 1996, 282–283, my italics).

Rawls's argument exposes his rather narrow focus on ideal theory, inquiring about what a just society would look like and considering what is demanded from different agents in these circumstances.[63] But since we cannot assume that our current social or global arrangements are already just, this account does not suffice: it remains silent when it comes to determining what agents are obliged to do under circumstances that are dramatically unjust. Pointing out that individuals may under favourable circumstances legitimately place value on the pursuit of their personal interests appears to me as potentially misleading and overly lenient in the face of the urgency of the problem of global injustice and in the face of the possible impact of individual action.[64]

Thus I contend that, if the institutions, laws and norms necessary for establishing justice are either inexistent or ineffective, the goal of justice should be directly taken on by individuals. The value of justice in itself is sufficiently important to demand action from *whoever* is able to do something about it. And even a possible division of labour that would provide individuals with more discretion, once just and effective institutions secure justice, would not let individuals off the hook.

5.3 Towards an egalitarian ethos

Cohen has criticised the implications of Rawls's theory of justice and the suggested division of labour. Against Rawls, he underlined the importance of an "egalitarian ethos" held by the individual members of a *just* society. Cohen famously asked, *if you are an egalitarian, how come you are so rich?*, and in doing so exposed the double standard applied by many rather affluent individuals when they hold egalitarian views but do not consistently act according to them (Cohen 1997, 2000, 2008). Cohen criticised Rawls for permitting individuals unlimited self-interest in economic choices, as long as it takes place within a just basic structure and respects the rules and laws of such a society (Cohen 1997, 16). Rawls's division of labour limits the demands of justice to institutional

---

[63] For the distinction between ideal theory and non-ideal theory, cf. Simmons (2010) and Valentini (2012).
[64] "If this division of labour can be established, individuals and associations are then left free to advance their ends more effectively within the framework of the basic structure, secure in the knowledge that elsewhere in the system the necessary corrections to preserve background justice are being made" (Rawls 1996, 269). This view has triggered Cohen's objection against Rawls, more on which in the following section.

agents and hence lets individual agents off the hook too quickly.[65] The "egalitarian ethos" defended by Cohen would motivate individuals to act according to the values endorsed in the theory of justice. Such an "ethos of justice" would then also "inform [...] individual choices" (Cohen 2000, 128).

But how should an "ethos" be understood? Wolff has offered a useful and concise characterisation of an ethos as

> a set of underlying values, which may be explicit or implicit, interpreted as a set of maxims, slogans, or principles, which are then applied in practice. As an idealization we can identify three levels: values, principles, and practice, all of which are part of the group's ethos. Typically the values and principles will be internalized by members of that group, and inform their behavior. We can talk of the ethos of a particular society, or of a smaller group, and can raise the question of whether, and how strongly, a particular individual shares the social ethos in question. (Wolff 1998, 105)

With this definition in mind, I agree with Cohen's views and stipulate an *ethos of cosmopolitan responsibility* as the appropriate and motivating attitude to be adopted by individual moral agents in the face of global issues. While Cohen originally showed the need for an egalitarian ethos under the condition of a society already organised according to principles of justice (and with coercive rules for institutional conduct and the economic transactions between individuals already in place), it should be clear that such an ethos is needed *even more urgently if such rules are absent*[66], and this holds true on the domestic as on the global level. Nevertheless, as I will argue below, promoting such an ethos does not have to mean that everybody has to take up every problem on this planet individually —even though, according to the idea of cosmopolitanism, all relevant problems in the global context do concern and oblige all agents in some way. A division and distribution of the required moral labour between different types of agents—different institutions and different individuals—will still be in line with cosmopolitan thinking, if the idea of a morall relevant community connecting all as equals is upheld. Possibly, it will even grant individuals choices— maybe along the lines of reasonings about feasibility and effectivity, but perhaps

---

[65] While I share Cohen's conclusion that individuals have to develop an egalitarian ethos which also informs people's private economic choices, his general criticism of Rawls seems slightly exaggerated to me, since Rawls repeatedly indicates (even though I feel that this aspect is underexplored in his institution-focussed theory of justice) that individuals also play a role in supporting just institutions and bringing them into existence (cf. Rawls 1999b, 93, 99, 231, 398, 415, cf. Scheffler 2010, 131).

[66] See also Young (2011, 67–68).

also taking into account contingent facts about personal preferences—about which issue to tackle with how much energy.

Such an understanding of a division of labour, however, differs significantly from Rawls's own proposal, insofar as my suggestion does not liberate individual agents from anything. Quite the contrary: in light of both the circumstances of our unequal world, and the obvious limitations of the Rawlsian division of moral labour under non-ideal conditions, it is part of the problem that individuals are too easily let off the hook and and that they quickly seize the opportunity to imagine their inaction as morally justifiable. These practical considerations will be explored further in the second part of the book.

This chapter introduced the long and rich tradition of cosmopolitanism and portrayed important concepts and distinctions from the current debate about global justice. Cosmopolitanism was presented as a distinctive normative stance that conceives of *all* humans as *morally equal citizens of the world*. This (self-) understanding can be employed to critically assess states of affairs and to guide and prescribe action and reform. With this, moral cosmopolitanism has been established as the first core element of a cosmopolitan ethos, that can shape and guide how agents feel, think, talk and act about global issues.

Chapter 2
Equality. Towards global relational egalitarianism

A commitment to the ideal of equality, as explained by an account of global relational egalitarianism, is the second constitutive element of the cosmopolitan ethos. Generally, the ideal of equality is central for both moral and political philosophy, for both theories of ethics and of justice. I will contrast two different understandings of equality and favour a relational interpretation over a distributive one. On this interpretation, equality is understood primarily as something agents *do* (and not primarily as a feature of persons or a pattern of distributions); a firm commitment to relational equality will shape the disposition of individual agents to feel and think, talk and act about global issues, making it a cornerstone of the cosmopolitan ethos and an important element of answering the question about the role and responsibilities of individuals in the face of injustice.

Thus, the following pages take up the question *What is the point of global equality?* and, given its importance for the project of developing a theory of *cosmopolitan responsibility*, discuss it at length. Today, many people tend to agree with the statement that all human beings have equal moral worth, a statement also enshrined in many constitutions and human rights documents. Nevertheless, extreme global inequalities persist in the living conditions of people around the globe, in how much access to resources they have, or in how well their basic needs are met, and in how much influence they have on decisions that matter most to their lives and well-being. Questioning the point of global equality calls for spelling out this widely held (but grossly underdetermined) view. How exactly is this notion of equality an issue of moral concern? Answering the question demands, in turn, a careful specification of just *which* inequalities between people matter, and *why*.

My attempt to answer this question turns primarily on—and ultimately promotes—a view that I call *global relational egalitarianism* that has not yet received much attention in the scholarly literature. I discuss whether and how this view provides a plausible and useful approach for spelling out the moral importance and implications of an ideal of global equality. Global relational egalitarianism is an extension of a theory of egalitarianism initially developed with a national setting in mind. Relational egalitarianism, both in its domestic and global variants, stresses that the crucial first implication of moral equality is that people should stand in relations of social equality to one another and interact with one another as moral equals. Equality then is a lived practice, something we *do*, not a static state of affairs. This view has implications not only for interpersonal relationships, but also for relations between groups. Here, a primary concern is with the domination, oppression, or exclusion of some within unjust structures that are instantiated or upheld also through individual behaviour. While domestic relational egalitarianism has been explicated in detail in the works of Anderson, Scheffler, and others, the idea of a *global* version of relational egalitarianism has not yet received much attention. Thus I undertake to explore whether such an extension is feasible, as well as plausible and helpful.

I contrast global relational egalitarianism with global *luck* egalitarianism (or global *distributive* egalitarianism), which is itself a global extension of domestic luck egalitarianism. Luck egalitarianism, as I will present it here, is fundamentally concerned with attempts to counteract unjustified inequalities in the distribution of goods between people.[67] The assumption that the crucial first implication of moral equality is that people are (with some qualifications) entitled to *distributive* equality, lies at the core of luck egalitarianism, in both its domestic and global forms.

I ultimately argue that the egalitarian core of *cosmopolitan responsibility* should be spelled out in terms of global relational egalitarianism, since that view is both theoretically more plausible and practically more relevant than global luck egalitarianism. One important argument for this claim is that some degree of economic inequality, if it occurs above a certain threshold of sufficiency, is not intrinsically morally problematic, even if it results from processes and factors beyond one's control. This holds true, I argue, because *some* distributive inequality in non-relational goods (with both a lower and an upper limit of how much of the relevant goods people have access to) does not necessarily conflict with the equal moral worth of people and still allows for social and relational equality understood as the possibility and reality of interactions among equals on a footing of equality. However, extreme forms of distributive inequality—absolute deprivation and extreme luxury—quite clearly conflict with the equal moral value of all, and undermine all possibilities for social equality. Generally, however, I do not contend that concern for global equality is based on a justified claim or entitlement to equal distributive shares or an equalising compensation of inequalities that result from brute bad luck. Instead, concern for global equality is a corollary of a justified moral obligation to see every person equally as deserving moral concern, and thus to take the interests of all—as moral equals—

---

[67] I am aware of the fact that, in following Anderson's critique, I somewhat selectively focus on resourcist and distributive variants of luck egalitarianism. (For a critical discussion of Anderson's presentation of luck egalitarian claims cf. Lippert-Rasmussen (2012, 2015).) This, however, will allow me to carve out the relevant contrast between both approaches in a clearer way, even though this inevitably comes at the price of not giving full justice to some of the more nuanced versions of luck egalitarianism.

into account. This in turn argues for the establishment of *relationships of equality* among all. These obligations, which can be said to be universalist or cosmopolitan in spirit and constitutive of the ethos of *cosmopolitan responsibility*, correspond with the entitlement of all to be treated with equal respect and to have access to what is necessary to function as equals in a global society.

Within this argument, sufficientarianism is not a competitor to egalitarianism.[68] Quite the contrary, the sufficientarian idea that all are equally entitled to live a sufficiently good life, even if some distributive inequalities persist above this (possibly ambitious) lower threshold of sufficiency, should be considered as strongly egalitarian. Moreover, it can be understood as a variant of *relational* egalitarianism, because the entitlement to have enough is not only justified by the equal moral standing or the basic needs of all, but also by the importance of being able to interact with one another on a footing of equality. While my account thus includes a non-comparative component of equality (the ambition to secure sufficiency for all), comparative inequalities above the threshold of sufficiency do matter as well, namely when they start to negatively affect the possibility of relationships of equality. The lower threshold of having enough must thus be complemented by an upper threshold of having too much. Thus, my account calls for a 'corridor' of justifiable distributive inequality compatible with relational equality: it demands that those those who have less are put in a situation in which they have enough; and that those who have more do not have too much (where 'too much' would be the amount of relevant advantages that would undermine relational equality).

The chapter consists of six sections. The first section introduces the reader to luck egalitarianism and relational egalitarianism as they were initially conceived, which is to say in their original domestic contexts. In the second section, I raise and animate the question *What is the point of global equality?* Global luck egalitarianism will be introduced in section three, while section four begins the argument establishing global relational egalitarianism as the appropriate answer to the question. I deal with some objections against global relational egalitarianism in section five, before offering a reconciliatory conclusion in section six.

Thus, the chapter explores and analyses the notion of "equality" as an essential normative concept in understanding the role and responsibilities of individual agents in the context of global (in-) justice and in determining the content of the ethos of *cosmopolitan responsibility* that can shape how indvidual agents feel, think, talk and act about global issues.

---

[68] However, it opposes a distinctive form of *distributive* equality which I introduce in the form of distributive and resource-centred luck egalitarianism.

1 Domestic luck vs. relational egalitarianism

Domestic egalitarians can broadly be separated into two schools: luck egalitarians and relational egalitarians. All egalitarian doctrines "tend to rest on a background idea that all human persons are equal in fundamental worth or moral status" (Arneson 2013, 1). The decisive and divisive question then is: What follows from the assumption that all human beings have equal moral status? Luck egalitarians deduce from this assumption a justified claim to distributive equality of the relevant goods; justice, on this account, thus demands the elimination of unjustified distributive inequalities. Relational egalitarians, on the other hand, deduce from the core egalitarian assumption that humans must "relate to one another on a footing of equality" (Scheffler 2015, 21); justice on this account thus demands that unequal relationships (those characterised by domination, exploitation, exclusion and so on) be transformed into relationships of equality. These two major views shall now be presented in some detail.

1.1 Domestic luck egalitarianism

Luck egalitarians[69] consider unequal distributions of (non-relational) goods between persons as unjust only when these inequalities are not in some sense the fault of persons themselves. Underlying this concern is the conviction that equal moral worth entitles all—generally speaking—to equal shares of whatever good is distributed. Distributive egalitarians come in different shades, according to which metric of justice they espouse, with the most common metrics being *welfare*,[70] *resources*,[71] a *combination* of welfare and resources,[72] or *opportunities*[73] or *capabilities*.[74]

---

[69] The term "luck egalitarianism" was coined by Anderson to describe the view she criticises (Anderson 1999, 289). The name has since been taken up by some of those who identify with the view Anderson criticises.
[70] E.g., Arneson (1989) and other thinkers in the utilitarian tradition.
[71] E.g., Rawls's basic primary goods, or the theory of Dworkin (Rawls 1971, Dworkin 2000).
[72] E.g., Cohen speaks of "advantage," which includes welfare, but is also sensitive to the distribution of resources (Cohen 1989).
[73] E.g., Rawls's principle of "fair equality of opportunity" (Rawls 1971) or again Arneson with his account of "equal opportunity for welfare" (Arneson 1989).
[74] Most prominently, Sen (1980) and Nussbaum (2006).

For luck egalitarians, the equal moral worth of all entails that no one should end up worse off than others for reasons beyond her or his control.[75] In order to determine which inequalities are acceptable, and which are not, it is hence crucial to the luck egalitarian position to plausibly define which reasons for being better (or worse) off are within an individual's control. Here, luck egalitarians generally rely on a distinction between "brute luck" and "option luck," a distinction first introduced by Dworkin (2000, 73–78).[76] Dworkin's canonic definitions are as follows: "Option luck is a matter of how deliberate and calculated gambles turn out—whether someone gains or loses through accepting an isolated risk he or she should have anticipated and might have declined." Brute luck, on the other hand, is defined as "a matter of how risks fall out that are not in that sense deliberate gambles" (Dworkin 2000, 73).

Instances of *brute* luck that lie beyond an individual's control include one's genetic endowment and handicaps, 'race', sex, gender, talents, and the social background of one's family, for example. According to luck egalitarians, if one is worse off than others due to such reasons, this counts as bad brute luck and entitles the person to raise justice-based claims for redistribution against society. Good fortune is also, and importantly, undeserved when it is the result of brute luck. Hence, those who are better off through no desert of their own cannot claim that they are entitled to additional advantages. The additional goods resulting from good brute luck should consequently be used to even out the shortage of goods that result from bad brute luck to others.

Underlying this account of brute luck is the fundamental intuition that equality has intrinsic value: those who are of equal moral worth should also be equally well off in distributive terms. Additional instrumental arguments for equality, such as the argument that an egalitarian society would be more happy or more productive, are not needed in such accounts. Defenders of this view are often called "teleological," "telic" or "non-instrumental" egalitarians. They hold that it is in itself bad if some people are worse off than others through no fault of their own (Parfit 1997, 204), and that no one should be better or worse off for morally arbitrary reasons.

---

[75] Proponents of luck egalitarianism of all stripes often refer to Rawls, who also argued that arbitrary inequalities are of important moral concern. Rawls points out that morally arbitrary inequalities are problematic, and argues that influences and inequalities that result from factors that are "arbitrary from a moral point of view" (Rawls 1999b, 63) or result from the "natural lottery" (Rawls 1999b, 64) should be eliminated. This has been used by some to claim a continuity from Rawls to luck egalitarianism. Yet, Rawls clearly is no luck egalitarian in the sense discussed here (see also Freeman 2007, 114–115).

[76] The two relevant chapters of Dworkin's book were first published as articles in 1981.

On the other hand, inequalities that result from voluntary risk taking (including gambling, or reckless behaviour), raise no such concern for the luck egalitarian. Such instances of so-called *option* luck do not entitle the person to justice-based claims against society, e.g. for redistribution or compensation, if she should end up being worse off as a result of a risk realised or a wager lost; conversely, people are also entitled to keep the additional advantages that result from their deliberate risk taking. Here is an example: an individual who works extremely hard to realise some entrepreneurial idea and yet fails, falls into professional bankruptcy and personal financial ruin, and, as a result, also into ill-health, has no justified claim to social compensation. It was the agent's proper, voluntary, informed choice that made him pursue his plan, and he must thus consequently himself face the burdens of a failure that cannot be fairly shifted onto others. Conversely, in the case of business success, she would be personally entitled to reap the benefits from it. Option luck hence trumps the telic egalitarian commitment to equality by providing the justification for acceptable inequalities.

This distinction between unchosen and arbitrary inequalities, and inequalities that result from voluntary and responsible choices has considerable appeal, for at least two reasons. First, it is consistent both with the plausible (and widely held) view that personal responsibility matters, and with the common intuition that it is unfair for individuals to be worse off as a result of factors beyond their control. Second, the view calls for a very sensible and reasonable pooling of individual risks in order to compensate people who are disadvantaged through no fault of their own.

A seminal contribution to luck egalitarianism was made by Arneson in 1989. He defends *equal opportunity for welfare* as the relevant metric of egalitarian distributive justice, and defends this against several alternatives. It is the fact that he argues for equal *opportunity* of welfare, and not straight equality in outcomes, that makes his account a luck egalitarian one. Equal opportunity, understood as equal starting conditions for all, allows for significant distributive inequalities at a later time, provided they result from the responsible choices of an individual.

Arneson introduces two independent distinctions in order to substantiate his view (Arneson 1989, 88). Generally speaking, choosing a metric of egalitarian distributive justice involves both a decision about whether justice is about resources or about welfare, and a decision about whether justice is about strict actual equality or just equality of opportunity. As a brief reminder: Resourcists count non-relational all-purpose goods (like money) as relevant goods, while welfarists see the actual achieved levels of well-being as relevant. The distinction between strict equality and equal opportunity also gets to the heart of what equal distribution means exactly. Strict equality is achieved if and only if all have exactly the same amount of whatever is to be distributed, while equal opportunity is best understood as a "starting gate" theory: the "only" guarantee it insists upon is that at some predetermined point in time, all had exactly the same opportunities to achieve whatever good is deemed most relevant.[77]

Arneson spells out his view further: "An opportunity is a chance of getting a good if one seeks it. For equal opportunity for welfare to obtain among a number of persons, each must face an array of options that is equivalent to every other person's in terms of the prospects for preference satisfaction it offers" (Arneson 1989, 85). Arneson concludes: "When persons enjoy equal opportunity for welfare in the extended sense, any actual inequality of welfare in the positions they reach is due to factors that lie within each individual's control. Thus, any such inequality will be unproblematic from the standpoint of distributive equality" (Arneson 1989, 86).

This account, Arneson argues, avoids two paradigmatic criticisms that are often raised against views demanding distributive equality. First, it can avoid the so-called "slavery of the talented"-objection. Attempts to realise strict distributive equality, the objection holds, would demand excessive redistribution which would place particularly high burdens on the talented, hard-working and successful individuals because the fruit of their labour will be continuously taken away from them in order to be redistributed to the untalented (Dworkin 2000, 90). Such burdening and punishing of people with high talent can be avoided, if equality is secured for all by a fair "starting gate" of equal opportunity. Second, Arneson's account upholds the importance of individual responsibility, and does not provide incentives for laziness: It is "morally fitting to hold individuals responsible for the foreseeable consequences of their voluntary choices, and in particular for that portion of these consequences that involves their own achievement of welfare or gain or loss of resources" (Arneson 1989, 88).

Arneson, especially in his paper from 1989, is thus something of a paradigmatic luck egalitarian. Although luck egalitarianism has significantly evolved since he first began writing about it,[78] the core elements spelled out by Arneson still apply: genuinely valuing equality means insisting that inequalities that follow from brute luck are morally problematic, and need to be compensated for,

---

[77] In this regard, equality of opportunity could be seen as a specific form of strict equality too, but the temporal extension is different. Equality of opportunity secures strict equality only at a single point in time, or at a single point in everyone's life (say when reaching adulthood), while strict equality aspires to uphold equal distribution over time.

[78] Arneson himself has developed his earlier view further and now defends a "responsibility-catering prioritarianism" (Arneson 2000) which, however, still endorses the core commitments of luck egalitarianism.

while those inequalities that are the result of people's responsible choices are morally acceptable.

It should be added that luck egalitarianism, as presented here, focuses on distributive questions with regard to non-relational goods and does not (at least not necessarily) aspire to offer a comprehensive theory of justice, let alone a comprehensive moral theory. In any case, luck egalitarianism in all of its forms has been met with intense criticism.

1.2 Objections against domestic luck egalitarianism

In spite of its initial plausibility, luck egalitarianism has been subject to intense and compelling criticism (Wolff 1998, Anderson 1999, Scheffler 2003). There are four main objections; namely that it misses the point of equality; is overly harsh to the victims of bad option luck; favours levelling down; and is disrespectful towards the victims of bad brute luck.

Anderson has written a fervent polemic against luck egalitarianism (Anderson 1999). Her *first* criticism is based on the reproach that luck egalitarianism *misses the point* of equality.[79] She argues that the luck egalitarian concern with equalising undeserved distributive disadvantages, and the corresponding focus on the difficult task of distinguishing which disadvantages result from brute luck and which from option luck (victims of which are not entitled to be compensated), is both misguided and ultimately alien to egalitarian (political) movements, which have been fighting for equality understood as a substantive *relational* value. And indeed, for the civil rights or women's rights movements, as in the fight for the inclusion of minorities, the unequal distribution of non-relational goods is not the primary focus of concern, but rather an indicator of the actual, more fundamental problem. The problem that motivated egalitarians in these cases was not, for example, that women were per se poorer than men, but that they had no right to vote and that distributive inequality was reflective of a much more profound relational inequality and power asymmetry; it was not only that Jews were materially disadvantaged, to take another example, but that they were disrespected and oppressed as inferior. Exclusion and disrespect often materialise in unequal distributions of opportunities or goods, but while *some*

---

[79] The following pointed discussion of luck egalitarianism stands in the tradition of Anderson's sharp critique. Thus, it does not cover all variants of luck egalitarian thinking and many luck egalitarians have as well directed their concern to the very inequalities that appear also as problematic from the relational perspective. The last section of this chapter will point towards this convergence and end on a more conciliatory note, but first, the two views will be contrasted.

degree of distributive inequality might be acceptable, the unacceptable, essential wrong in question lies deeper than the unequal distributions at the level of relationships between persons and groups of persons. Thus, the call for equal recognition and for full inclusion within society for the members of disadvantaged or excluded groups was and still is of prior concern for egalitarian political movements (cf. e.g. Young 1990). From this perspective, many challenges that are widely discussed in the luck egalitarian literature appear misguided: Why should it be of prior concern for an egalitarian to determine whether a lazy Californian beach bum is entitled to food stamps (a much discussed example in the recent luck egalitarian debate), if the problem persists that certain groups in society are seen as inferior, are met with disrespect, have significantly lower opportunities, and are excluded, oppressed etc.? Here, a shift in focus in egalitarian attention is required.

Anderson sums up her problem with luck egalitarianism, and hints towards a preferable alternative understanding of the ideal of equality, when she writes "that in focussing on correcting a supposed cosmic injustice, recent egalitarian writing has lost sight of the distinctively political aims of egalitarianism. The proper negative aim of egalitarian justice is not to eliminate the impact of brute luck from human affairs, but to end oppression, which by definition is socially imposed. Its proper positive aim is not to ensure that everyone gets what they morally deserve, but to create a community in which people stand in relations of equality to others" (Anderson 1999, 288–289).

A *second* much discussed objection is the so called *harshness* objection, which takes issue with the attitude that luck egalitarianism express towards those who end up worse off through their own fault and choices (Voigt 2007). Anderson again offers up the core of this objection in detail: if only those who end up worse off due to reasons beyond their control are entitled to compensation, all others who suffer as a consequence of voluntary risk-taking cannot raise any justice-based claims for compensation and support against society (Anderson 1999, 295–302). Standard examples include a biker choosing to ride without a helmet and suffering an accident, and a person choosing to smoke who develops lung cancer, both of whose medical needs might be viewed by the luck egalitarian as their own responsibility. Hence such persons are not entitled to public medical care on the grounds of justice since their ill health is the result of self-incurred option luck, and not of morally arbitrary brute luck. Society may of course offer help on the grounds of pity, charity or benevolence, and does not have to choose to let the biker die by the roadside, but it is not obliged to do so on the grounds of justice. To state it clearly: by luck egalitarian reasoning justice does not *entitle* the reckless biker to get medical support: she has to hope for the generosity of the community, because it would be unfair if all were to cover the costs of her individually reckless behaviour.[80]

As a side note, the most radical version of luck egalitarianism would posit that a society would have to intentionally withhold medical care from reckless drivers, even if some in that society were prepared to offer it out of pity or charity. This version of luck egalitarianism claims not only that no compensation is owed in cases of self-incurred risk taking gone awry, but that people who behave irresponsibly *should* in such cases be worse off than the responsible ones, who in turn *should* be better off.[81] Here, the harshness of luck egalitarianism seems entirely obvious, and verges on callousness.

While luck egalitarianism thus is rightly subject to the objection of harshness, some have argued that this objection has been overstated. Voigt, for example, claims that luck egalitarians can avoid it, at least in non-fictitious cases. She states that "because luck egalitarians are sensitive to the influence of unequal brute luck on an individual's choices, it is unlikely that there will be any real world cases in which the luck egalitarian would not have to provide at least partial compensation" (Voigt 2007, 389). But even if this is true, the fundamental intuition of luck egalitarianism will persist and will speak—on the grounds of justice—in favour of a *rejection* of justice-based claims made by those who end up worse off through their own choices. Demands to ease the "unforgiving perspective that has become the recent credo of egalitarians" and allow people one—or even several—"second chances" cannot easily be accommodated by luck egalitarianism (Fleurbaey 2005, 60).

A *third* important criticism of luck egalitarianism has to do with its telic commitment to the intrinsic value of equality, and is known as the so-called levelling-down objection. This critique ascribes the following reasoning to luck egalitarians: if equality is indeed an important intrinsic value, then it should be realised even if that comes at the cost of bringing everyone down to an equally low, or equally bad, level.[82] But, as Parfit has put it, there is nothing good about

---

[80] A longer discussion of such examples can be found in fn. 99 below, expanding on the alternative relational view.

[81] Stemplowska discusses, albeit critically, such an "additional principle" within a version of luck egalitarianism that she calls "equality of opportunity for maximum advantage" (Stemplowska 2011, 124). This principle requires "that opportunities should be structured in such a way that people who make different—better or worse—choices end up with different—better or worse—outcomes" (Stemplowska 2011, 125).

[82] Of course, this objection applies only to those who endorse this telic commitment; not all luck egalitarians do so.

securing equality through making some worse off.[83] Increasing equality in this way would in fact be better for no one, as well as worse for some, and potentially for a great many. This cannot be in the interest of justice.[84]

As an example, imagine a society in which all existing inequalities result from brute luck, and in which some are much worse off than others, others are somewhat worse off, and some are actually very well off. Possible metrics of justice could be well-being, wealth or health. Luck egalitarians would obviously condemn the existing inequalities, since they result from factors beyond the control of individuals. If an intervention were possible by which existing inequalities could be reduced, albeit at the price of reducing the general level of well-being, wealth or health, would this be morally required, permissible, or neutral? In other words, is reducing inequalities more important than, say, overall welfare levels, or overall rates of health, sickness and disease? Larry Temkin, a fervent defender of telic egalitarianism, specifies his view in this way: "The essence of the egalitarian's view is that comparative unfairness is bad, and that if we could do something about life's unfairness, we have some reason to" (Temkin 2003, 775). He continues by attempting to tackle the leveling down objection directly: "But, the anti-egalitarian will incredulously ask, do I *really* think that there is some respect in which only some being blind is worse than all being blind? Yes. Does this mean that I think it would be better if everyone else was blind? No. [...] equality is not all that matters. But it does matter *some*" (Temkin 2003, 780).

Unchosen inequalities are what Temkin calls a "comparative unfairness," and such unfairness provides an important moral reason to reduce the inequality in question. However, few telic egalitarians would endorse that leveling-down is indeed a demand of justice, to the degree that in a society where some are blind and others are not, everyone would have to be blinded. The ability to see has great value, and this has to be taken into account when making deci-

---

83 "Our objection must be that, if we achieve equality by levelling down, there is *nothing* good about what we have done." (Parfit 1997, 211). Temkin illustrates and reconstructs this "slogan" in the following terms: "The claim is not merely that the all-blind world is worse than the half-blind world, *all things considered*, as if the value of equality in the all-blind world is outweighed by the greater disvalue of blinding the sighted. Rather, the claim is that since there is no respect in which blinding the sighted is better for anyone—by hypothesis it isn't better for either the sighted or the blind—there is *no* respect in which the situation is better. *A fortiori*, the greater equality in the all-blind situation does not make that situation in *any* way *better*. Hence, equality has *no* intrinsic value, and non-instrumental egalitarianism must be rejected." (Temkin 2000, 136–137).
84 Versions of the levelling-down objection are discussed e.g. by Nozick, Temkin und Parfit (Nozick 1974, 229, Temkin 1993, 247–248, Parfit 1997).

sions: Equality is not all that matters, but it matters *some*. Consequently, in at least some cases, the telic egalitarian will hold it to be preferable to reduce overall levels of welfare, wealth, opportunity (or whatever the metric of justice will be) *in order to* realise a more equal society overall. This claim quite evidently appears to be more appealing with regard to certain metrics of justice, but not others. Imagine a society in which the distribution of resources above a sufficiency threshold is such that—while all have enough—some have only minimal means to enjoy costly but particularly rewarding recreational activities while others indulge in them freely. Here, some degree of leveling down targeting the most advantaged group may be acceptable in order to increase equality in society. With regard to health-related rather than leisure-related metrics however, attempts to equalise by leveling down—even if above a sufficiency threshold—appear less appealing: it seems difficult to convince people to morally justify interventions to end peoples's lives after a certain age, or to mutilate healthy members in a society, even when such measures would lead to a more equal society.

Even if one is willing to admit some plausibility to the intrinsic value of equality, this appears to hold only under very specific circumstances, and telic equality will certainly not work as a fundamental, general, or prior rule in the distribution of all goods. Stressing the intrinsic value of distributive equality is thus shown to come at the risk of making equality appear to be "merely arithmetic, instead of being a properly intelligible political value" (O'Neill 2008, 139). This, again, appears to support Anderson's diagnosis that luck egalitarianism is fundamentally misguided and that a richer account of egalitarian justice is needed.

A *fourth* criticism of luck egalitarianism is not so much concerned with the victims of bad option luck, but with the victims of bad brute luck, i.e. those who end up worse off through no fault of their own. What could be wrong with offering aid, support, and compensation to those who are blamelessly worse off? Examples could be people who, because of their outward appearance, cannot find mates or romantic partners, or those who, for lack of talent, do not find satisfying and well-paying employment. Anderson argues that in spite of its humanitarian claims, luck egalitarianism ends up having to identify those who are blamelessly worse off, but must in the process resort to reasons for granting aid to them that are deeply disrespectful (Anderson 1999, 302–307). An argument for entitlement to compensation would then be made in the following manner: 'You are worse off due to brute luck and indeed the disadvantages you have to suffer make your life poor and miserable. That is why we, the community, officially acknowledge your status of inferiority and come to your aid. We do not want to have anyone live under such miserable circumstances and out of pity we come to your aid.'

While this description of the luck egalitarian reasoning is admittedly coarse, it does seem to capture the experience of the recipients of aid, when such aid is given on the basis of such a luck egalitarian reasoning. If personal disadvantage —such as handicaps, poor outward appearance, lack of talents, etc.—are officially assessed, and in some cases classified as marks of inferiority, the administration of even well-intended aid becomes an official judgment of inferiority, and an official expression of disrespect for difference. According to Anderson, self-respecting citizens cannot but feel insulted by such attitudes.

Anderson's criticism is based on an important distinction between pity and compassion. While both of these emotions can motivate people to act altruistically, pity is condescending, as it presupposes a comparison between the worse off (the recipients of aid) and the better off (the benefactors). Compassion, on the other hand, is based on the awareness of suffering as an intrinsic state, and it is directed at acknowledging suffering wherever it exists, and at taking steps to diminish it, irrespective of the relative situation of the agent (Anderson 1999, 307). With this distinction in mind, Anderson concludes that luck egalitarianism is based more on pity than on compassion; consequently, its judgmental attitude towards persons becomes inescapable, and luck egalitarianism (in the version under discussion here) is revealed to be intrinsically disrespectful toward some members of society.

Moreover, in order to make the necessary distinction between instances of pure brute luck and option luck, a detailed scrutiny of a person's development and behaviour becomes necessary. This, however, inevitably means an intrusion into the private sphere of persons that is based on an assumption of irresponsibility, insofar as it is about finding out whether a person may, or may not, be personally responsible for his misery. The social institutions established in order to regulate the distributive questions would have to perform intrusive inquiries into the private sphere of people (Wolff 1998). The public assessment of lack of responsibility for disadvantage would not be able to respect the privacy, individuality and vulnerability of those under scrutiny, and might in fact add stigma to that disadvantage.

Furthermore, if the mechanism for granting aid and benefits depended on official acknowledgement of the effects of bad brute luck, this could ultimately create perverse incentives to deny individual responsibility for one's life and welfare. It might turn out to be attractiveto shift blame from oneself to others or to background conditions in order to qualify for support.

In conclusion, Anderson argues firmly that luck egalitarianism "reflects the mean-spirited, contemptuous, parochial vision of a society that represents human diversity hierarchically, moralistically contrasting the responsible and irresponsible, the innately superior and the innately inferior, the independent and the dependent. It offers no aid to those it labels irresponsible, and humiliating aid to those it labels innately inferior" (Anderson 1999, 308). While certainly harsh, this criticism nonetheless does point to problems inherent to the luck egalitarian view, even while it underplays the good intentions and serious arguments of many luck egalitarians.

Yet, as Anderson points out, it is still quite astonishing to find so many elements of conservative thinking in contemporary egalitarian reasoning: "If much recent academic work defending equality had been secretly penned by conservatives, could the results be any more embarrassing for egalitarians?" (Anderson 1999, 287). This prevalence of conservative elements in luck egalitarianism, however, can be explained, at least in part, by the time and the circumstances under which these theories were developed: Dworkin and others elaborated their theories in ways that account for the dominating political ideologies of the 1980s and 1990s—ideologies dominated by conservative political realities relentlessly pursued by the likes of Thatcher and Reagan.[85] Under political and ideological circumstances in which the general willingness was to scale back and dismantle the welfare state, Dworkin and others saw in luck egalitarianism a form of *defence* of the idea of a caring state that places value on equality. On the defensive due to the rise of conservative thought, some of the more ambitious aims of egalitarianism were perhaps set aside in favour of securing at least a minimal provision of support for the disadvantaged members of society.[86]

1.3 A relational alternative to luck egalitarianism

In light of the above-mentioned objections to luck egalitarianism, an alternative egalitarian theory has emerged. The main mistake of luck egalitarianism, from this alternative egalitarian perspective, is its exclusive focus on distributive questions, which comes at the expense of neglecting the quality of *relations* and *interactions* between individuals. This is a central concern, since it was precisely the unequal social relations and interactions—influenced by hierarchies, domination and disrespect—that initially triggered egalitarian political movements in the first place. Relational egalitarianism hence turns toward a re-interpretation of the ideal of equality as a feature of social relationships, namely as *rela-*

---

[85] While Rawls delivered, in the 1970s, a more ambitious ideal theory of justice that was in a sense a reflection of the general willingness in his time to build and strengthen the welfare state, his views came under severe fire in the following years for being too lenient on reckless and irresponsible individual behaviours.

[86] See also below, section 1.5. in this chapter.

tionships between moral equals with mutually respectful interaction. Such a relational understanding of the ideal of equality does not implicitly or explicitly suggest that distributive questions lack moral importance. But it does mean to suggest that the ideal of relational equality is different from the ideal of distributive equality, and that concern for equality cannot be reduced to a concern only for the distribution of different goods in society.

The egalitarian ideal in relational egalitarianism is *social* equality. A useful starting definition is that social equality has to do with relationships that are unaffected by status hierarchies (Fourie 2012). The underlying view, that all are fundamentally of equal moral importance, is of course still the familiar one, shared in common with all egalitarians (including luck egalitarians) and also underlying many constitutions, forms of legislation and the international human rights discourse.[87] Despite this unanimity, however, genuine social equality has been, and remains today, an extremely elusive goal. In order to spell out the ideal of social equality, it may be most useful to begin with clear instances of social *in*equality.

The central problem for relational egalitarianism: inequality as oppression

In a seminal paper, Young approaches the problem of social inequality as a form of "oppression". Understanding her argument and the phenomenon of oppression, even though she developed it originally in the domestic context, will help to understand social inequalities and injustices also on the global level; providing an important account of the wrongs that should be of concern for those endorsing the ethos of *cosmopolitan responsibility*.

Young argues that "all oppressed people suffer some inhibition of their ability to develop and exercise their capacities and express their needs, thoughts, and feelings" (Young 1990, 40; first publ. in 1988). Because Young does not think that any single set of criteria exists for identifying instances of oppression she argues instead that oppression designates a "family of concepts" that consists of five types. Matters of distribution are often relevant in these contexts, but oppression in Young's sense also includes many other matters "that cannot easily be assimilated to the logic of distribution: decision-making procedures, division of labour, and culture" (Young 1990, 39). I call the different contexts in which social equality (or inequality) exists frameworks of interaction. And it will be obvious that inequalities in these interactions extend far beyond questions pertaining to the distribution of non-relational goods.

---

[87] For critical discussion, however, cf. the contributions in Steinhoff (2015).

To employ the terminology of the capabilities approach, one could say that *socially caused* restrictions on the development of "capabilities" and their exercise ("functionings"), as well as restrictions on communicating one's wants, needs, preferences, emotions, etc. are what make a *structure*, an institutional framework, or a communicative setting oppressive. Oppression, for Young, more specifically designates "the disadvantage and injustice some people suffer not because a tyrannical power coerces them, but because of the everyday practices of a well-intentioned liberal society" (Young 1990, 41). These practices are not intentionally generated and upheld, but they are systematically reproduced in the major institutions of a society, as well as in the individual interactions that take place within such structures.

Indeed, it is necessary to employ Young's concept also in cases other than that of a "well-intentioned liberal society". Often enough, oppressive social structures match mean-spirited intentions and prejudices or they occur in illiberal or autocratic or other types of societies. Yet it is certainly the case that oppression often occurs also in liberal societies even in the absence of evil intentions, a phenomenon opon which Young has elaborated elsewhere under the label of "structural injustice" (Young 2006b, 112–116).

Young distinguishes "five faces of oppression," each of which is of concern to social and relational egalitarianism, since replacing each with relationships of equality constitutes the proper goal of promoting relational equality:[88] "Social justice [...] requires not the melting away of differences, but institutions that promote reproduction of and respect for group differences without oppression" (Young 1990, 47). All five forms of oppression can be found in both institutional settings and in individual interactions. Groups and—within groups—individuals can be oppressed; groups, institutions, structures, and—within them—individuals can oppress, according to Young. The five faces of oppression are exploitation, marginalisation, powerlessness, cultural dominance, and violence.

Exploitation, in Young's understanding, takes up the original Marxist idea of class domination.[89] As Marx argued exploitation occurs in a capitalist, class-based society when the benefits of the labour of workers are steadily and disproportionately transferred to the owners of capital. For Marx, however, the concept of exploitation was descriptive, rather than normative. It designated one of the central characteristics of a capitalist society, which would—according to Marx—eventually implode and disappear. Young, on the other hand, understands ex-

---

[88] See below, section four of the present chapter.
[89] For a helpful overview of "exploitation" in the Marxist tradition, and in analytical Marxism, see Kymlicka (2002, 177–187).

ploitation as a normative concept and widens its scope from the market economy to cover other social processes as well.[90] Exploitation, for Young, generally consists in the social processes that systematically lead to an unequal distribution of advantages. This happens most often by constraining a majority of people, and transferring the advantages that result from the constraint of those people's efforts to others who have contributed less (or not at all) to the generation of the respective advantages. Yet, distributive inequality is ultimately only a result and symptom of oppression; the oppression itself lies in the ongoing exploitative interaction that constrains the exploited.

Examples of exploitation can be found in the large amount of unpaid carework within families for children or the elderly, work mostly performed by women; or menial labour like garbage collection which is often performed by members of minority groups or immigrants. Other examples include academic systems wherein departments and senior researchers rely on the work of junior researchers who are frequently insufficiently acknowledged, and often overworked and underpaid, not to mention without any serious chance of ever occupying a permanent university position.[91]

Marginalisation is the second face of oppression, and for Young it is a particularly dangerous one. Marginalised people are those "the system of labor cannot or will not use" (Young 1990, 53), and who are thus systematically excluded from participating as full members in the cooperative practice of a society. The problems with marginalisation are at least threefold: it leads to material disadvantage and deprivation, even when mitigated by a state welfare system. This is particularly troubling, for Young, since the provision of welfare is itself problematic, as it establishes a dependency that limits the rights and liberties non-marginalised people can enjoy. "Dependency in our society [...] implies, as it has in all liberal societies, a sufficient warrant to suspend basic rights to privacy, respect, and individual choice" (Young 1990, 54). An example can be found in the Hartz IV laws in Germany, or in the way that refugees are all too often treated. When the welfare and support people receive is in kind rather than in cash, they cannot choose for themselves how to lead their lives. Permanent monitoring of individual activities and finances, the threat to withhold allowances if certain

---

[90] Here, her writings are close to a normative and political reading of Marx as developed by "analytical Marxists" like Cohen and Roemer (two prominent voices stressing that justice demands the elimination of bad brute luck), and against Marx himself, who understood his theory as a "scientific" theory of historical necessity.

[91] One can easily find examples also with a global scope, but I postpone this discussion for later sections of this chapter.—For a careful recent analysis of "anonymous" exploitation, i.e. exploitative structures involving groups, not individual agents, cf. Wollner (2019).

jobs are refused, and so on, are severe and disrespectful intrusions into the realm of personal privacy, and constitute an additional injustice that compounds the material inequality and deprivation meant to be remedied. Indeed, even where the provision of welfare succeeds in avoiding severe forms of material deprivation, marginalisation unjustly prevents people from becoming active, recognised members of society. Marginalisation blocks them from using their capabilities to contribute in a way that is recognised as being socially meaningful.[92]

Powerlessness, as the third face of oppression, for Young consists in the fact that some people in society lack the authority (or power) to make decisions about their lives and work, while others hold power over them. The workplace is a particularly pertinent example where professional workers can enjoy (albeit to admittedly varying degrees) the liberty to make autonomous choices. Those made powerless lack this liberty; they also lack the experience of intrinsically rewarding work, as well as perhaps the possibility of further developing their skills during a working life; they also generally lack the social recognition that comes along with working a "respectable" professional job. Countless people work under such conditions, all over the world. Yet, the phenomenon of powerlessness can be also found beyond the workplace. In May 2015, former US-President Obama referred to a "sense of unfairness and powerlessness" that has spread in some communities and which, together with an absence of any feeling of "hope and opportunity," raised social tensions and conflict.[93]

Cultural imperialism, the fourth face of oppression, pertains when dominant social groups impose their perspective of "the norm" on other groups, which are then considered deviant or inferior, groups which as a result find themselves stereotyped and silenced. Many examples can be provided for cultural imperialism: refugees, Jews, Muslims, blacks, or people with diverse sexual or gender identities have experienced such imperialism from the majorities of citizens, Christians, whites, or heterosexuals respectively.

The most direct form of oppression is actual, systematic *violence*, the fifth type of oppression on Young's list. Cases of police brutality against minority groups or attacks on refugee shelters are examples for such violence, but there are also less physically obvious appearances of oppressive violence, such as the persistence of "jokes" and idiomatic expressions that belittle homo-

---

[92] Another example, from the context of academic philosophy, can be found in the marginalisation of non-standard approaches in philosophical scholarship (Dotson 2012).
[93] Implicit or explicit racism, of course, importantly adds to this problem in the context of the US. https://obamawhitehouse.archives.gov/the-press-office/2015/05/04/remarks-president-launch-my-brothers-keeper-alliance [last accessed: 1 July 2019].

sexuality. As Young points out, it is not the actual violence alone, but the fact that such violence appears to be socially acceptable in certain contexts, that makes it an oppressive social practice.

The five faces of oppression obviously often overlap and cluster. Cultural imperialism often appears in the form of violence; the powerless are marginalised and exploited etc.[94] The "faces" are types of oppression, and they are together meant to provide a heuristic to identify different and diverse instances of social injustice, and particularly of those that go beyond easily measurable distributive issues.[95]

These social dynamics that Young identified and analysed as social injustice provide the background against which it will, below, become possible to identify structurally similar dynamics of oppression that apply on the global level.

The positive demands of relational egalitarianism

This section focusses on the versions of relational egalitarianism as presented by Anderson.[96] Anderson's criticism of luck egalitarianism shares features with Young's, particularly the diagnostic orientation towards identifying instances of social injustice, and the therapeutical ambition to promote justice by addressing the quality of social interactions within a society. For Anderson, oppression, in all its various shades, is an expression of fundamental inequalities in moral status and value. The aim of relational egalitarianism—or as Anderson prefers to call it, "democratic egalitarianism"— is to put an end to socially imposed oppression, and to create communities in which relationships and interactions take place on a footing of equality (Anderson 1999, 289). Equal respect for all, based on the equal moral worth of all, is made evident primarily in the way

---

[94] One among a great number of possible examples that could be given is the caste system in India. Cf. the recent critical edition of Ambedkar's classical incriminatory text and the call for the abolition of caste with a book length introduction by Arundhati Roy (Ambedkar 1936/2014).
[95] I have introduced oppression as the central problem from the perspective of relational egalitarianism by relying on the pioneering work of Young. And indeed, seminal contributions to this analysis stand in the tradition of feminist philosophy. Other traditions in moral, political and social philosophy have identified and analysed such oppressive social structures and processes as well, among them critical theory (Fraser and Honneth 2003) and Pettit's neo-republican view of freedom as non-domination (e.g. Pettit 1997).
[96] Forst (2014) and Scheffler (2015) have also elaborated on this alternative view.

agents interact with one another, although it also inevitably has implications for distributive patterns (Scheffler 2015, 27).[97]

Scheffler, accepting and building on Anderson's views, further specifies the characteristics of a society of equals. Central to such a society is a "reciprocal commitment on the part of each member to treat the equally important interests of every other member as exerting equal influence on social decisions" (Scheffler 2015, 35–36). Scheffler is aware of the fact that such relationships of equality in a society go far beyond individual face-to-face interaction, and must also include large scale, collective decisions. However, he spells out the core convictions of relational equality along the lines of face-to-face interaction between people, and moves on from there to expand his argument to include all interactions, face to face and collective, in a society of equals. The constant across all interactions is that all those participating in a communication or a framework of interaction must be able to participate on equal terms, which Scheffler explores under the rubric of a "deliberative constraint".

Anderson has a slightly different, though compatible, take on the necessary elements of the ideal of a "community in which people stand in relations of equality to others," and in which all competent adults are equally recognised as moral agents (cf. Anderson 1999, 312–315). Concretely, the egalitarian commitments of such a community must include a list of relevant goods to which citizens must have effective access over their life time in order to enjoy a wide range of capabilities. As a consequence, securing sufficient access for all to fundamental capabilities guarantees that all can function not only as *human beings* (i.e. their basic needs are fully met), but also as *participants in a system of cooperative production* (i.e. they contribute in a meaningful way to society as a complex system of interaction), and as *citizens of a democratic state* (i.e. they are able to voice their opinions, and see those opinions have an impact on collective decision-making). The goods necessary for realising these fundamental capabilities must be provided unconditionally, and without resort to any form of paternalism or disrespectful inquiry before they are granted. If injustices are identified, the remedies offered in response must match the type of injustice being corrected.[98]

---

[97] For relational egalitarianism, any concern for (re-) distribution, aid and compensation comes only as a result of equal concern for all, and does not result from pity or presumption of inferiority.

[98] Anderson's examples here include "the disabled, the ugly". For democratic equality, compensation in the form of another "metric" is inappropriate: If the injustice suffered by "the disabled and the ugly" is exclusion, the appropriate remedy is not giving them money or more elegant flats, but to secure for them social inclusion. "Democratic equality does not attempt to use private satisfactions to justify public oppression" (Anderson 1999, 334).

None of this should be interpreted to suggest that the egalitarian principles governing a society of equals do not uphold the responsibility of individuals for their own lives. In fact, Anderson argues that the collective is not in charge of compensating for all sorts of losses that people suffer, and in doing so calls for individual responsibility; however, she demands that collective responsibility be understood as a form of insurance against the loss of certain *types of goods*, namely those included in the list of relevant goods for functioning. This still allows the possibility for people to end up worse off when they behave irresponsibly, but avoids the pitfall that some of them will end up so badly off that they will no longer be able to fulfill their core functions (as a human being, cooperative member of society, and democratic citizen), because the community has a duty to prevent this from happening.[99]

---

[99] Since this is where Anderson's relational egalitarianism conflicts directly with luck egalitarianism, she explains in detail how her view avoids inviting personal irresponsibility (by compensating only for certain types of losses), avoids subsidising irresponsible behaviour (like smoking, by, for example, the imposition of heavy taxes on tobacco products in order to generate funds so that resulting medical costs can be absorbed publicly), avoids paternalistic interferences with individual freedoms (like choosing to smoke, too stay with this example, by distinguishing between what people *want* to do and what other people are obligated to *give* them) or by imposing one particular conception of the good (by justifying the promotion of certain goods through "collective willing"). Altogether, she argues that her democratic egalitarianism does incentivise people to behave responsibly, since ultimately—not only for luck egalitarianism, but also for relational egalitarians—prudent behaviour will lead to less losses. All this is illustrated well in Anderson (1999, 326–331).

To spell this out in one example, consider the reckless biker suffering injuries from an accident. Relational egalitarians will argue for the provision of medical care, even in this kind of case, because the idea of a community of equals includes the idea that no one will be left alone and denied urgent medical care. However, the entitlement the reckless biker has to community support does not include all medical treatments that could possibly be given to her, according to Anderson. Indeed, the entitlement only extend as far as what is necessary for her to re-secure her functioning as an equal citizen in society, and no further. Other acquired advantages, like the prior possession of excessive fortunes, are not collectively insured. Furthermore, the sheer possibility of having to undergo unpleasant medical treatment, and to be less healthy than prior to an accident incurred through risky behaviour, should also serve as a disincentive to irresponsible behaviour. This means that, according to relational egalitarianism, there is a limit to entitlements. This threshold of equality remains ambitious, but it also seeks to avoid being overly generous, so as not to create perverse incentives for reckless behaviour.

But would such costly support for reckless drivers not be unfair to those acting more responsibly, who will then ultimately bear a burden in order to help meet the medical (and other) needs of the reckless? Anderson suggests that there is an egalitarian, and non-discriminatory, way to make sure that those who end up with higher needs and thus also social costs, will have already contributed more to the collective insurance scheme: the way, very simply, is to heavily tax risky activities (like motor bike driving, skiing, smoking, etc.) *beforehand*. This creates further disin-

Anderson's community of equals is furthermore understood as "a system of cooperative production" in which different functions are met by different members of society in order to generate the goods that can be then distributed among all its members. Such an understanding of society, and the division of labour, clearly owes much to the ideas of Rawls's *Theory of Justice:* there is to be reciprocity among free and equal democratic citizens, who are socially productive, and who are continuously engaged, in a mutually respectful way, in social and political cooperation. A division of labour is required to produce such benefits, for the simple reason that social organisation is complex, and involves many different (functional) hierarchies, as both Rawls and Anderson agree. The reality that all such tasks must be fulfilled in one way or another for society to continue functioning—the judge cannot get to the courthouse if the surrounding roads and streets are not in good repair, and parents, be they road construction workers or senior vice presidents, cannot spend all day at work if they have no one to mind their children—means that so many different people must contribute somehow to that joint functioning. What is thus needed is a just division of labour, as well as a just division of the (jointly generated) fruits of that labour, which means appropriate *recognition and remuneration* for all.[100]

In contrast to the luck egalitarian ideal of an equal distribution of goods in a just society (where only inequalities that result from informed choices are morally acceptable), relational egalitarians hence defend a quite different ideal. Justice for the latter consists in the absence of (non-functional) hierarchies and oppression. A just society, for relational egalitarians, is characterised by relationships of equality. Distributive equality is not what matters, at least not primarily.

Both types of egalitarianism differ substantially, perhaps even attempting to meet quite different types of challenges. Is it then appropriate to compare and contrast them against a single yardstick? Or is it possible to merge the impulses from both approaches into a pluralistic account?[101] If yes, which of the perspec-

---

centives for engaging in such acts, yet preserves the freedom to do so for all agents who choose to engage in such risky pursuits (and can afford them), without having to resort to paternalistic scrutinising of individual behaviours. This would, according to Anderson, help the realisation of equal respect for different preferences, while upholding disincentives for risky behaviour, as well as the necessary means for covering the costs of accidents and illness resulting from such behaviour. Treating individuals in this manner, she thinks, fairly expresses on behalf of society the equal, inalienable, and fundamental moral worth of every person. Note, finally, that this is just one of many instances of dealing with diversity within the model of "democratic citizenship".

100 Cf. Anderson (1999, 332–326).
101 For an attempt to combine luck egalitarianism intuitions with the aims of democratic or relational egalitarianism cf. e.g. Brown (2005).

tives should take the lead? I will reconsider this possibility at the end of this chapter. Now, I proceed by presenting the differences established so far between domestic luck egalitarians and domestic relational egalitarians.

1.4 Major differences between luck and relational egalitarianism

The contrast between luck and relational egalitarianism can be illustrated by looking at four major differences,[102] even though such a binary analysis can only help broadly demarcate the two poles of the debate, and is unable to fully capture the intricacies of the debate along its entire spectrum. The *first* major difference between them is that the former understands equality in terms of the equal distribution of *non-relational* goods.[103] Which non-relational goods should matter exactly, or which *metric* of justice is the most appropriate, has emerged as an enduring topic of debate, decisively triggered by the publication of Sen's Tanner lectures on the question *Equality of what?* (Sen 1980). Major candidate metrics include, among others, welfare, opportunity for welfare, resources, and rights.

Against this view, relational egalitarians hold that equality is a *social and interactional value* that is realised when relationships of a certain type exist between all members of a community. Distributions of non-relational goods matter only secondarily, and only insofar as they have an impact on relationships of equality.[104] Relational egalitarians see the excessive concern for the "equality of what?" debate to be fundamentally misguided, as it seems to assume that a *single* non-relational good can be identified that captures all morally relevant features of inequality (Anderson 2012, 55). Relational egalitarians, however, are in a sense pluralists about equality; they claim that relationships based on equality have many implications on many dimensions of human experience, including (but not restricted to) the distribution of non-relational goods (Scheffler 2015).

A *second* point of difference between luck and relational egalitarians lies in the more specific choice of which inequalities in non-relational goods are of moral concern. For luck egalitarians the answer is of course obvious: the commitment to telic egalitarianism renders, in principle, unjust *all* distributive inequalities that do not result from voluntary, responsible individual choices.

---

[102] For the following section cf. Anderson (1999, 313–314, 2010, 1–6).
[103] For a more nuanced version of luck egalitarianism that accommodates also relational goods, cf. Lippert-Rasmussen (2012).
[104] For this, cf. the discussion in Parisi (unpubl. ms.).

For relational egalitarians, however, distributive inequalities of non-relational goods are of moral concern only if and when they cause or uphold relational inequalities. Concretely, relational egalitarians are not, in principle, against even quite substantial differences in income and wealth, as long as all persons posses *sufficient* means for allowing them to function fully as citizens and as long as those having more than others do not have *so much* that they begin to dominate and thus undermine the possibility of relational equality.[105] There is no conclusive answer to the question of what it means exactly to live fully as a citizen and to what exactly is required to be able to do so, but regardless of how ambitiously any particular relational egalitarian defines sufficiency, economic inequalities raise a relational egalitarian's moral concern if they result in status hierarchies, or exclusive political advantages (which imply unjustified disadvantages for others), as for example with the purchase of political influence, which so often seem to come along with extreme wealth. In this scenario, a material inequality—which is of no intrinsic concern, if an ambitious threshold of sufficiency has been assured, and is thus otherwise acceptable to a relational egalitarian—turns into a morally unacceptable political and relational inequality.[106]

This example points to a *third* important difference between these two poles on the egalitarian spectrum, which is how each one conceives of what is truly *foundational* for equality and justice. Luck egalitarianism holds that distributive equality has intrinsic value (see above, "telic egalitarianism"), and thus that the fundamental demand of justice is to secure that the relevant goods' distributions are equal, and that inequalities result only from individual and responsible choices. For relational egalitarians, the foundation of justice lies in the quality of the relationships and the interactions between individuals. Equality is a characteristic of interactions that fully acknowledge the fundamental equal moral worth of all. Equality is a lived practice, something we *do*, not a static state of affairs.

The *fourth* major difference regards the justification of standards of equality and justice. Luck egalitarians defend their principles of justice and equality from the assumed external "moral point of view" of a neutral spectator. If distributive equality has intrinsic value, this intrinsic value can be said to exist *sub specie aeternitatis*, which is to say that it does not depend on concrete settings, persons,

---

105 This claim refers to the core commitment of relational egalitarianism and its central distributive commitment (which I call the 'corridor' between having enough and having too much) and is not meant to preclude the possibility of developing more fine-grained pluralist accounts.
106 This argument stands in the tradition of Rawls who also demanded that "excessive concentrations of property and wealth, especially those likely to lead to political domination" have to be prevented in a just society (Rawls 2001, 44).

or interactions. Against this somewhat detached view, relational egalitarians hold that their standard of justice is justified from the perspective of concrete persons who interact with one another. This is indeed perhaps why Scheffler's account of relational equality is so compelling: he develops it by way of describing an interaction between two persons, between "me" and "you," an interaction that has immediacy and tangibly resonates with the universal human experience (Scheffler 2015). The concrete lived human experience of those involved, and the reasons and opinions they exchange in this setting, provide the ultimate justification for relational egalitarianism. The concern of relational egalitarians for the experiences and concerns of actual people in concrete settings might make the view appear more messy, and less parsimonious, than other theories, but it also makes it far more relevant for most of us, as well as more consonant with egalitarian political causes and movements, both historically and contemporaneously.[107]

Despite these differences, I do not want to rule out the possibility of reconciling insights from both poles of the spectrum into a comprehensive egalitarian account. Ultimately, both fairness *and* respect, both the distribution of non-relational goods *and* the quality of interpersonal interactions, are important issues of moral concern.[108] The main problem with luck egalitarianism is that, in seeking to stress the relevance of fairness and personal responsibility, too much attention is directed towards the possibility that people will benefit from *unfair advantage*. The standard example here is the irresponsibly lazy Californian beach bum with her expensive taste for surfing instead of working, which has generated an astonishing amount of scholarly literature. While this possibility, of course, cannot be ruled out, and does indeed have to be accounted for, luck egalitarians seem to have forgotten somewhere along the way that their main concern should not be unfair advantage, but *unfair disadvantage*. Determining which of the egalitarian concerns—about relations and respect on the one hand, and unfair disadvantage on the other—is of greater moral importance is straightforward: unfair advantage is a far less common and less morally troubling occurrence, and it should not dominate the debate. Unfair disadvantage, however, is in urgent

---

[107] Luck egalitarians might object against these four distinctions that follow Anderson's own favourable presentation of the ideal of relational equality. Cohen, for example, a self-identifying luck egalitarian, engages with issues of equal distributions not from a detached perspective, but generates justifications for his views also from an interpersonal and interactional perspective when he demands an "interpersonal test" or directs attention to the speaker-audience-relativity of arguments (Cohen 2008, e.g. 36–28, 42).

[108] Suggestions to narrow the gap between the two rival accounts have been made among others by Gheaus (2016) and Seidel (2013).

need of address. Alas, this shift in attention has not sufficiently taken place. Current debate about luck egalitarianism seems still largely focussed on the narrow issue of *unfair advantage*. Historical reasons may partly explain this myopia.

1.5 The historical context of the theoretical development

Taking into account the temporal (and broader socio-political) dimension permits a better understanding of how the two rival views, not as exact opposites but as two poles of a debate, have morphed over time in relation to one another. It also permits a better understanding of the subtle shift in the *questions* that are addressed by each view. The difficulties in directly comparing luck and relational egalitarianism can be, at least in part, explained by the fact that their different central questions seemed to be the most politically important ones in the respective decades of the past century during which the poles were formulated.

The liberal egalitarian theories developed by Rawls from the 1960s onwards engaged systematically and critically with the emerging welfare state in the 20th century, for which no recent political theories were available at the time. Rawls repeatedly alludes, in his justificatory method of "reflective equilibrium," to the shared intuitions ("considered judgements") of citizens, and his theory is an attempt to spell out the content of such intuitions and judgements in a comprehensive way. The immense success of his *Theory of Justice* shows that Rawls filled a gaping lacuna in Western political philosophy by capturing the political realities of his time and by proposing a philosophical justification for its ongoing social and political processes.

The relative historical congruence between the political mainstream and the dominant theories of institutional justice (as offered by Rawls) did not last long however. In the 1980s and 1990s, criticism of the welfare state mounted, and a shift from (left) liberalism to (right) libertarianism took place, a shift particularly visible in the Thatcher government in the UK, the Reagan administration in the USA, and the Kohl and Schröder governments in Germany. A central criticism of the time *against* the idea of the welfare state was that it encouraged people to deny responsibility for their own lives, and that it encouraged the view that "circumstances" or "society" were ultimately responsible for individual successes and failures, rather than the individuals themselves. The call for constant government intervention to equalise the circumstances in which people act—if necessary by heavily taxing the successful—was gradually replaced by a call to focus on individual, instead of governmental, responsibility.[109] An egalitarian ideal is still found in this newer call, but it appears in the more limited form that equality is to be secured only with regard to minimal starting conditions. The rest of one's life should depend on what one made of one's equal starting conditions. The assumption was that the prudent and wise would fare well, and that they would thus also deserve that well-being. The converse assumption—that the reckless and lazy would fail, and that this would be no one's fault but their own—was also relentlessly promoted. Compensation, financed by taxing the better off, was considered to be deeply unfair, since it certainly could not be the task of the majority to subsidise an irresponsible minority. Right leaning conservative politicians and pundits also began promoting and repeating the message that welfare systems will never work, since they have never managed to eradicate poverty in any country, even those with the most generous benefits. Over time, the dominant view became that the poor are poor because of the so-called "poverty trap," which generous welfare provisions only aggravate, and so an alternative must be found.

It is from this political and ideological context, described here in admittedly abridged and necessarily simplistic terms, that the core commitment of luck egalitarianism emerged. The interesting point here is that the development of luck egalitarianism was led by left-leaning philosophers (such as Dworkin and Cohen), who were alarmed by the emergence and ferocity of the new conservative political landscape.[110] It is a sign of how urgent things seemed at the time that luck egalitarianism was born of the desire to *defend* egalitarianism (and the popular commitment to the welfare state) against the formidable forces aligning themselves against it. It is indisputably from such a defensive position that Dworkin, Cohen and others developed their theories. Alas, in attempting to defend egalitarianism, the philosophical and political agenda came to be dominated by examples meant as criticism: more and more discussion turned exclusively to the irresponsible surfer who might benefit from unjust advantage, and less and less to the marginalised single mother in a neglected and remote rural area who clearly suffered from unjust disadvantage. In hindsight, it does indeed seem clear that these embattled left egalitarians failed to uphold the full breadth

---

[109] A careful reconstruction of this shift, and an analysis of its implications, can be found in Young (2011, ch. 1). The question how many luck egalitarian elements were already foreshadowed in Rawls's theory is discussed by Freeman (2007, 111–142).

[110] In the words of Cohen, Dworkin showed how egalitarianism could incorporate "within it the most powerful idea in the arsenal of the anti-egalitarian right: the idea of choice or responsibility" (Cohen 1989, 933).

of the egalitarian values they claimed to hold dear.[111] Yet, one must also concede that it may not have been possible for anyone to have done otherwise in light of the rapid advance of a conservative climate which put them deeply on the defensive.[112]

Anderson's unsparing criticism of luck egalitarianism marked—along with several other papers published around the year 2000—a turning point for egalitarian theorising: the reconsideration and return to classical egalitarian commitments got under way, and it continues today.

2 What is the point of global equality?

This chapter has thus far been concerned with contrasting domestic luck (or distributive egalitarians) with domestic relational egalitarians. This analysis provides the basis for extending the debate from the domestic to the global level that is relevant for *cosmopolitan responsibility*. I will now turn to the following question: Does a similar contrast between luck egalitarians and relational egalitarians exist also at the global level?

Global luck egalitarianism is already a prominent and established stance in the contemporary debate about global justice, but global relational egalitarianism has not yet received much scholarly attention and is still in a rather early stage of development. Anderson does not spell out the international implications of her view, though she does mention this as a challenge (Anderson 1999, 321, fn. 78). Scheffler, similarly, merely hints at the global application of relational egalitarianism (e.g. in Scheffler 2010, 192, fn. 42). Others have taken some steps to positively spell it out: Koggel offers a relational approach to global inequality analysis (Koggel 2002); and Brock mentions a relational view of global justice inspired by Anderson's theory, but is also critical about a simple extension of it (Brock 2009, ch. 12)[113]; and Miller has referred to and criticised an assumed variant of global relational egalitarianism, albeit only very briefly and with much scepticism (Miller 2007, 77–78). Recently, however, Nath has sketched an account of Global Social Egalitarianism (Nath 2011, Nath 2015), Cloarec has

---

[111] This led Anderson to the provocative introductory question of her seminal paper: "If much recent academic work defending equality had been secretly penned by conservatives, could the results be any more embarrassing for egalitarians?" (Anderson 1999, 287).
[112] For this chronological presentation cf. also Kymlicka (2002) and, with a special focus on health issues Wikler (2004).
[113] Brock distinguishes a "relational cosmopolitanism" from a "distributional cosmopolitanism".

discussed the implications of the demands of social equality in the global society (Cloarec 2017), and Ip has provided the first book-length analysis of global egalitarianism from a relational perspective (Ip 2016).[114] The remaining part of the present chapter adds to this still relatively small body of literature about *global* relational egalitarianism and advances this understanding of equality which will then be employed as the second central element of my account of *cosmopolitan responsibility*.

A crucial challenge is again to specify "the point of equality," i.e. the right reasons for moral concern about the relevant forms of global inequality. It stands to reason that, as with the contrast explored in previous sections at the domestic level, it may be helpful to begin by opposing *global* luck egalitarianism with *global* relational egalitarianism. Is *global* equality about the equalising compensation of bad brute luck, or is it about establishing relationships of equality? Is it about unequal distributions, or is it about unequal—i.e., hierarchical or oppressive—relationships? I begin by surveying and discussing the already better established account of global luck egalitarianism, before directing my attention to the possibility of global relational egalitarianism.

3 Global luck egalitarianism—a critique

There are two connected reasons why global luck egalitarianism is appealing. First, it focuses on the obvious and crass inequalities of non-relational goods like material wealth (and subsequently levels of well-being, development etc.) that exist between people in different countries. From a luck egalitarian perspective such inequalities obviously constitute severe injustices, since no one chooses one's country of birth. Second, it avoids engaging with the numerous and extremely complex past and ongoing relationships and interactions that influence current levels of wealth, well-being, development etc. between countries and people, thus generating a rather straightforward diagnosis of injustice.

Above, I have already elaborated on the plausibility of the fundamental intuition of luck egalitarianism, which is simply that no one should be worse off through no fault of his own. This intuition suffers no loss of appeal or power when the perspective is shifted to the global level. The non-relational 'arbitrariness objection' in the global domain focuses on the place of birth of a person, and identifies the country of one's origin as one among several morally arbitrary factors that are beyond one's control but which have a huge impact on the

---

[114] Cf. also Heilinger (2016b).

amount of resources, welfare or opportunities available to someone over a lifetime (Shachar 2009, Milanovic 2015). This can be illustrated, for example, by the fact that the richest 5% of the population in India have the same per capita income as the poorest 5% of the population in the USA (Milanovic 2011, 116).[115] This means that—notwithstanding individual cases—for the morally arbitrary reason of one's birthplace, Indians in general have essentially no chance of ever becoming richer than the very poorest Americans (in monetary terms at least). Furthermore, there are many other poor countries in which even the richest groups are poorer than the poorest groups in affluent countries (Milanovic 2011, 188). Global differences linked to birthplace also occur with regard to health prospects (Segall 2010), as well as educational opportunities,[116] and many other dimensions of life (Satz 2003). So the widely shared concern about the unfairness of the huge impact of birthplace is both empirically supported and morally warranted.

Nagel shares this intuition: "The accident of being born in a poor rather than a rich country is as arbitrary a determinant of one's fate as the accident of being born into a poor rather than a rich family in the same country" (Nagel 2005, 119). Caney mentions a historical parallel to support moral concern for global distributive inequality on the grounds of a luck egalitarian intuition:

> If [...] we object to an aristocratic or medieval scheme that distributes unequal opportunities according to one's social standing, or to a racist scheme that distributes unequal opportunities according to one's race, we should, I am arguing, also object to an international order that distributes unequal opportunities according to one's nationality. In short, then, the rationale for accepting equality of opportunity within the state entails that we should accept global equality of opportunity. (Caney 2001, 114)

For Caney, the global extension of the objection against morally arbitrary inequalities is already entailed in its domestic application. One can understand citizenship as an inherited privilege, and draw a parallel to the medieval feudal system which systematically conditioned peoples' lives, as Carens did (Carens 1987, 252); a thought reinforced also by Shachar. On this account, the inherited privilege of citizenship should be of far greater concern to egalitarians than actual distributions and inheritance of material wealth (Shachar 2009). Global luck

---

[115] Of course, the richest persons in India are not poorer than the poorest in the USA. Some—relatively small—overlap can be found, when comparing percentiles (Milanovic 2011, 118).
[116] See the impressive tool for making comparisons between countries at: https://www.education-inequalities.org [last accessed: 1 July 2019].

egalitarians take this arbitrariness as the central justification for the demand to fight such unequal life prospects.[117]

There is much debate about what exactly would follow from taking the arbitrariness objection and the egalitarian commitment to the intrinsic value of equality seriously at the global level.[118] But before I engage in more detail with the question of what should be done, and by whom and according to which standards, a more general and theoretical level survey is needed in order to properly ground such details.

In spite of its initial appeal, there are several important *objections* against global luck egalitarianism, largely paralleling the four objections that Anderson had raised against its domestic variant (Anderson 2010b). While these objections do not lead to a rejection of global luck egalitarianism, they indicate some shortcomings to the view which motivate the search for a better alternative.

First, one can object that global luck egalitarianism simply *misses the point of equality* when it limits itself to comparing actual distributions of resources, well-being or opportunities of people in different countries. This criticism asserts that a focus on distribuenda, and patterns of (re-) distribution necessarily remains only at the surface of the problem. What is wrong is that distributive inequalities are symptomatic for ongoing social and interactional dynamics that stand in need of change. Such relations and interactions tend to escape the luck egalitarian's attention; even though they cause and perpetuate the unequal distributions that raise the luck egalitarian's concern.

Second, global luck egalitarianism could turn out to be *overly harsh to the victims of bad option luck*, especially if it is understood to argue that the economic well-being of countries counts as a result of the gamble a population made when selecting a certain leadership. For even if it is granted that elections (or broad economic policy choices by elected officials) can be understood as wagers for which an electorate must take responsibility (of course, in many cases it is implausible to assume this, in light of both the democratic deficits in many countries, and the danger that minorities are seriously and negatively affected by the

---

117 This presentation indicates that it is possible, also on luck egalitarian grounds, to take into account relations and relational goods. However, my discussion here aspires to lay out the contrast between both views, thus I read the luck egalitarian concern here as being primarily about the unequal distribution of advantages.

118 Some defend a global difference principle (Beitz 1979, Tan 2004, 109); still others the idea of global equality of opportunity (Caney 2001). For a helpful overview over contemporary theories of global egalitarianism (with a focus on contemporary luck egalitarian theories), cf. Armstrong (2009).

outcomes of the majority votes), no population or individual should be forced to live under conditions of absolute deprivation or below a reasonable sufficiency threshold, even if past actions and "responsible choices" have contributed to bringing about this very state of affairs.[119]

Third, placing intrinsic value on equality runs the risk of *favouring a levelling down* which, particularly in the international comparison of, for example, health standards and life expectancy, appears to be implausible: If the Swedish live longer than the Germans, this does not per se constitute an important concern for global egalitarian justice. If, however, life expectancy at birth differs by more than thirty years between Japan and Sierra Leone, this is indicative of a fundamental and grave problem of justice.[120] Shortening the lives of the citizens in the better off countries does not appear a morally acceptable and viable option. The normative challenge rather consists in justifying an ambitious threshold of sufficiency or adequacy that defines and aims to secure what people should have in order to live a decent life, no matter where they were born or happen to live.

The *fourth* criticism is precisely the danger of a misguided and ultimately counterproductive tendency which results from global luck egalitarianism's preferred focus on *current* distributive inequalities: Interventions to establish distributive equality as a "starting gate," e.g. by providing aid or redistributing goods, tend to be blind to *ongoing* structural inequalities and processes which, if they remain in place, will continue to bring about these objectionable distributive inequalities. Equalising the starting conditions for all agents (i.e., particularly persons in the domestic setting, and particularly states in the global context) is thus likely to be insufficient for bringing about lasting distributive equality, since even a temporalily equal redistribution of non-relational goods would leave the background conditions of interaction unchanged. In other words, if unequal power-relations substantially contribute to distributive inequality, then material redistribution will at best alleviate the worst *symptoms*, but certainly not eradicate the *roots* of, the relevant inequalities that would reemerge after a short time. In distributive terms, a permanent redistribution would be necessary, although such a move would, as we saw above, not only be open to some variant of the "slavery of the talented" objection, but would miss the point of equality as well, since the fundamental moral wrong (social inequality) can-

---

[119] A parallel objection could be raised against Rawls's claim that the economic situation of a country results largely from the choices and cultural preferences of its citizens (Rawls 1999b, 108).

[120] See the discussion by Segall (2010, ch. 11). Data about life expectancy are taken from the 2015 WHO report published in 2016: http://www.who.int/gho/publications/world_health_statistics/2016/EN_WHS2016_AnnexB.pdf?ua=1 [last accessed: 1 July 2019].

not be righted by a proxy measure of such (distributive equality). Indeed, even if one could establish permanent resource transfers that would secure the long-term material well-being of the currently disadvantaged, such material well-being would still fail to establish genuine (social or relational) equality, because the resulting equal distribution both depends on the willingness and capacity of the advantaged to "support" the disadvantaged, and fails to offer the disadvantaged the hope of eventual independence. All this can be said to express disrespect towards the disadvantaged.

A *fifth* objection is that global luck egalitarianism is implausibly insensitive to the different historical origins of the arbitrary inequalities between people and consequently fails to assign moral obligations in a justified and effective way (cf. Schemmel 2007). In short, global luck egalitarianism, at least in my pointed presentation, appears to be a-historic; it takes the status quo as a starting point and is narrowly forward-looking, at the expense of insufficient attention paid to past dynamics, historical events and experiences. History, however, is essential to understanding why certain types of injustice are currently experienced by certain people, and what sort of remedies should be provided by whom.[121]

The combined moral weight of these objections makes global luck egalitarianism little appealing for my theory of *cosmopolitan responsibility*. The objections call for an alternative understanding of equality—and an alternative approach to assigning responsibility for remedying inequalities—at the global level.

4 Towards global relational equality

How plausible then is a global variant of relational egalitarianism? In this section, I will argue that it is not only possible, but also rather straightforward, to deploy relational egalitarianism internationally. As with its domestic variant, global relational egalitarianism rests on two core claims, a negative one (opposing hierarchical relationships of domination and oppression), and a positive one

---

[121] To anticipate already here a possible objection against my own account, which also has a focus on forward-looking assignement of responsibility: First, past contributions of *individual* agents to causing a problem differ significantly in size from major historical events such as, e.g., colonialism. Second, insofar as individual agents are responsible, in a backward-looking way, for the existence of a problem, my account allows for assigning particular forward-looking responsibility to address the urgent problem in question. But such forward-looking responsibility exists also in the case that *no* such past contributions exist and in the case of culpable inaction of those who brought the problem about and should be the primary bearers of forward-looking responsibility. Cf. the concluding chapter below.

(endorsing the ideal of relationships of equality in the global society). The grounds for these claims lie in the multiple different connections between people across the globe and their important effects on how the lives of people go. Concretely, I argue that a relational account of egalitarianism is not confined to parochial or intranational interactions and relations. This makes an account of *global relational equality* an attractive element of my theory of *cosmopolitan responsibility*.

It has already been established that there are numerous interconnections between different agents across the globe. Often such connections are particularly intensive on a local or near range scale, but—under what I called the circumstances of cosmopolitanism—they are not confined to one's immediate surroundings as it might have been the case in earlier times. Agents interacting with one another include not only governments and their representatives, but also NGOs and corporations, and, of course, individuals. At first sight, one can list intergovernmental communications; multiple economic interactions, including individual consumer decisions; friendships, communities pursueing a particular interest such as, say, collecting butterflies, following soccer, and academic collaborations around the globe. Connections include also joint reliance on clean air which presupposes particular ways of behaviour elsewhere, as much as those living downstream of a river will depend on the behaviour of those living upstream. Here, global political interaction becomes increasingly important. The connections also include increasing knowledge about how other lives go elsewhere on our planet. Of course, such a diverse and inclusive account of relations that may transcend borders stands in need of further differentiation with regard to the intensity of the collaboration or the degree of its institutional mediation. Yet, all these examples firmly establish that our contemporary world is shaped by multiple transnational interconnections—through *knowledge*, through the *assumption of the existence of others*, e.g. when buying something that has to have been produced by someone, or through *cooperation* and *exchange*. Some of these connections and relations are institutionally mediated, others not. This, however, is, as I will argue, secondary with regard to the question whether they provide a ground for egalitarian demands. What matters is that they indicate a shared frame of coexistence and cooperation, that they massively impact on the life prospects of individuals and that they sometimes even exercise coercion upon individuals.

The perspective of relational egalitarianism now stresses the demand that all humans, because of their equal moral worth, should be able to and actually relate to one another as social equals; i.e. that all persons matter equally, and that interactions should be free from oppressive hierarchies between individuals and groups. As within a country, this perspective is applicable also to the multiple relations and interactions between individuals and groups across borders mentioned above. From this perspective, many severe moral wrongs can be identified and the distributive inequalities are often only an indicative symptom of such underlying relational inequalities within the inevitable sphere of influential global connectedness. Here are three examples.

– The presupposition that it is acceptable to buy products manufactured under exploitative conditions elsewhere: When buying all manner of consumer goods (and perhaps particularly apparel and electronic devices) it is obvious to consumers that such goods have to have been produced somewhere. One cannot deny or ignore this fact, which, however, is only tacitly assumed and not considered any further. However, it has been increasingly documented and known that such manufacturing often occurs in disgracefully exploitative ways. Individual consumer decisions hence establish links connecting consumers to those who produce, transport, and trade in such products. The fact that many of us consider it to be entirely inevitable, as well as morally unproblematic, to buy products manufactured under exploitative conditions, shows how consumers discount the importance of other people's legitimate claims to decent working conditions and place higher weight to their interest in buying stuff cheap. The many links in the commercial trade chain obscure but do not diminish the clear fact consumers are inescapably socially connected to these other far away and exploited persons, persons whose legitimate interests we rarely even acknowledge, let alone respect.

– The treatment of migrants and refugees arriving at the borders of the European Union: The way that migrants attempting to enter the EU are treated indicates a form a dramatically unequal relationship that is accepted as legitimate by affluent Europeans, despite being so disrespectful towards the massively disadvantaged, many of whom have legitimate moral and legal claims.[122] This is a complex issue that cannot be fully explored appropriately here, but the conclusion that persecuted people attempting to enter the EU are not treated as moral equals is undeniable. Whether or not status distinctions (between refugees, asylum seekers, and other groups of migrants) apply, it is clear that interactions, communications, and relations exist, and that those who are seeking assistance to escape desperate conditions ought to be treated as the human beings worthy of a equal and respectful treatment that they are. There is little doubt that a great many individuals working at the EU's outer borders attempt, daily and courageously, to live

---

[122] Cf. Heller et al. (2018).

up to such treatment standards, but there is also no doubt whatsoever that migrants arriving at the borders are, in many instances, and often even systemically, treated in morally unacceptable ways.
– The treatment of the representatives of poor nations in discussions with rich and powerful nations, as e.g. within the United Nations: If the voices from poor countries are heard at all in such venues as the UNGA, it is often with a level of disrespect verging on reprehensible: representatives of the powerful, affluent nations routinely dismiss the views and claims of representatives from poorer countries. Simply being allowed to speak is held up as a great concession by the powerful (when in fact it is an established international legal right), but rarely is it heard from a representative of a poor country that they feel they are considered and treated as equals, on a footing of equality, within global institutions and negotiations.[123]

These examples indicate several forms of unequal relationships and the apparent assumption of status hierarchies that shape global interactions. It is important to stress that not all hierarchies are problematic, some functional and also some social hierarchies inevitably shape human co-existence and are an undeniable fact of human life (Scheffler 2010, 225–226). Such hierarchies, say, between parents and children, between different types of workers in a society, accommodate differences in our ontogenetic development or allow more complex and beneficial cooperation. The problem, from the perspective of global relational egalitarianism, is hence not the existence of any hierarchies, but of particular social hierarchies that endorse the assumption of superiority and inferiority of particular individuals and groups.[124] In the examples mentioned above, the workers in countries of the Global South, migrants, and representatives of poorer countries are looked down upon. The relations displayed in these examples are objectionable because they presume, and express the assumption of, the lower status of some, which will often be vividly felt by them (although not always and not in each case be intended by those occupying the privileged position).

---

[123] This admittedly general remark stands in need of further proof, but here let me simply refer the reader to the experience of René Préval, president of the République d'Haïti, following the earthquake that hit the Port-au-Prince area in 2010, at the United Nations, as documented in Raoul Peck's film "Assistance mortelle" (2013).

[124] The types of hierarchies mentioned are not immune to be transformed into hierarchies of status. If children are seen as the property of parents, or if workers in particular professions are seen as inferior because of their work, such ontogenetic or professional differences—which are in themselves inevitable or conducive to a better coordination and cooperation in society—are perverted. Cf. Young (2006a).

I argue that these hierarchies in status are in the relevant sense structurally similar to the one's which can be found on the local or domestic level, when e. g. people of a particular sexual orientation or with a particular ethnic background are subject to disrespectful treatment, have limited opportunities, or are in other ways worse off. The suggested expansion of the scope of egalitarian concern hence is just a matter of scope, not a matter of type.

Taken together these examples can be quite plausibly understood as evidence of a wide web of social interactions and relations, a web that by its very existence establishes the scope of global relational egalitarian justice—even though it often goes beyond inter-individual face to face-interaction. Just as social *cooperation, coercion,* and the *pervasive impact* of the "basic structure" of a society determine the domestic scope of justice in Rawls's theory, *these same three features* determine the scope of justice on a global level.[125] Existing global structures and patterns of interaction have a social, political and economic dimension. They can be instrumental for securing *fair* cooperation and interaction on a footing of *equality*, as they can also be implicated in the imposition and persistence of relations characterised by domination, oppression, coercion, and exploitation. If such preconditions can be shown to exist both on the domestic level *and* the global level, it then makes perfect sense to extend the scope of egalitarian justice to the global level.

That I take up arguments from the Rawlsian tradition to support my view of global relational egalitarianism may appear surprising to some, since Rawls is known for limiting his concern to the *domestic* setting, as we saw earlier. However, the three arguments for the importance of the basic structure as a pre-condition for justice in a domestic setting can also be deployed on the global level.[126] The relevant relations that occur on both levels should count as instances where relational justice or relational injustice can reign. In the following I will expand on this view by transferring Rawls's arguments about cooperation, coercion and pervasive impact from the domestic to the global level in order to lend further support for my argument.

---

[125] In a thorough critical discussion of Rawls's basic structure argument, Abizadeh has shown that a global basic structure can—against Rawls's own views—be identified with regard to *global* social cooperation, *global* coercion, and *global* pervasive impact (Abizadeh 2007). In what follows, I will discuss these three dimensions of interaction. The pervasive impact criterion, moreover, is pertinent for global luck egalitarians.

[126] As noted above, I will follow arguments from Abizadeh (2007), but cf. also Van Parjis (2007). With regard to the extension of relational egalitarianism, building on Rawls's basic structure arguments has also been suggested by Cloarec (2017).

A *first* Rawlsian account of the relevance of the basic structure for justice analyses the basic structure as the determination and regulation of *social cooperation*, coming along with both a *division of labour*, and a *division of the fruit of this labour* in society. Society is here understood to be a set of persons engaged in a scheme of recurrent institutionally regulated social interaction and cooperation. Rawls writes that the basic structure of society is comprised of "the way in which the main political and social institutions of society fit together into one system of social cooperation, and the way they assign basic rights and duties and regulate the division of advantages that arises from social cooperation over time" (Rawls 2001, 10). But is it plausible to assume that similar institutional forms affect individuals, albeit perhaps in a wider (less direct) sense, at a global level as well? Consider the following comparison.

For Rawls, the paradigm of a society as a system of cooperation is a nation (like Germany), where cooperation includes the joint production of a variety of goods. It is important that some manage factories, that others work in those factories, that others raise children, that some take care of the elderly, that some invent and innovate, that some educate and train while others entertain, that others cook and run shops, etc. The interactions in society are thus multiple and manifold, but in order for a society to work well, and to generate and guarantee the desired goods—be they security, well-being, wealth, or capabilities, etc.—*all* essential functions, according to Rawls, have to be fulfilled. If no one takes up one task or another, everyone has less time for doing their own jobs. If everyone had to dispose of or recycle their own rubbish, instead of being able to rely on public waste management, for example, or if there were no child care, then people simply couldn't work effectively. Individual roles make no sense in isolation, in other words, since it is only within the context of society that these roles have meaning. And this context as such is shaped by—sometimes explicitly stated, sometimes implicit—institutions that influence the distribution of advantages and disadvantages in society.

Acknowledging that no one can manage an enterprise, or run a department of philosophy, without relying on the support provided by others (by food production and preparation, child and elderly care-taking, and cleaning maintenance, etc.), means recognising that any success one person achieves (as a manager or philosopher) cannot be exclusively credited to that person alone. The obverse conclusion hence is: "lower skilled" work is just as essential to individual and collective success as is "higher skilled" work. Acknowledging this conclusion exposes the massive injustice in paying extremely low wages for "low skilled" or "menial" work: It is an abuse of power to deny the fair share of the advantages, brought about collectively, to those who are less able to make their voices heard, to defend their interests vigorously.

Precisely the same logic, however, applies on a global scale, where a *global division of labour* quite obviously exists. Were it not for the availability of products imported from other countries, many of the needs of the German population would have to be satisfied by domestic production. But the possibility to import staples, electronics, entertainment devices and many other goods from abroad allows Germany to specialise in other, often much more profitable, manufacturing and design activities. The global traffic in goods, raw materials, and finished products, etc., shows that a global scheme of interaction and cooperation is already in place.

However, what is already glaring at the domestic level (unfair wage differentials between so-called low and high skilled work) is galling at the global one: powerful affluent countries, seeking their narrow self-interests, successfully claim nearly the entire global economic pie, and often grumble about leaving even crumbs for the less powerful countries. Although this outcome is often claimed to be a result of "market decisions" influenced by an invisible hand, the reality, known broadly by all, is biased favourably towards the already powerful and advantaged players. One might think of the negotiations about TTIP, the trade agreement between two world leading economic regions, that excludes all those not part of the treaty from benefits; or the TRIPS Agreement administered by the World Trade Organisation. Pogge, among others, has convincingly demonstrated how the TRIPS Agreement systematically protects the benefits of companies based in affluent countries at the cost of systematically excluding the citizens of poorer ones from access to modern pharmaceutics (cf. Banerjee, Hollis et al. 2010). This is a particularly egregious case of injustice, for the pharmaceutical studies that precede the admission of new medicines on the Western markets are often tested on research-participants in low-income countries, as it is much cheaper to run medical trials in the latter (Ganguli-Mitra 2013). Although both highly trained research personnel and untrained research participants are indispensable for clinical trials of new drugs, the latter group, despite its essential contribution, is often lastingly excluded from benefiting from the outcome of such efforts, if the trial is taking place in a low-income setting. Here we have a clear case for global relational inequality resulting from unjust institutional arrangements about how a system of cooperation should work.[127]

---

[127] Some might try to frame this problem exclusively in distributive terms. After all, they might say, what is unfair here is the *distribution* of the advantages that result from cooperation. Against this view one can point to the fact that the situation would remain unfair, even if some more money or some more pharmaceutics would be made available to ill people in poorer countries out of generosity of the pharmaceutical companies. Indeed, the question here is not simply about poor people getting treatment, but about poor people being treated as equals, as well

Rawls's *second* argument for the relevance of the basic structure understands it insofar as it has a right to *coercive power and interference*. Coercion and (political) authority is not under all circumstances morally questionable for Rawls, since some forms of such are justified, if and when for example, individual autonomy and liberty can be secured only through (the threat of) coercion. This is, in the end, quite a familiar argument for the legitimacy of political power: the threat of interference is justified if all people affected share equally in creating and controlling the form of coercive power that secures the conditions for individuals to flourish.[128] For Rawls, however, such a justification must always respect the principle of subsidiarity: coercion can be justified only up to the degree that is necessary to allow for individual autonomy, and because coercion is meant to ensure the possibility of autonomy, it must meet the reasoned approval of the autonomous subjects who agree to be potentially coerced, should the need arise.

The presence of such coercive structures is, for Rawls, an indication of a shared basic structure that legitimises the application of the principles of justice. Rawls himself, as well as Nagel (2005), argued that the absence of a globally coercive framework speaks against the applicability of the principles of justice at that level (Rawls 1999a). Indeed, it must be conceded that, at the global level, there are no structures similar in coercive power to the domestic monopoly over law enforcement and violence held by national governments. Nevertheless, there are international political bodies with coercive structures, including one particularly striking trans-national example where the problem culminates and becomes particularly visible in the form of the border regime in place around the European Union.

At the outer border of such political entities, individuals are continuously subject to coercion. The standard reasoning to justify state coercion, mentioned above, however, comes to its limits when force is employed to keep others out of

---

as the right to appropriate care of citizens in poor countries when such care is available elsewhere, since no one's need for that care counts morally more than anyone else's. Existing intellectual property protection regimes, however, prevent this from happening, and they do so in order to maximise profit margins. Since these protections have been codified into international law, and since that law has a profound effect on related global interactions as well as distributions, the example stands as a clear instance of global relational inequality.

128 A prominent element of justified authority and coercion is that those who run the possibility of being coerced can consent to such coercion, at least under 'normal' circumstances. Cf. e.g. the "normal justification thesis" suggested by Raz who argued that authority is justified when the agents that are subject to authority, are by this very fact more successful (in comparison with a setting without such authority) in conforming their actions to the reasons they have themselves (Raz 1986, 53–57).

the group that justified coercion in the first place in order to secure its autonomy. The problem becomes particularly pertinent, if such coercion is not exercised occasionally but permanently: Subjects attempting to enter the community that justified coercion will be subject to such ongoing coercion without ever being allowed a possibility to consent to or object against the coercion. An ongoing exercise of coercion and domination over people without offering them—at least eventually—a perspective to participate in the justification of this coercion perverts the justification of this coercion. If the coerced subjects gain nothing with regard to their autonomy, the justification for coercing them fades away.

The frontiers of the European Union—for example in Ceuta and Melilla and on the Greek islands as in the Mediterranean Sea generally—are visible examples for such coercion, as there are many other instances of coercion that restrict the movement of people across the borders of states (Abizadeh 2007, 348–349).[129] All such areas represent clear examples of relationships and interaction that are in a very real sense permanently cross-border: relations between individuals in border zones reflect fundamental relational inequalities: some individuals are systematically excluded from the possibility of becoming members of the advantaged in-group, whose collective consent is the only legitimate source of the coercive powers to which they find themselves subject. Such situations are thus yet another clear instance of the existence of global relational injustice.

Rawls's *third* argument for the relevance of the basic structure for justice in the domestic context focusses on a feature which exists at the global level, as well, namely the *profound impact* that the basic (global) structure has on an individuals' chances for leading a life of flourishing. This far-reaching condition goes well beyond the narrow distribution of goods, and the arbitrariness-objection, as becomes clear with Rawls's explication of "profound impact" as "the effects of the basic structure on citizen's aims, aspirations, and character, as well as on their opportunities and their ability to take advantage of them, are pervasive and present from the beginning of life" (Rawls 2001, 10). In a domestic caste system, to take a paradigmatic example of what Rawls means here, the very aims and aspirations of people are shaped by the social strata to which they belong: from the very outset of an individual's life, it is clear what options are available to him or her, and which are out of reach. Indian Dalits, for example, as a result of the caste system, tend to internalise as givens such social restrictions. Because of these restrictions they will rarely even imagine or aspire to take up a higher

---

[129] The objection that these persons are only coerced if they choose freely to attempt to enter certain territory can be met by the rejoinder that the reasons motivating people to leave their countries of origin are often connected to the prior decisions of those more powerful players who now coercively deny them refuge and entry.

social position, and instead will adapt their aspirations to what is said to be achievable by them by the caste traditions (cf. Roy 2014). This self-limiting mechanism, which results in highly constrained personal expectations and preferences, is known as the problem of adaptive preference formation (Elster 1983).

Obviously, much the same pattern of constraint, and of profounding limited adaptive preference formation, holds true at the global level, where birthplace and citizenship profoundly impact on an individual's judgement about what is possible, what could be achieved, and what might be available in the future. There is, plainly put, an obvious hierarchy of countries with regard to their political, economic, educational, military (and other) powers, that directly shapes their citizen's outlook on life, and in a manner not dissimilar to the caste system in India. This argument will resonate particularly with global luck egalitarians, since they understand birthplace to be morally arbitrary. I now turn my attention to spelling out this argument beyond the luck egalitarian focus, and pointing to its distinctive relational implications, by way of anecdotal evidence.

Generally, my students in Haiti (where I teach regularly) do not aspire to reach the same social or professional positions, or material levels of wellbeing, as my students in Germany generally feel will be their due, even though neither group is more skilled nor more laborious on the whole.[130] Clearly, this tempering of expectation is an example of the pervasive impact of the basic structure of the global order, which, it turns out, is a distinctive problem not only for distributive justice and luck egalitarianism, but also for *relational* egalitarianism. After all, relationships of equality may exist *within* the respective groups of, say, Haitian and German students, but a pervasive and permanent form of relational inequality is plainly tangible when actual, cross-group interaction takes place. For my Haitian students, I am, in a very tangible way, an alien: I grew up and was educated under truly privileged circumstances, and the fact that I regularly travel to Haiti to teach, but then leave again afterwards, is just an additional indicator of my privilege. In fact, my presence makes the very unequal options which are available to different groups of people even more visible, as travelling outside one's country of origins is not an option for all. This awareness, and the many other profound differences that result from the arbitrary fact of being born a German or a Haitian, affect the relations between Haitians and Germans; and while it is fully possible to attempt to interact on a footing of equality, and to be mutually respectful, the massiveness, and the pervasiveness

---

[130] This general claim can be defended even though some do indeed leave their socially pre-assigned frame of possibilities.

of the inequalities in our background conditions, regularly present a challenge to establishing and upholding such relationships.[131]

These anecdotal remarks are meant simply to illustrate the challenges of realising *relational equality* where contact and interaction takes place, but where arbitrary factors (such as nationality) exert pervasive and persuasive impact on individual perspectives.

It is time to sum up: I have argued so far that evidence of global relational inequalities is not difficult to find, and thus that it is important to develop an ideal of global relational equality that applies to a broad range of situations and contexts. Global connections, relations, and interactions are not in short supply: a full spectrum of entities, from official international institutional interactions to informal interactions among individuals, can be subject to an analysis according to the standard of relational equality. We live in a globalised world, which is very plausibly understood as a complex system of cooperation. The border regimes—but also the international rules—often exercise coercive force over individuals and groups who are and remain systematically excluded from participating in the shaping and justification of such powers. And the pervasive impact with which birthplace, which is truly arbitrary, inevitably influences individuals' and groups' outlooks on life, as well as conditions the interactions between them.[132] These numerous actual and ongoing interactions and relationships indicate the scope to which the ideals of global relational egalitarianism can and should apply.

A classification of the negative and positive abstract demands of global relational egalitarianism might at this point be clarifying: *Negatively*, it is about avoiding (and overcoming) the five faces of oppression introduced and developed by Young as the standards for (domestic) justice: exploitation, marginalisation, powerlessness, cultural dominance and violence.[133] My illustrations have made it clear that these faces of oppression pertain also to the international level. *Positively*, it is about securing equality for all human beings, as equals, such that they can fulfill the three interactional functions, in different dimen-

---

131 That I mention my students may appear misleading, since the student-teacher-relationship, with its inherent functional hierarchy, adds an additional layer of inequality. Yet, this functional hierarchy also exists with my students in Germany, where it does not have the same impact. And also in other contexts where people from different countries meet, the privileges and disadvantages attached to nationality impact on the characteristics of interpersonal relations.
132 I point again to the illuminating article by Scheffler, who deconstructs the concrete practical interaction between two individuals in order to construct the ideal of social equality (Scheffler 2015).
133 Cf. p. 80–84 above.

sions over their lifetimes: as *human beings* (i.e. having sufficient means to lead decent lives), as *participants in a system of cooperative production* (i.e. being able to contribute to the global system, even if only in minuscule ways, without being exploited or marginalised or disempowered), and as *citizens in a democratic state* (i.e. being capable of developing and voicing their views on issues that regard them) which includes (given the inevitable acknowledgment of the circumstances of cosmopolitanism and the resulting global scope of my argument) functioning as *global citizens*. With regard to this last element, with which I amend the list offered by Anderson (Anderson 1999, 312–315), the concrete requirement is also that all people are respected of having equal value and that all can make their voices heard in the matters that are of concern for them on a global scale.

Where there is global relational equality, people are able to meet and interact with one another without feelings of inferiority or superiority, because all have enough of the relevant goods and opportunities to realise the mentioned functions, no one would have so much that she could dominate or unilaterally impose her will on others (through masses of wealth, through inherited social status, privileged class membership), and all would be able to contribute through their abilities, thus in different forms, to realising the relevant social goods that can be brought about through interaction and cooperation.[134] Such relational equality is as relevant at the global level as it is at the domestic level, for in both cases it is not the case that all people—citizens and global citizens alike—*actually* interact. What matters is that relational equality is secured *whenever* individuals interact and also when social *institutions* shape the interaction between different (groups of) people or their representatives. Relational equality, however, is compatible with quite some degree of functional differentiation and functional hierarchies that are necessary for an advantageous division of labour in the (global) society: manager and worker, parent and child, even prison-guard and prisoner, can in their interactions respect relational equality by treating the other as a person, with respect, and not as inferior.[135]

---

[134] Those in need of support to realise as much as possible the described functioning as (global) citizens in this way, are entitled to it. The possibility that some will try to free-ride has to be taken into account, but it seems not to be the challenge primarily in need to be addressed when discussing global (in-) equality.

[135] This claim seems to be most controversial in the case of the treatment of those who have committed horrible crimes. But even here (and these cases are certainly not the most pertinent one's for discussing global relational equality), I contend that respectful treatment—that includes a right to a fair trial, to decent conditions in jail, and that precludes self-administred vigilante justice or draconian punishment—must not be denied.

And while (quite some) resulting distributive inequalities may be acceptable, limits to such distributive inequalities apply where they negatively impact on the outlook to realise and uphold relational equality. The permissible degree of distributive inequality is determined by both a lower and an upper threshold, forming a 'corridor' of acceptable distributive inequality: those who have less must have enough to realise the relevant functions; those who have more must not have so much that their advantages undermine the possibility of all to relate and interact with one another on a footing of equality.[136]

The ambition of relational egalitarian justice, on my account, then is not confined to the narrower and direct interactions within any given community alone; instead it extends globally.

5 Global relational egalitarianism—for and against

Having sketched an account of global relational egalitarianism, I will ask, in this penultimate section of the chapter, first, if global relational egalitarianism can avoid the criticism that has been voiced against global luck egalitarianism. Sec-

---

136 Sufficientarianism is generally characterised by comprising of a *positive* thesis, that all should have enough, and a negative thesis, that inequalities above the sufficiency threshold are not relevant to justice (cf. e.g. Shields 2016). My own sufficientarian account endorses the positive thesis and specifies that all should have enough to function as human beings, participants in a system of cooperative production, as citizens in a democratic state and as global citizens. Unlike the dominant views among sufficientarians, however, I reject the negative thesis by demanding that a second threshold limits the acceptable supra-threshold inequalities, because in a massively unequal and unjust world as ours, having much more than enough cannot be considered to be morally unproblematic. Morally acceptable is only the state between having *enough* and having *too much*, where both thresholds of course cannot be determined in absolute terms and instead will be characterised by significant indeterminateness. Nevertheless, the additional second, limiting threshold, located above the first sufficiency threshold, will—on my relational account—secure such that having more than enough will not negatively impact the possibility to relate to all others as equals. Having powers to realise one's own preferences at the expense of others, having more political influence than others, or being able to dominate others will be examples for morally unacceptable degrees of having more than enough. Since such relational inequalities are often the result of distributive inequalities in terms of income and wealth, a regulation of such goods is necessary also on relational grounds.—As I will argue in later chapters, endorsing (global) relational egalitarianism commits oneself to self-limitation because using one's resources excessively for oneself—above the second, limiting threshold—is morally unjustifiable. Where institutional arrangements to secure such limitations are still absent, self-limitation is morally required.

ond, I will raise and discuss two objections directed particularly against global relational egalitarianism.

I contend that the ideal of global relational equality does not display the shortcomings of the ideal of global distributive equality as pointed out above. Global relational egalitarianism has no problem taking into account the distinctive historical origins of inequality and injustice because such antecedents of the current status quo are understood as relevant *relations* and *interactions,* and hence fall rather directly within its scope (Schemmel 2007). While global luck egalitarianism must begin with an assessment of the status quo to decide between instances of brute-luck and option-luck and is predominantly "forward-looking," global relational egalitarianism explicitly takes up a diachronic perspective in order to analyse current inequalities (in relations, interactions, and distributions) as the outcome of past relations and interactions, and on the basis of such, is able to then formulate distinct and concrete remedial obligations.

Such a temporal broadening of the analysis is appropriate, necessary even, when the absurdity that results from neglecting it is contemplated. Think, for example, of the disadvantaged social status of, say, African-Americans in the United States, of the Romani people in Europe, or the Dalit in India, etc. There is no natural law that explains their relative disadvantage, which is instead quite clearly the result of cultural, economic, and political decisions and processes. Failing to take this into account, by focusing on the fact that their being worse off is a result of bad luck beyond their control, potentially obscures the necessary analysis of *why* their disadvantage exists as well as *what* should be done about it, and by *whom.*

Taking into account such historical causes of current disadvantages does not mean insisting that the only explanations for current inequalities are historical, but it suggests that disadvantages need not be seen as simple facts, but as the result of social processes. The corresponding remedy then will lie not only in redistribution, but in addressing the very social processes responsible for the persistence of the disadvantage in question. Think, for example, about the different levels of economic and social prosperity of the colonial powers and their former colonies. Some decades after the end of colonial rule, it seems implausible to pin all current disadvantages in former colonies exclusively on the events that took place many years ago. Additional factors and events have occurred in the meanwhile that have clearly had an impact on these inequalities—and in many cases have even exacerbated them. Nevertheless, the lasting negative impact of colonial rule, along with the ways it eventually withdrew in different regions, cannot be eliminated from a comprehensive analysis of existing inequalities. The relational account of global egalitarianism thus is not subject to the two objections that applied to a distributive account.

Two further objections against a theory of global relational egalitarianism need to be mentioned. The first one doubts the existence of the preconditions necessary for establishing reciprocal relations of democratic equality; the second argues that global "equality of status" simply does not matter for people who have, on a global level, no direct interaction with one another. Both objections can, by explaining my own account further, be refuted and thus do not, I contend, undermine my project of advancing the ideal of global relational equality.

The first objection ties the existence of legitimate claims about egalitarian justice to the existence of a basic structure of a (domestic or global) society or to the existence of democratic institutions. Anderson's account of "democratic" egalitarianism seems to be a clear target for this criticism. Tan, for example, contends that relational egalitarianism has the distributive implication "to ensure that the gap between the rich and poor in a society stays within the limit consistent with the ideals of democratic polity, and this objective is quite independent of the luck principle. A democratic society, fundamentally, is understood as a fair system of social cooperation, and a fair system of social cooperation must in turn honour the ideal of reciprocity" (Tan 2011, 397). I can agree with this description of the distributive implications of relational egalitarianism, but if it is used to tie claims of egalitarian justice (in terms of both relations and distributions) to the condition of an actual all-encompassing basic structure or an actual global democracy, this condition seems too strong to me.

According to Tan, the absence of a global democratic order within which reciprocal interactions reign will lead to the fact that there are no such claims for egalitarian justice. He writes that under "democratic equality, since distributive justice is derivative of the ideal of a democratic order, unless it can be shown that the global order is a democratic social order in the appropriate sense (or that there is some commitment to bringing such a global order about), considerations of *global* distributive justice do not even arise" (Tan 2011, 398, cf. also 409, 412). I disagree and contend, instead, that the quite specific demand for a democratic order as a precondition for legitimate demands of egalitarian justice be replaced by an, admittedly more vague but sufficiently specific, account of 'frameworks of interaction', i. e. contexts within which individuals, groups, or institutions can or do interact and can do so on more equal or on more unequal (potentially oppressive) terms. Global relational egalitarians might agree that the ideal of relational equality can be realised best within a democratic global society in which not only its members understand themselves as equally important participants and contributors in a joint scheme of cooperation but within which also the institutional arrangements mirror this commitment. But it is possible (even though maybe less realistic) to uphold and apply the ideal of relational equality to contexts and settings within which any such democratic set-up is absent. The undisputed fact that the current global reality lacks a great many democratic features and institutions thus does not undermine the ideal of global relational equality.[137]

Furthermore, one can reproach Tan with applying a double standard when considering the conditions for legitimate claims of egalitarian justice. In his own institutional framework, Tan presupposes for his variant of global luck egalitarianism the existence of a global basic structure, in a roughly Rawlsian sense.[138] Whether such a global basic structure already exists, is debatable (Nagel 2005); as debatable as is the existence of the relevant forms of global relationships/interactions/connections needed by relational or democratic egalitarians. However, in my view, both sides—global luck egalitarians as well as global relational egalitarians—can find in the actual global interactions (whether mediated through institutions or not) a sound basis to justify their respective egalitarian concerns and demands.

A second objection against the plausibility of global relational egalitarianism has been advanced by Miller, who, in a brief passage in his book *National Responsibility and Global Justice* (Miller 2007, 77–78)[139] doubts whether the ideal of "equality of status" or "social equality" can ever claim relevance on the global level. Miller has strong sympathies for equality of status in the domestic setting (where he thinks people ought to interact, in spite of all their differences, as equals), but he does not see how this should matter on the global level: "Equality of status is important among people who are in daily contact with one another, and who share a common way of life" (Miller 2007, 77). The type of relationships that individuals have with their interacting counterparts is much more important to them, Miller holds, than the relationships their group has with other groups. When they are treated as equals in their immediate surroundings, intergroup comparisons with regard to social status lose their im-

---

[137] My own account does not stress the *democratic* or institutional aspect of relational equality as strongly as Anderson does, and focusses instead on the ethical *cosmopolitan responsibility* of individuals in any frameworks of interaction within a globalised and interconnected world, irrespective of the question whether a global democratic order already exists. Thus, it may escape the mentioned critique even easier.

[138] Not all global luck egalitarians presuppose a joint basic structure or global connectedness. Caney, for example, argues that the requirements of global equality of opportunity should exist even in the absence of such institutional connections (Caney 2001, 124–127).

[139] Miller himself does not defend global egalitarianism in any form, though he does stress the importance of national responsibility.

portance: differences in status that matter to people in their everyday interactions do not bother them in the diffuse, distant, and more abstract form they take internationally, or so Miller argues.

This claim may be true as a descriptive statement about human dispositions, because indeed inequalities in the near range tend to bother people more than inequalities in comparison with those far away. However, as a normatively relevant statement it becomes morally problematic: The fact that the globally privileged do not care very much about the global poor may be generally true, but this disinterest and apathy is exactly the moral problem that needs to be addressed. Pointing out that the global poor also care more about the inequalities in the near range would be, even if true, rather cynical, because their disinterest in such rather remote inequalities could arguably count as an additional indicator of disadvantage that limits their attention on concern on the more pressing issues in the near range.

My argument against Miller's claim is based, once again, on the importance of being able to make one's voice heard, and to have one's voice count for something. Most will intuitively understand this requirement, since most—even the relatively affluent citizens of relatively affluent countries—have on occasion personally felt what it means to have one's voice go unheard. In functioning democracies, however, most adult citizens at least have the right to vote, and this right should be freely exercised, without interference or coercion, and without domination. People may be dissatisfied with the outcomes of general elections, and they may feel disempowered by crude majority-rule, but as imperfect as the system of voting may be, at least every person in a functioning democratic setting has one vote and no one has more or less than one vote. With the right to vote comes at least a minimal certainty that one's voice is accounted for when it comes to political representation. And, in democratic countries, political representatives are not only occupied with domestic issues: they also make sure that the voice of "their" constituents is heard when it comes to decisions with international import. Here, affluent citizens can also be sure that their representatives defend the national interest (and often even with a particularly vicious ruthlessness). Indeed, the straightforwardly nationalistic, zero-sum interventions of national representatives in international negotiations demonstrate just how much it is accepted in international politics that national interest be pursued above all else. Contrast this vigorous defence of interest, and expression of voice (even if that voice cannot hope to capture the full diversity of belief and value of all represented individuals), with how people in poorer countries that lack functional democratic institutions are twice duped: not only are their legitimate interests not taken into account domestically, but they are also left without adequate representation internationally.

I take this to be a relevant inequality in status that is obvious to every person with some access to information about domestic and international political processes—through TV, the internet or social media. Knowing that one's interests are represented in political processes is, I argue, also connected with the self-esteem and the self-perception of one's social status. Knowing of one's lack of representation may indeed add further to feelings of inferiority and marginalisation, insofar as it shows just how much the issues that are of relevance to such a person lie within the exclusive domain of the powerful to decide upon.

The lack of direct interaction between individuals hence does not speak against the importance and pertinence of equality of status on the global level, as Miller suggests. The wide-spread absence of political representation for the legitimate interests of many people (from countries of the Global South, for example, or from future generations), should instead be understood as a morally problematic indication of their presumed status inferiority. True, there may be no actual interactions and no adequate (institutional) representation. This, however, does not speak against the normative claim that there *should* be representation and that all interaction, however direct or mediate, should respect the equal moral status of all.[140] Thus, such actual *absence* of interaction can even be perceived as a *denial* of relations, where such interactions and relations could and should exist.[141] Pointing to the fact that there are no interactions with those in dire need far away, or with those in the future who will have to suffer from the negative effects of climate change, is hypocritical and must not serve as an excuse for inaction. The effects on these peoples' lives are multiple and significant, and must not be ignored. This problem is clearly captured from the perspective of global relational egalitarianism and comes with an urgent call for responsible action.

---

140 Tessman makes a similar claim: "a vulnerability and the moral requirement to which it gives rise may still be said to be relational even when no *existing* relation is identified as one that hosts the moral requirement. In such a case, the need or vulnerability is relational in the sense that it *seeks* a relation. One person's need is a call for response" and she further specifies that such "vulnerability-responsive moral requirements can exist regardless of whether they can be satisfied" (Tessman 2015, 247–248). For further discussion of this claim, cf. chapter six below.
141 In a disturbing essay on migrants drowning in the Mediterranean Sea, Frances Stonor Saunders wrote in 2013 that a relationship exists between the privileged "us"—i.e. myself, those I know, and those somehow nearer and dearer to me—and unknown others who drown while attempting to cross the sea. She writes about an unknown refugee who drowned while giving birth that: "it's this, her lack of known identity, which places us, who are fat with it, in direct if hopelessly unequal relationship to her." (https://www.lrb.co.uk/v38/n05/frances-stonorsaunders/where-on-earth-are-you [last accessed: 1 July 2019]).

To expand: the absence of actual interaction, even if true, can not serve as a general denial of connection or relation—and subsequently of responsibility. *Knowing* about a harm or wrong suffered by some person or group is already a form of relationship which can be sufficient to justify a *demand to establish a more tangible relationship*. Knowing, combined with an ability to help, further develops this relationship within which moral demands then emerge. Thus, it is already an expression of disrespect if one remains fully untouched and fails to react when learning about some harm or wrong suffered by someone else.[142] Such failures to respond and act are highly indicative of one's moral commitments, and while it would be absurd to demand that all constantly address all instances of moral wrongs they have ever learned about, no one endorsing the view that all humans are of fundamentally equal moral standing can ignore human suffering and social inequalities, even if she is not directly connected to it by personal relations or close proximity. Both on the individual and also on the institutional level, such wrongs morally trigger a (prima facie) demand to respond and act.

6 The priority of relations, the relevance of distributions

The relationship between global luck egalitarianism and global relational egalitarianism has been brought into much sharper focus, and in summing up what has been covered in this chapter, I would like to strike a conciliatory note, one that stresses how much luck and relational egalitarians share in common despite their points of disagreement. After all, I think that much of the debate is best understood as a family quarrel among egalitarians, all of whom share similar —and good—hopes and intentions.[143]

First, it is important to remember that both relational and distributive egalitarians have common ground with regard to the equal moral worth of all human beings, despite drawing different conclusions from this crucial commitment. While global luck egalitarians focus on equal distributions as the appropriate expression of equal moral worth of all, relational egalitarians focus on so-

---

142 Neglecting to support or save a person in existential need, where extending help would be possible, clashes with relational equality not only because of the fact that the people involved have such radically unequal abilities, but primarily because in denying support, the advantaged person weighs her own preferences, goods etc., even if above the threshold of sufficiency, higher than the the existential needs of the other.
143 Cf. also Lippert-Rasmussen's recent suggestion of an "ecumenical form of egalitarianism" (Lippert-Rasmussen 2018).

cial or interactional equality, and are only indirectly interested in distributive questions. Yet, both should have—at least outside of the academic disputes where differences should be carved out in a clear way—sympathy for the other's position, since relations are sensitive to different distributions, and relations influence distributive outcomes. Since both these aspects clearly do matter, and are often rather inseparable in practice and in policy, the question of assigning comparative relevance to distributive and relational issues is really one of degree.

Second, it is probably more difficult to find common ground *within* the field of different types of global luck egalitarianism than between some luck egalitarians and relational egalitarians—, since it is possible to justify luck egalitarianism for very different reasons. Indeed, *some* have defended luck egalitarianism in order to *avoid having to intervene* in the face of distributive inequalities, since the view can set aside even massive ones, provided they are the result of "responsible choices".[144] For those, giving up their version of luck egalitarianism would lead to a costly call for redistribution to poorer countries and peoples. Helping the poor who are in a disadvantaged situation presumably because of their own behaviour and choices would mean, on this account, to provide *unfair advantage* to some. *Other* global luck egalitarians, more convincingly, defend their view with the aim of drawing attention to the arbitrariness by which some groups are *worse* off than others, and this position sits more easily alongside a more general willingness to call for redistributive interventions, even very costly ones. Here, *unfair disadvantage* lies at the core of the luck egalitarian concern, but the global luck egalitarians endorsing this variant of luck egalitarianism will generally be prepared to bite the bullet and concede (out of consistency alone) a more prominent role to concern for unfair *advantage*, as well. Reconciling the tensions between different luck egalitarian background convictions may thus, at least in some cases, be more difficult than reconciling the luck egalitarian concern for unfair disadvantage (in distribution) with the relational egalitarian concern for respect in relations on a footing of equality.

Global relational egalitarianism, as I understand it, is not opposed to distributive interventions, even costly ones, when they are a necessary condition for the possibility of relations of social equality, but they would not target distributive questions as problematic in their own right. Relational egalitarianism may in fact allow for quite a lot of distributive inequality (as long as those who have

---

[144] I refer again to Cohen's diagnosis that Dworkin, by directing attention to luck and choice, has integrated into egalitarian thinking the most powerful idea of the anti-egalitarian right (Cohen 1989, 933).

less have enough and those who have more do not have too much, which would undermine the possibility of relational equality). Yet, it seems to be more ambitious than luck egalitarianism, insofar as moral concern is not restricted merely to the distributive symptoms of global inequality, but explicitly includes the root causes of these inequalities; namely the structures that cause and perpetuate inequalities in power, influence and wealth.

In sum, in this chapter I have sought to show the possibility of understanding the dispute between global distributive and global relational egalitarians as a rather productive disagreement about the relative importance of two unquestionably important aspects of justice. I also hope to have shown that a problematic disagreement exists between some global luck egalitarians and all other egalitarians, be they relational or luck egalitarians.

I contend that global relational egalitarianism is the best available theory for spelling out the point of global equality, since it is distribution-sensitive without being narrowly focussed on distributive issues. In this regard, global relational egalitarianism can be called a pluralistic account of equality. Working towards global relational equality will go along with increasing global distributive equality, since massive distributive inequality is often a symptom and indicator of social inequality. Increasing social equality should, one would imagine, then also reduce the symptomatic distributive inequality to more morally acceptable levels.

I cannot but admit that, in the shadow of current realities on our planet, the entire dispute presented in this chapter appears to be somewhat academic. The catastrophe of widespread *absolute* human deprivation, which continues to fatally limit the lives of so many persons, goes on, while egalitarians talk about details of elaborate definitions of justice and equality in the greatest abstraction. Yet, even increasing agreement *that* help should be provided and that absolute deprivation should be eliminated should not hide the problematic fact that the underlying justifications for such help are very different: some argue for it as a duty to be charitable, others as a duty to even out unjustified distributive inequalities, and only global relational egalitarians call for realising an ambitious and complex ideal of social relations of equality. Global relational egalitarianism, in this sense, is a fine match for the ambitious moral ideal of cosmopolitanism, in the way that it sees individuals not as a disconnected mass of individuals living on this planet, but as a society of equals.

This chapter has introduced the second essential feature of the ethos of *cosmopolitan responsibility:* a firm commitment to the normative ideal of equality as explained by an account of *global relational egalitarianism*. This ideal applies —in both a diagnostic and a prescriptive function—to the numerous connections and interactions between people across the globe. It demands, negatively, to end the identified instances of structural injustices in its different forms; furthermore, it demands, positively, that all can make their voices heard and count, and interact with one another as moral equals. This relational ideal has distributive implications: all must have *enough* to be able to function as citizens of the world; and no one must have *too much* so that he or she is able to dominate others, thereby excluding them from participating in the social processes that influence their lives. When endorsed by individual agents, the ideal of global relational equality will shape dispositions, habits, and acts: even if resulting concrete action is local, it can be done with the ambition to honour the ideal of global relational equality.

Chapter 3
Pragmatism. Practice and the possibility of progress

> "The ethical life belongs to human beings, living together in ever larger groups, and working out their shared lives with one another. Philosophy's task is to facilitate this working out." — P. Kitcher

1 Cosmopolitanism as a personal way of life

Cosmopolitanism and egalitarianism are not only theoretical normative ideals. They can become a lived practice when they are endorsed by individual agents, shape their ethos, and influence how agents feel and think, talk and act about global issues. The third essential feature of my theory of *cosmopolitan responsibility* is its pragmatic nature for which I take some inspiration from the rich and diverse philosophical tradition of US-American pragmatism, notably from the works of John Dewey.[145] Although the inspiration is more general than systematic, the following chapter will introduce several elements of a pragmatist approach to ethics that I suggest to integrate into the proposed theory of *cosmopolitan responsibility*. To be clear, I do not aspire to develop a comprehensive account of pragmatic ethics, which is admittedly in itself less a coherent moral philosophical theory than a specific perspective on the means and aims of ethics.[146] Neither do I propose a full pragmatist account of (global) justice.[147]

---

[145] The fact that Dewey's biography shows him personally an active cosmopolitan, involved in many progressive social movements around the world, shall only be briefly mentioned here. For his engagement in Turkey, China, Mexico and elsewhere, cf. the biography by Martin (2002).– Dewey himself does not particularly stress the cosmopolitan implications of his *ethics* himself. Nevertheless, there have been several attempts in the literature to read him as a cosmopolitan in general, as well as a valuable contributor to the project of a global ethics (Waks 2009, Hickman 2010). Particularly fruitful, in this regard, were attempts to take up Dewey's thinking in political theory and theories of international relations (Cochran 1999, Bray 2011).

[146] Good overviews are provided by LaFollette (2000), Anderson (2010a), Pappas (1998), Serra (2009) and Welchman (1995).– Yet, even for a single pragmatist philosopher like Dewey, it is difficult to identify the concrete content of his ethics. As Pappas has it: "When reading Dewey […] it is important to resist the philosophical habit of trying to find a 'system.' A better approach is to become acquainted with his moral vision. But this task is complicated by the fact that Dewey did not consolidate his ideas about ethics in a single work. He scattered his ideas throughout his many books and essays. In some cases he even presented them in a paragraph or two placed

In a somewhat piecemeal approach then, I simply seek to present selected elements of pragmatist and neo-pragmatist reasoning about ethics which together point towards a plausible alternative to a variety of conventional philosophical thinking about the role and goals of ethics. Central to the pragmatic approach is the role of individual experience, the importance of personal habits and patterns of conduct as a way to turn considered values into justified action, a systematic method for moral inquiry that makes room for normative pluralism, and an optimistic belief in the possibility of progress in living together. These elements also shape the ethos of *cosmopolitan responsibility*.

Pragmatism is often met with reproach of refusing to provide a substantial normative criterion for decision making and assessment and being concerned instead simply with 'whatever works'. If true, a narrow focus on 'whatever works' would make for a very uninteresting view, particularly in ethics, since ethics should provide appropriate reasons for the normative views held and actions undertaken. While a strict 'whatever works' hence cannot constitute a worthwhile aim of the ethical project (nor of any philosophical undertaking), the reproach against pragmatism nevertheless catches well one distinctive feature of pragmatist ethics: namely that philosophical reasoning in ethics should take into account how the theoretical tools employed make a difference in practice. A central claim in pragmatism is that ideas, including norms and values, cannot prove their "truth" independently from practical implementation, i.e. they have to be put to 'work'. In the words of James: "truth happens to an idea" (James 1909, 574). Truth, on this understanding, is nothing but the successful use of ideas in practice. Pragmatism is hence concerned, first, with the acute circumstances under which certain problems appear; and, secondly, with the impact theories and ideas actually have in such circumstances, i.e., how they work with regard to overcoming or dealing with perceived problems.

In this pragmatic sense, morality is not a detached intellectual enterprise of establishing a determinate and substantive set of rules and principles to guide human behaviour, but should be understood as a collective, social undertaking, as a continuing process, an ongoing challenge to figure out how to deal best with the given problems in the context of humans living together.

---

almost parenthetically in the midst of a passage devoted to another philosophical topic" (Pappas 1998, 100).

147 It has been noted that the notion of justice is largely absent in Dewey's writings (Dieleman, Rondel et al. 2017). While recently some have started to address this lacuna (Talisse 2017, Rondel 2018), my own attempt to advance the project of a global political ethics can, as is explained in this chapter, draw directly from many pragmatist insights.

This first, tentative characterisation invites a brief recapitulation of the concrete problem for which the turn toward pragmatism seems to me particularly useful. At issue in this book is, ultimately, the problem of how humans should live together under conditions of globalisation, which are currently shaped by enormous inequalities in distribution, massive asymmetries in power and influence, and persisting domination and structural injustice. In this context it is still unclear how exactly individuals should act and institutional arrangements should look like in order to allow and support good lives for all and a good living together of all. This is the massive, current ethical challenge of the ethical project. In addressing it, Kitcher, for example, foresees also a role for moral philosophy: "The ethical life belongs to human beings, living together in ever larger groups, and working out their shared lives with one another. Philosophy's task is to facilitate this working out." (Kitcher 2012, 2). I agree and my writing thus aspires to contribute to the task of figuring out how individuals should think and act in order to live well together under the de facto circumstances of cosmopolitanism.

These global circumstances generate a jointly shared sphere of interaction that can also be caputured in pragmatic perspective. For Dewey, the actual interactions between people who live together, be it in smaller or larger groups, give rise to what he calls "the public". The public is constituted by all who are in one way or another influenced or affected by the other's actions. In *The Public and Its Problems*, Dewey writes

> We take then our point of departure from the objective fact that human acts have consequences upon others, that some of these consequences are perceived, and that their perception leads to subsequent effort to control action so as to secure some consequences and avoid others. Following this clew, we are led to remark that the consequences are of two kinds, those which affect the persons directly engaged in a transaction, and those which affect others beyond those immediately concerned. In this distinction we find the germ of the distinction between the private and the public. When indirect consequences are recognized and there is effort to regulate them, something having the traits of a state comes into existence. (Dewey 1927, 244)

This distinction gives a lay of the land in which problems of global justice and global ethics are embedded: the fact that some of our actions impact on others, even if this is in a mediated and indirect manner, generates a wide-ranging and inclusive field of interaction in which there is a need for individual actions (and thus their consequences) to be regulated. I am less concerned here with Dewey's notion that this brings about already something similar to "a state". The establishment of a joint interactional sphere—in which there is mutual influence, the consequences of which are perceivable, and hence at least some effort is made to regulate individual actions—is sufficient. Dewey further specifies "the public" by stating that it "consists of all those who are affected by the indirect consequences of transactions to such an extent that it is deemed necessary to have those consequences systematically cared for" (Dewey 1927, 245–246).

Such a definition of "the public" as unconstrained by national boundaries is of fundamental importance to my purpose here. The relevant form of a public is created by the interactions and relationships between agents; and particularly so when the impact of some agent's action on others is harmful or damaging.[148] Dewey defends a universal egalitarianism when he assumes that all persons matter equally, since "other persons are selves too" and "the good is the same in quality wherever it is found" (Dewey 1922, 202). All this points to a potentially global scope of the Deweyan public—albeit one comprised of several subsets of particularly intense interaction and influence.

Dewey can plausibly be regarded as a "relational egalitarian" for the combination of his commitment to a global public, constituted by the relations and interactions between people, and his commitment to the equal moral importance of all.[149] Anderson, for example, ascribes to Dewey the idea "that a free society of equals is a society of mutually accountable individuals who regulate their claims on one another according to principles that express and sustain their social equality" (Anderson 2010b, 3, fn. 4).[150] And Dewey himself writes, in the context of an early defense of an *Ethics of Democracy*, "The true meaning of equality is synonymous with the definition of democracy [...]. It is the form of society in which every man has a chance and knows that he has it—and we may add, a chance to which no possible limits can be put, a chance which is truly infinite, the chance to become a person. Equality, in short, is the ideal of humanity; an ideal in the consciousness of which democracy lives and moves." (Dewey 1888, 246).

---

[148] As I argued above, in chapter two, also abstaining from certain (inter-) actions can be of moral relevance.
[149] Cf. chapters one and two above.
[150] Cf. Young, in a similar spirit, on the link between individual experiences with the complexities of a social life and the need for a 'democratic' engagement among equals: "We make our moral and political judgements, then, not only by taking account of one another's interests and perspectives, but also by considering the collective social processes and relationships that lie between us and which we have come to know together by discussing the world. [...] Just because social life consists of plural experiences and perspectives, a theory of communicative ethics must endorse a radically democratic conception of moral and political judgement. Normative judgement is best understood as the product of dialogue under conditions of equality and mutual respect. Ideally, the outcome of such dialogue and judgement is just and legitimate only if all the affected perspectives have a voice" (Young 1997, 59).

Dewey's claim about the role of the ideal of democracy can also bear on the ideal of moral cosmopolitanism: democratic ideas and ideals should, he claims, translate into "a personal, an individual, way of life," which includes "the possession and continual use of certain attitudes, forming personal character and determining desire and purpose in all the relations of life. Instead of thinking of our own dispositions and habits as accommodated to certain institutions we have to learn to think of the latter as expressions, projections and extensions of habitually dominant personal attitudes" (Dewey 1939, 226). This is as important in a domestic as in the global setting.[151]

In the balance of this short chapter, I hope to draw attention to certain key features of the (neo-) pragmatist tradition that appear to me to be helpful with regard to the project of contributing to a theory of global ethics by developing a more nuanced understanding of moral cosmopolitanism which can serve as the core of such an ethics. Yet, all this is meant only as a modest proposal. Nothing hinges on the distinctive historic influence of the pragmatist tradition when it comes to assessing whether the arguments I develop in later parts of this book are sound.

2 From criterial monism to pragmatic pluralism

Before illustrating the distinctively pragmatic approach to ethics that underlies my account of a cosmopolitan ethos, it is important to sketch what could be considered the 'standard view' of ethics, and to identify some of its troublesome features that motivated the early pragmatists' efforts to define an alternative view. The features of the 'standard view' are still very widespread in modern philosophical ethics, even if they are often held more implicitly than defended explicitly.[152]

The core of the pragmatic criticism of the standard view in ethics is that it understands moral theories to be "about abstract structures that sort agents, actions, or outcomes into appropriate categories" (Jamieson 1991, 477). The job of the philosopher or moral theorist within this view is to "make particular moral theories explicit, to describe their universality, and to make vivid their coercive

---

[151] Cf. also Green (2011, 61–62).
[152] Among others, Kitcher has distinguished such two different "visions in normative ethics" (Kitcher 2011, 285–288), one being what I call the 'standard view,' the other the pragmatist alternative (cf. also LaFollette 2000). A similar critique to the one developed here on pragmatist terms has been suggested by Hutchings, who builds on resources from virtue ethics, feminist ethics and postmodernist traditions for her account of global ethics (Hutchings 2018).

power" (ibid.). Often, a single basic moral principle is identified that functions as the morally relevant criterion; for example the categorical imperative or the principle of utility. Such "criterial" views establish the relevance of a particular perspective (or paradigm) for moral thinking at the cost of other morally salient aspects with the promise of a conclusive, transcendental account of morality. Such an approach to making ethical judgements can be described as top-down, or the direct application of abstract theory to concrete problems (Arras 2010): theory comes first, and then in a second step it is applied to concrete moral problems to yield justified moral judgements.

Such universalistic, criterial moral theories standardly assume—in one way or another—that their morally relevant criteria are logically prior, fixed, complete, and directly applicable (LaFollette 2000, 401). LaFollette pointedly illustrates the assumption, using utilitarianism as an example:

> Although the principle of utility might be revealed through experience, its truth is thought (a) to be logically prior to experience and (b) to provide a measure for determining what is moral for all people, at all times. Moreover, this principle (c) does not need to be supplemented, and (d) can be directly applied to specific cases. (LaFollette 2000, 401)

Problems with moral theories of this criterial type are at least threefold. First, the standard view is based on de-contextual thinking, wherein moral principles are deduced from "pure" thought and under idealised circumstances, rather than developed from real world situations and plausible approaches to their amelioration. This transcendental approach relies on forms of ideal theory that are frequently rather remote from, and even alien to, the problems people face in real life. Second, the standard view does not allow for amendment or correction. Its criteria are static, and are by definition forever right and thus inflexible and never evolving. All alternative ways of reasoning are hence neglected and excluded as being morally irrelevant. But if there remains, as there does, always the possibility that a theory has it partly or wholly wrong (falsifiability), yet amendments and corrections are ruled out by it, these theories reveal themselves to inhabit the realm of dogmatic absolutist ideological thinking. Third, theories of the standard view type are (most often) incapable of applying their theoretical insights to real world situations in a way that actually helps agents to solve the moral problems at hand. Instead, a moral method that is both intellectually and practically responsible should not rely on a monistic standard of moral judgment but integrate the complexity of the initial challenge into the moral method.

In addition to these fundamental internal problems that plague all variants of the standard view, the incommensurability of competing criterial views causes even more problems for such theories. What reason could one provide to adhere to *only* one or the other of say deontology and consequentialism, for example? Should one not aspire to put the different available tools to use when it comes to understanding the moral complexities of right and wrong?

Dewey pointedly summarises the net effect of these objections against standard moral theory and starts to identify an alternatie approach:

> Moral theory cannot emerge when there is positive belief as to what is right and what is wrong, for then there is no occasion for reflection. It emerges when men are confronted with situations in which different desires promise opposed goods and in which incompatible courses of action seem to be morally justified. Only such a conflict of good ends and of standards and rules for right and wrong calls forth personal inquiry into the bases of morals. (Dewey and Tufts 1932, 164)

Dewey here embeds moral theorising in concrete circumstances in which agents, confronted with challenges in their own personal experience, have to make up their minds about what to do. Applying one single type of moral consideration, as stipulated by all the standard moral theories, shuts out entirely the insights offered by the others. From a pragmatic ethical perspective, such thinking is too narrow, too constrained to single criteria assessment, in order to be of any actual use in the making of moral evaluations in response to complex moral problems. Because of their complexity, the moral challenges almost invariably have different salient facets so that only a plurality of normative perspectives will be able to capture them.[153]

3 Elements of a pragmatic ethics

In the following section I point out four key elements of a pragmatic ethics, as suggested in the writings of Dewey: the role of individual experience, a pragmatic focus on acts and habits, a distinctive pragmatic method of inquiry and a belief in the possibility of progress.

(1) *The role of individual experience.* The "ordinary experience" of people lies at the centre of Dewey's philosophy (cf. Jung 2014). Experiences are an anthro-

---

[153] The task for pragmatists consists not in integrating alternative criterial views into one which is considered to be fundamental, as it is undertaken in the attempts to "consequentialise" moral theories (Portmore 2007) or to stipulate a "threshold deontology" (Alexander 2010). Such approaches retain their distinctive theoretical affiliation to consequentialism or deontology respectively. From a pragmatic perspective the different types of moral reasons should, however, be considered as genuinely different, "independent factors" in morality (Dewey 1930), requiring thus for a genuine plurality in normative perspectives.

pological universal and as such fundamental to the human existence. Experience is the bridge between individual persons and the world around them. In *Experience and Nature*, Dewey analyses in great detail the intricate relationship between mind and world, and shows the relevance of experience in many dimensions of human lives—such as in art, in science, and in society (Dewey 1925). Dewey's notion of "experience" is immensely rich and in the present context I can only shed some light on the role of experience in the realm of human action. Starting from the experience of people matters in several different ways for the present exploration of *cosmopolitan responsibility*. The complex experience of deprivation, disadvantage, oppression, etc. lies at the origin of what causes moral concern; the experience of irritation and uncertainty about how to respond to such triggers of moral concern shapes the situation of all those who become aware of it and could be doing something about it. Concretely, according to Dewey, the trigger for doing ethics is the experience of conflict, of "being torn between two duties," such as of having to "make a choice between competing moral loyalties and convictions," often because of a conflict between "incompatible values" (Dewey and Tufts 1932, 165). This distinctive moral experience is initially characterised by uncertainty and irritation, it disrupts the usual orientation guiding an agent's habitual conduct, and thereby, for Dewey, calls for moral "inquiry". On the role of moral theory with regard to the experience of conflicts, Dewey writes:

> Moral theory can (i) generalize the types of moral conflicts which arise, thus enabling a perplexed and doubtful individual to clarify his own particular problem by placing it in a larger context; it can (ii) state the leading ways in which such problems have been intellectually dealt with by those who have thought upon such matters; it can (iii) render personal reflection more systematic and enlightened, suggesting alternatives that might otherwise be overlooked, and stimulating greater consistency in judgment. (Dewey and Tufts 1932, 166)

It is important to stress that, for Dewey, the experiences that call for moral analysis are ordinary experiences of agents going about their lives, affected by some state of affairs (Pappas 1998, 102–104, Jung 2014). Dewey further stipulates that the means for dealing with identified problems can also be found with the help of such ordinary experience: the three abilities of moral theories quoted above do not result from esoteric expert knowledge and competencies; rather, they are based in the ordinary capacities of ordinary people in ordinary circumstances.[154] Dewey argues that within an appropriate institutional framework, ordina-

---

[154] Kitcher has, following Dewey, questioned the need for or existence special ethical expertise

ry citizens (equipped with qualitative resources stemming from their experiences) are fully capable of deliberation about complex moral and social issues.[155]

(2) *Acts and habits*. Moral action is only rarely the result of abstract rational deliberation; most often, it is embedded in collective as well as individual habits, which are mostly pre-conscious. This is not meant to downplay the role of reflexivity and reason, but its importance for most of an agent's (moral) actions must not be overestimated. For Dewey, reason standardly does not precede moral action but reason is only deployed in problematic situations to help shape the formation of new, intelligent (as opposed to unreflected) conduct that may turn into habit over time.

Consequently, a pragmatic ethics focusses generally much less on single acts and more on patterns of action, which are called habits (Dewey 1922). Habits are dispositions to respond to certain stimuli in a specific way and most often our acts, no matter whether they are of a particular moral quality or take place outside of the moral realm, are shaped by habits. These habits mirror our commitments as well as the expectations of our social environment. The important insight underlying the focus on habit is that habitual action is executed in a stable way and with little, if any, reflective effort. We just act and do not have to engage in time- and energy-consuming reflection before we do so. Habits shape our conduct as long as they are not perceived to be problematic, but in some situations agents start to experience frictions and the formerly unquestioned patterns of behaviour fail to satisfy. Here, a reconsideration and restructuring of one's habits becomes necessary—not only a one time execution of a different type of action.[156]

Thus, the central question of pragmatic ethics is not the narrow 'what action should I take?' but 'what *habit* is appropriate for addressing problems of this type, how can it be developed, and how can it be incorporated as the stable future of conduct?' (cf. Hildebrand 2008, 68). Analysing a concrete, single challenge about what to do in a given situation only serves as a proxy for addressing a general problem. And if the solution to the problem at hand is found and successfully enacted, this counts in favour of acting alike in similar situations. Here is an example: Should one come to the conclusion that it is morally demanded to donate some percentage of one's disposable income to charity, it is not enough

---

that goes beyond what "ordinary" citizens can do guided by an intelligent method of ethical inquiry (Kitcher 2001, 2011).
155 Cf. Cochran who explains how for Dewey "a public is an instrument through which problem-solving is socially coordinated" (Cochran 2010, 325).
156 In this regard, Dewey agrees with Aristotle who, in *Nicomachean Ethics*, argued that "one swallow does not make a summer" (Aristotle NE, 1098a17).

to donate once. For a single such act does not sufficiently address the relevant ethical challenge, which deals with *patterns* of (inter-) action. Ethics for Dewey is not about one-off choices, but about forming stable character traits, dispositions to act in a certain way, for the origin of many of the social problems—also and particularly in the context of global structural injustice—do not result from single acts but from repeated acts and patterns of action that result from morally problematic habits. Since the single individual act alone is too meagre to bring about lasting change, only change in the habits can.[157]

This point demonstrates how a pragmatist ethics takes an important interest in the entire character of the person who is acting, rather than in individual acts alone. Pragmatists emphasise the importance of persons acting as the person *they want to become* also in the light of their considered moral judgements. As Dewey has it:

> it is proper to say that in choosing this object rather than that, one is in reality choosing what kind of person or self one is going to be. Superficially, the deliberation which terminates in choice is concerned with weighing the values of particular ends. Below the surface, it is a process of discovering what sort of being a person most wants to become. (Dewey and Tufts 1932, 287)

Concretely, acts are hence on the one hand voluntary consequences of knowing and choosing, and, as such, are also contributions to and expressions of a rather stable yet constantly evolving character (Dewey and Tufts 1932, 166, 167). In this light, even seemingly trivial acts—the everyday acts we perform without any explicit decisions—matter a great deal morally, since they result from character. Dewey specifies: "If we omitted from our estimate of moral character all the deeds done in the performance of daily tasks, satisfaction of recurrent needs, meeting of responsibilities, each slight perhaps in itself but enormous in mass, morality would be a weak and sickly thing indeed." Hence: "Such acts, non-moral in isolation, derive moral significance from the ends to which they lead" (Dewey and Tufts 1932, 168).

Generally, the pragmatist perspective thus places significant weight on the relatively stable dispositions of people to respond in certain situations with a specific sort of action. Identifying and then cultivating the right kind of disposition—also through intelligent structuring of the social and factual environment

---

[157] "Our moral measure for estimating any existing arrangement or any proposed reform is its effect upon impulse and habits. Does it liberate or suppress, ossify or render flexible, divide or unify interest?" (Dewey 1922, 202).

of an agent or a group in order to support the considered habit—is an important goal of pragmatic ethics.

(3) *Method of inquiry.* In order to address a problem, to find out how to act and which habits to form, Dewey advocates a pluralist method of inquiry. This method, that is applicable also to the realm of ethics, was originally developed to analyse and guide the process of solving problems in the context of the sciences (Dewey 1938, 105–122). Inquiry is for Dewey, a "rule governed activity—an activity of developing hypotheses, predictions, and explanations; of assessing what is to count as evidence for or against a hypothesis or prediction; of deciding which explanations should be adopted and acted upon" (Misak 2013, 129).

What are the steps of this sort of—moral—inquiry for Dewey? First, an agent experiences some general unease in a situation, a diffuse irritation, without being able to concretely delineate the source of that feeling. The second step consists in attempting to identify and specify exactly the concrete problem that is so vexing. This step is particularly important, since often it is unclear what exactly was at the origin of the initial experience of unease and irritation. This second step is for Dewey already experimental, insofar as it is by definition tentative, always open to further revision. The third step consists in considering one or several possible solutions that may promise to overcome the initial confusion. After this heuristic step, the next one consists in experimentally imagining the implications of the candidate solutions by predicting and comparing their different multidimensional consequences and implications. This is the point at which Dewey proposes to use conventional moral philosophical principles: He acknowledges that these principles and rules contain important ethical knowledge that should be taken into consideration when it comes to anticipating the implications of certain acts. It is only the last, fifth step, that leads to actual action performed by the deliberating agent. Action, however, is also experimental and as such provisional. Only after acting does it become possible to assess the factual consequences and implications of an act. The experiences gained by actual action become, in turn, crucial for orienting future actions in analogous circumstances. If such actions are positively assessed, they may as a result contribute to the formation of a helpful habit.

To locate vexing problems and identify (moral) conflicts, it is essential to be able to identify and to name the respective values that may clash. Interestingly, as I pointed out, the existing moral principles can function here as heuristic tools in the moral inquiry, even for pragmatists. However, the "all too human love of certainty" (Dewey 1922, 242) should not lead to the isolation of principles from empirical investigations which acknowledge the contingency of concrete situations. For pragmatists, principles are only indispensable empirical generalisations in need of a constant readjustment to changing conditions.[158]

This is only the roughest sketch of what Dewey has spelled out in his *Logic* and I will not discuss it further.[159] It remains simply to be stated that much of the work I will undertake in later chapters is best understood as contributing to the second and third steps of Dewey's pragmatic moral method: I attempt to locate the problem, and then to reveal the conflicting values that gave rise to the initially diffuse experience of irritation, the "healthy dissatisfaction with the familiar," as Nagel has called it (Nagel 1991, 8).

(4) *The possibility of progress.* I would like to conclude this brief introduction to pragmatic ethics with a word on the role of ideals and ends. In pragmatism, and particularly in Dewey's version, one finds a sophisticated account of meliorism, perfectionism and progress. The fundamental idea of pragmatic progress, however, is not one of teleological progress where humanity would constantly get closer to some fixed ideal end state. Instead, progress is understood in pragmatic terms: it consists in (evolutionary, not necessarily revolutionary) incremental improvements of the human capacities to live together by overcoming limitations and problems. This can occur in the form of progress in our abilities to reason about the relevant challenges at hand and, of cours, importantly also of progress 'in practice', in the form of improved individual behaviour or political and institutional reform. Pragmatic progress hence does not have to be understood as progress *to* some ideal, but as progress *from* an imperfect and problematic status quo (Kitcher 2011, 288, Kitcher 2016).[160]

For its belief in the possibility of achieving meaningful progress, pragmatism can also be called a "philosophy of hope." It trusts that thoughtful inquiry and the joint search for solutions in a cooperative, multi-perspective effort can actually help make things better (Rondel 2018, xii). Defending the possibility of progress in this sense amounts to the optimistic assumption that solutions to social problems can eventually be found, despite the fact that currently available

---

158 Cf. also Hildebrand: "Dewey promotes the capacity of pragmatic moral inquiry to sort out the nature of a problem and its possible solutions. Inquiry also has the ability to reconsider and reconstruct even the moral values and ends at stake, questioning the purposes people use to direct their conduct, and why such purposes are good [...]. Moral inquiry not only discovers morality, it *makes* it" (Hildebrand 2008, 79).
159 But cf. also Hildebrand (2008, 53–58) and Heilinger (2016a, 155–158) for a more detailed presentation. For a critical take on the transfer of Dewey's general method of inquiry to the field of ethics, cf. Grimm (2010, 120).
160 Sen, for example, has distinguished in a similar way his own "comparative," "non-ideal" approach to justice from Rawls's "transcendental," "ideal" approach (Sen 2009).

patterns of thinking and action fall short of providing them. The rejection of both the possibility of, and the need for, perfect, complete, converging and final answers—an imaginary illusion according to Dewey and his followers—is what permits this confidence in the never-ending search for stepwise improvements.[161]

4 The role of philosophy

With regard to the present problems of global injustice and global inequality, what is the role of philosophy? Mightn't it be just plainly absurd to turn to philosophers for answers to such urgent and pressing ethical questions, and for solutions to the unknown challenges that lay ahead? In a sense, it is hard to disagree with such a suggestion, for several reasons. First, philosophy is not directly concerned with practical solutions to concrete problems. It would be folly to turn to a philosopher qua philosopher in order to identify what exactly should be done by whom, for example, to fight food shortages or drought and starvation in a particular region of the world. Philosophers have few skills related to such matters; vast amounts of empirical knowledge are needed that they generally do not possess. Secondly, it would be similarly absurd to turn to philosophers alone with an expectation of receiving conclusive answers even to the conceptual theoretical questions (such as about how responsibility should be distributed or which social and political institutions should generally exist on the global level) in which philosophers do specialise, and for which they do possess pertinent skills, or to expect philosophy to decree solutions to acute chal-

---

[161] I find these ideas helpfully spelled out in Moody-Adams's work on *The Idea of Moral Progress* which also stands in a pragmatist tradition (Moody-Adams 1999). She distinguishes between two forms of moral progress, one being moral progress "in belief" the other moral progress "in practices". The former consists in a deepened understanding of particular moral concepts, such as equality or justice; the latter consists in bringing such newly deepened moral understanding to influence individual behaviour or shape social institutions. In both cases, as Moody-Adams points out, progress is local, i.e. it always proceeds by departing from and improving upon a given status quo. The willingness and ability for critical self-scrutiny of numbers of individuals is a condition sine qua non for actual progress in practice, yet, on her view, academic philosophy and progress "in beliefs" alone will only have a very limited impact here. Even the important "advocacy of engaged moral inquirers" who put to use "the richness and complexity of their conceptions of rationality and rational persuasion", can be successful only if the "main obstacle to moral progress in social practices" is overcome: the tendency to "widespread affected ignorance of what can and should already be known". Yet, such self-scrutiny in an examined life is frequently avoided, particularly if people "expect it to yield insights that [they] are not prepared to obey" (180).

lenges. Here, a broader cooperation involving others—politicians, political and social scientists, and the public—is needed.

Nevertheless, philosophers can and should play a distinctive role in the context of cosmopolitan and other ethical challenges. But not for their specific ethical knowledge, nor for their ability to provide answers and solutions. Instead, the role of philosophy is more modest. For Kitcher—and others, including Socrates—philosophy should be understood to provide a form of dialectic midwifery:

> Philosophers can make proposals, attempting to facilitate the conversation that would deliver answers. [...] The most obvious forms of philosophical midwifery consist in proposing topics for consideration (places on our common vessel where planks might deserve attention) and suggestions about those topics (specific ways of rearranging the timber in those places). (Kitcher 2011, 370)

The allusion to Otto Neurath's comparison of the epistemological challenge of improving knowledge with sailors constantly rebuilding the vessel on which they sail, underlines the anti-foundational views of pragmatism: the constructive role of philosophers lies primarily in a careful contribution to identifying worthwhile topics and facilitation of processes for discussing them. Prior ethical knowledge can help here, but it is not on the grounds of such ethical knowledge that answers to new challenges will be found.

The role of philosophy as midwifery hence consists mostly in bringing certain ideas into the conversation, in explaining, exploring, developing, and nurturing them, so that they matter for ongoing challenges and debates and are alive and available to be put to use when the time is ripe.

Implicit in understanding philosophy as dialectic midwifery is the view that philosophy is no single man or woman's work, but a joint undertaking, a never-ending pursuit to improve the status quo. What is necessary to deal appropriately with the challenges at hand is a coordinated and socially embedded approach. Philosophers contribute to it, but philosophers alone are in no way able or expected to provide definitive solutions. Progress can only occur in incremental steps, and, if it takes place at all, that will be because certain ideas and solutions gain broad acceptance: truth then, to quote James again, happens to an idea (James 1909, 574). Such a pursuit, to improve the human lot, is not an elitist project, but an inclusive and collaborative one involving all, and all on equal terms. Intelligence, in a pragmatic understanding, is not a feature of individuals but a cooperative praxis. If there are intelligent solutions to problems, they cannot but be found experimentally and cooperatively. Prior established knowledge alone, be it philosophical or scientific, is insufficient.

It is in this spirit that I will pursue my reasoning in this book. Central ideas—equality, impartiality, rights, and responsibility—are here understood as tools for tackling the problems of a cosmopolitan scope. The minor contribution I hope to make to larger related debates will consist of scrutinising philosophical ideas in order to assess their meaning and relevance in the context of a global ethics. If these ideas are helpful, and if they gain somy acceptance among those affected[162] by the problems at hand, they hold the potential to inform choices and motivate action, both in individual agents and in collectives. They are thus presented here as potential part of the larger project of finding better ways for humans to live together.

This short chapter was meant to provide an explanation for how I came to hold some of the views underlying the reasoning in the following chapters, namely the views that morality is an ongoing, collective social undertaking in which the experiences of all individuals matter and in which all those who are affected should have an equal say in the matter; that attempting to find solutions for contemporary challenges of global justice and global ethics will require a plurality of moral standards, since only such a philosophical buffet will be sufficient to capture the many ethical dimensions of the many complex social problems at issue; that moral progress, in the sense of an improved social practice, is actually possible, most likely as incremental progress that builds upon actual experiences both positive and negative and a better understanding of the normative concepts employed; and that the progressive change will be advanced by people coming jointly to hold certain views and to endorse a certain type of ethos that promotes coordinated, collective action and institutional, systemic change. Furthermore, acting together can function as an external social scaffold which promotes and supports the newly acquired, intelligent habits by ultimately taking the psychological burden of acting in unusual ways from the shoulders of individual agents.

On a pragmatic account it is not necessary to spell out how an ideal world would look like or to provide principles that, if respected, would make the world perfectly just. But it is necessary and possible to identify instances in which the lives of many people are hindered by removable, social obstacles that prevent them from pursuing their lives. Domination and exclusion from participating in the social processes that influence their lives are among them. Here, a change in the habits of the more powerful, whose behaviour, even if without malevolent intent, frequently is at the origin of such social exclusion and domination, is urgently needed. A pragmatic ethics can hint towards changes in acts and habits of individuals, and subsequently also towards social reform, that would count as

---

[162] In the present context of our globalised world, arguably *all* are affected in one way or the other, as agents, patients, disadvantaged or advantaged etc.

progressive insofar as more people will be enabled to live as equals in the global order.

This chapter has introduced a pragmatic perspective as the third central characteristic of my proposed theory of *cosmopolitan responsibility*. Conceiving of humans as citizens of the world that morally ought to relate to and interact with one another as moral equals is not primarily a theoretical exercise, but has a distinctively practical side to it. This side can be captured well from a pragmatic perspective: the normative commitments we have, plural as they may be, should support the living together of all humans by shaping also individual habits and patterns of action. Without an ambition to discover moral truth, but in search of solutions to practical problems that appear in the living together of humans, the pragmatic side of *cosmopolitan responsibility* offers guidance for action and the formation of habits, and points towards the need and the possibility to make cosmopolitanism a personal way of life.

Part II Challenges

Part II discusses three important challenges in moving from the cosmopolitan ethos to responsible action. How does individual action matter, given its limitations and the size of the problems? Does a cosmopolitan ethos leave room for preferential treatment of those particularly near and dear to us? Can we ever hope to live up to the apparently excessive demands of the cosmopolitan ethos? In discussing these challenges, further details are added to elaborate the theory of *cosmopolitan responsibility*.

Chapter 4
Impact. Do my acts matter?

Anyone morally concerned about the massive global injustices and unhappy with the unwillingness or inability of—national or international—institutional agents to coordinate and effectively tackle them, will eventually wonder about her or his own role and responsibility. But anyone considering taking action to address the oversize problems that dominate our world, will wonder how her or his actions will matter: Can I make a difference at all? This is the first challenge for my attempt to work towards a theory of *cosmopolitan responsibility*.

The present chapter is organised in five sections. The first briefly mentions climate change, world poverty, and unfair global trade as instances of cosmopolitan concern where, however, the impact of individual acts seem not to make a difference. Section two explains how small, bad contributions can cause great harm. Section three explains how small, good contributions can yield tremendous benefits for other individuals, even if the structural problem is not solved. Both section two and three engage with and accept a broadly consequentialist perspective, as an important normative element in determining how to respond to global injustice. Section four then introduces, in some detail, the social connection model of responsibility as developed by Young. This model further supports the claim that individual agency matters in contexts of injustice. Section five concludes.

1 Competing problems

The challenge of the limited impact of individual action applies to different large and complex global problems calling for moral attention, such as the changing climate, world poverty, and global trade, among others. I will briefly explain the challenge in the context of each of these.

Anthropogenic climate change

Global warming and climate change[163] are prominent and morally urgent examples of large scale though unintended global phenomena brought about by the

---

[163] Global warming and climate change are often used as synonyms but they have distinctive

aggregation of many acts and decisions—individual, political, economic etc.—that on their own would not have caused harm. Yet, together with other like acts and decisions they do cause a severe problem. One of the most important causes of global warming is the emission of greenhouse gases into the atmosphere as a result of human activities, and particularly those that are related to the burning of fossil fuels.[164] Climate change will lead to severe disadvantage and extreme harm for many people around the globe, and mostly among those that are already relatively worse off: harsh weather phenomena and rising sea-levels, for example, have already made it more difficult and even impossible for many communities to continue living how and where they used to.[165]

Today, there is widespread agreement that the major global players could and should reduce the output of greenhouse gases in order to prevent average global warming from exceeding 2 °C, or, as a more ambitious aim, 1.5 °C[166] (relative to average global temperatures around the year 1850, i.e. before the advent of industrialisation). Actions that could potentially mitigate global warming in-

---

meanings. Global warming refers to the increase in average temperatures of the planet due to increase in greenhouse gas emissions since the industrial revolution. Climate change refers to a broad range of different phenomena, including increasing temperatures (global warming) but also including rising sea-levels, the melting of polar ice, extreme weather conditions and changes in the flora and fauna of the planet.

164 The question of *whether* anthropogenic emissions have had a significant effect on global warming should be considered to be settled. Since the Intergovernmental Panel on Climate Change published its first report in 1990, more evidence has further solidified this claim. The COP21 meeting in Paris in 2015 concluded with a breakthrough agreement signed by nearly all countries based on such an understanding, reconfirmed recently at the COP24 meeting in Katowice. Of course, it remains an interesting scientific question to determine *exactly* the contribution of *anthropogenic* emissions to global warming and climate change, since other factors also influence the global climate. In any case, it is beyond doubt that anthropogenic emissions play a crucial role, and that the anthropogenic emissions can and have to be reduced in order to prevent severe harm for the environment and existing ecosystems with potentially disastrous consequences for large numbers of humans.

165 The last report of the Intergovernmental Panel on Climate Change from 2014 states about the assumed impact of climate change on human health: "The health of human populations is sensitive to shifts in weather patterns and other aspects of climate change (*very high confidence*). These effects occur directly, due to changes in temperature and precipitation and occurrence of heat waves, floods, droughts, and fires. Indirectly, health may be damaged by ecological disruptions brought on by climate change (crop failures, shifting patterns of disease vectors), or social responses to climate change (such as displacement of populations following prolonged drought). Variability in temperatures is a risk factor in its own right, over and above the influence of average temperatures on heat-related deaths" (IPCC, Smith et al. 2014, 713). The next report is being produced and due in 2022.

166 IPCC (2018, in press).

clude the significant reduction of emissions—which would eventually require both the widespread implementation of fossil fuel alternatives, even the full replacement of using fossil energy, as well as increased sequestering of CO_2 already in the atmosphere (e.g., through reforestation or carbon capture and storage). Since it is highly unlikely that global warming can be fully halted, given the lack of political will, it also becomes important to prepare for the adverse impact it will have on many people. It is most probable that climate change will further increase global inequality, since vulnerable and poor populations tend to cluster in areas where the negative impacts of climate change are likeliest to be disproportionately high.[167] Since the tremendous costs for such action simply cannot be afforded by poor countries, the moral obligation to fund such interventions falls to the capable, more affluent countries.[168]

In the light of the magnitude of the ongoing processes of climate change, and the scale of the steps necessary to mitigate its expected negative outcomes, focusing on the role of individual acts (and individual responsibility) may seem absurd, trivial, or even out of touch with reality: Any single individual seems to be neither causally responsible for global warming, nor able to contribute in any significant way to significantly reducing the emission of greenhouse gases nor to mitigating the expected negative outcomes of a changing climate (Dwyer 2013). But to what extent is this true? And even if this was true, can the apparently negligible effect of my personal behaviour to prevent or mitigate climate change serve as a justification of inaction and continued greenhouse gas emissions?

Much of common morality, in agreement with a broadly consequentialist reasoning, has significant difficulty capturing why individual moral acts in this context may matter morally, and how individuals can be said to bear some sort of personal responsibility for diffuse global phenomena like climate change. After all, no single act that contributes to global warming causes the climate to change: no single act alone—not my decision to drive a car instead of taking public transportation, nor my decision to skype into an ethics conference rather than fly across the world for it, nor even one politician's decision to build another huge coal plant—makes a relevant difference to the *general* problem of climate change, nor to the already harmful and foreseeably catastrophic further consequences thereof. Yet, taken together, the aggregate effects of individual acts and decisions constitute the anthropogenic contribution to climate change (Peeters et al. 2015).

---

[167] Some have argued that global warming "is all about inequality, both in who will suffer most of its effects and in who created the problem in the first place" (Roberts 2001, 501).
[168] For weighing a 'polluter pays' principle against an 'ability to pay' principle, cf. Shue (1993) and Caney (2005a).

World Poverty

Until today, many millions of humans live under conditions of deprivation and extreme poverty. They lack the necessary means to meet their most basic needs and remain under any reasonable minimal standard of living along different economic, social and political dimensions. And in spite of some significant progress,[169] incredibly large numbers of people continue to die prematurely every year of poverty related causes. The 2015 UN Sustainable Development goals have again acknowledged this and set out the aim to eradicate severe poverty and hunger by 2030. This is at least an indication that global leaders do not assume that world poverty is an unchangeable fact, one that must be accepted as an inevitable feature of the world. Poverty today is not a natural disaster: it is a result of human activities and omissions, and it could be diminished or even eradicated, provided political will is up to the task of committing the financial means, organisational skills, and institutional reforms necessary for a better distribution of the available resources (cf. also Sachs 2005).

If we conceive of an adequate standard of living—including, importantly, freedom from poverty—as an international human right, the primary holders of the rights-corresponding obligation are the contracting partners, i.e. the nation states that have signed the relevant legislation.[170] But when the primary bearers of responsibility so clearly fail to live up to their obligations and do not secure the rights of those who live under their sphere of influence, then individual agents become directly bearers of rights-corresponding moral duties, as well.[171]

---

[169] Cf. the overview on global extreme poverty at https://ourworldindata.org/extreme-poverty [last accessed: 1 July 2019].

[170] Such as the United Nations' Universal Declaration of Human Rights and the two subsequent Covenants (the International Covenant on Economic, Social and Cultural Rights, ICESCR, and the International Covenant on Civil and Political Rights, ICCPR, multilateral treaties adopted by the United Nations General Assembly in 1966 that came into force in 1976); as well as regional and national human rights documents.

[171] Here, a distinction between a political or institutional view about human rights and rights-corresponding obligations on the one hand and an interactional or moral view is frequently made. The *political* view focusses on actual documents signed by contracting partners as the basis for obligations and sees human rights as a political and legal tool. Individual persons have, on this institutional account, only indirect obligations: "All persons have a duty to bring about and maintain institutions that ensure that persons can enjoy their human rights" (Caney 2007, 287). The *moral* view, on the other hand, focusses on human rights and corresponding obligations among individual human agents. When appropriate legitimate legislation does not (yet) exist or when existing legislation is disrespected, these moral rights exist nevertheless

And yet again, when individuals donate, speak up and campaign to address poverty, will any individual contribution have a meaningful impact? The size of the problem of world poverty seems incommensurate to the ability of any one individual action. Unless one is a politician in a leading and influential position, or becomes a leader of a political movement, my personal contributions pale in comparison to the size of the problem.

Consumer choices and economic injustice

Sweat shops are manufacturing facilities, generally located in developing countries, where products for Western markets are made by people working under conditions of systematic threat, domination, deprivation and exploitation.[172] This triggers the following questions: Are we, the end consumers who buy products manufactured under sweat shop conditions, morally responsible for the systematic exploitation of workers far away? Do we harm them? Is it morally wrong to buy such products? What should we do in order to address the wrong of exploitative working conditions in sweat shops?

With Young one can understand the problem of sweat shops as a paradigmatic instance of "structural injustice", that is, as a problem that is anchored in patterns, rules and routines of interaction that together cause a severe wrong. Such structures have, in one way or another, a huge impact on the lives of most if not all humans. They distribute opportunities and constraints, advantages and disadvantages, albeit in a very inequitable way, frequently including violations of basic rights. Yet, if I, as an individual consumer, change my behaviour, this will generate no tangible effect on these overall structures. The power of the individual seems to be negligible.

With these examples in mind, we can soon turn to some philosophical analysis of responsibilities in situations where individual contributions seem to be so

---

and oblige all those who are able to contribute to securing them. For further discussion cf. also Mayr (2012).

172 Occasionally, such sweat shops receive international attention, as for example the Rana Plaza factory complex where more than thousand workers died and more than two thousand were injured, when the ill-maintained eight floor factory building collapsed in April 2013. I will not go into further detail here. For an illustration of the working conditions in sweat shops, and their role in the production chain of goods for the global market, see Young (2006b, 107–111).—For the debate, whether sweat shops should be welcome, because they also bring new choices and advantages to the workers and the countries where they are located, cf. e.g. Zwolinski (2007); critically McKeown (2017).

small that they do not matter given the size of the problem that needs to be dealt with. The following discussions will show that agency in the global context requires a different understanding from agency in a direct, near-range context.[173] The understanding of individual agency in the near range was characterised by a "conception of human social relations as consisting primarily in small-scale interactions, with clearly demarcated lines of causation, among independent individuals" and by a "characteristic way of experiencing ourselves as agents with causal powers" (Scheffler 2001, 39). This, however, does not apply to the global context where numerous direct and indirect connections and interactions that are realised through individual acts as well as through repeated patterns of action have to be taken into account with regard to both their short-term and their long-term (aggregate) effects. Such an understanding of agency, however, will complicate matters significantly. An unambiguous assessment of the moral quality of acts and patterns of action, and a straightforward identification of moral demands will become more difficult because of complex networks of actions, relations and social dynamics that provide the inevitable background for each single act and each pattern of behaviour.

2 Making no difference? Imperceptible harm and threshold effects

Particular influence on this debate has been sparked by Parfit with his seminal book *Reasons and Persons* in which he discusses the moral quality of individual acts that seem to make "no difference," or where the harms, if any, caused by individual acts are "imperceptible" (Parfit 1984, 67–86). Parfit establishes, through a series of thought experiments, several widespread "mistakes in moral mathematics" to show that one must *not* ignore the negative effects of individual acts, even if the effects of any single act are imperceptible.

One of Parfit's pertinent thought experiments to support this view imagines a group of a thousand "harmless torturers" who are inflicting pain on a thousand victims by controlling a complex device. This devise administers the pain each torturer causes not to a single person but disperses the effect to the thousand victims. The effect of any single torturer's act on any victim is imperceptible, because moving on a scale of pain just one of a thousand possible steps between "no pain" (0/1000) and "severe pain" (1000/1000) cannot be distinguished by the victim. Yet, since a thousand torturers are using this device simultaneous-

---

[173] Cf. Scheffler 2001, 38–39; also Parfit 1984, 85–86, Kitcher 2012, 2–7.

ly, the state of pain in each victim reaches the full level of severe pain. Parfit writes about the torturers using this complex device:

> Each of the thousand torturers presses a button, thereby turning the switch once on each of the thousand instruments. The victims suffer [...] severe pain. But none of the torturers makes any victim's pain perceptibly worse. (Parfit 1984, 80)

With this, Parfit shows that one can be harmed and be worse off, even if one cannot trace the harm back to the distinctive contribution of individual persons. Conversely, acts can be harmful (and hence morally wrong because of their effects), even if no one feels specifically worse off, if they are part of an aggregate which together causes harm. Parfit explains that one is mistaken in the

> belief that imperceptible effects cannot be morally significant. This is a very serious mistake. When all the Harmless Torturers act, each is acting very wrongly. This is true even though each makes no one perceptibly worse off. The same could be true of us. We should cease to think that an act cannot be wrong, because of its effects on other people, if this act makes no one perceptibly worse off. Each of our acts may be very wrong, because of its effects on other people, even if none of these people could ever notice any of these effects. Our acts may together make these people very much worse off. (Parfit 1984, 83)

Parfit's aim is to show how individual acts can be parts of sets of acts which together bring about severe harm, and how, in being parts of such harmful sets, even seemingly non-harming individual acts can and do in fact contribute to bringing about severe harm.

However, pointing out this flaw in moral reasoning is not the same as overcoming it, because this way of thinking is deeply ingrained in a morality that has its roots in small communities of directly interacting individuals, where obvious complaints were the indicator of having harmed someone. Yet, Parfit argues that conditions have changed significantly and everyone now can affect others through the widely dispersed effects of our behaviour. Exposing the mentioned mistakes debunks the questionable illusion of innocence to which many individuals adhere.

> For the sake of small benefits to ourselves, or our families, each of us may deny others much greater total benefits, or impose on others much greater total harms. We may think this permissible because the effects on each of the others will be either trivial or imperceptible. If this is what we think, what we do will often be much worse for all of us.
>
> If we cared sufficiently about effects on others, and changed our moral view, we would solve such problems. It is not enough to ask, 'Will my act harm other people?' Even if the answer is No, my act may still be wrong, because of its effects. The effects that it will have when it is considered on its own may not be its only relevant effects. I should ask, 'Will my

act be one of a set of acts that will together harm other people?' The answer may be Yes. And the harm to others may be great. (Parfit 1984, 85–86)

This account allows the attribution of causal responsibility for negative outcomes to agents even if this negative outcome would have existed without their individual contributions. Instead, it is about identifying a jointly sufficient set of acts and conditions that bring about the relevant effect. This understanding is an important development in establishing responsibility for outcomes: It is not about establishing a necessary connection between a single act and the relevant effect which would constitute a "but-for condition." Instead, it is about establishing that an act constitutes, under given circumstances, a necessary part of a complex of conditions which are together sufficient to cause the relevant outcome. In the legal debate about causation, Wright has called this a "NESS condition," because it identifies the single act as a "necessary element of a sufficient set" (Wright 1985).[174]

This inclusion of single acts into sets of acts in order to identify causal responsibility for harmful effects on consequentialist terms is an important expansion of a narrow focus on the direct consequences of single acts. Here, it can be said, that the act—as part of a set of acts—has harmful consequences.

Nevertheless, a critic might ask, aren't there cases where it could very well be true that my act might or might not make any difference? For it could very well be that a relevant threshold of causing a new level of harm for some will only be reached if, say, exactly fifty more people engage in a certain kind of activity. Only then, my personal contribution will cause the next level of harm—and if the others do not act in this certain way, my act might indeed have no (and not only an imperceptible or dispersed) effect. Kagan has studied such cases and offered an extended act-consequentialist analysis to secure a negative assessment of such acts, even while admitting the possibility that an individual act might truly not cause any effect and hence does not make any difference (Kagan 2011).

Kagan's alternative hinges, in brief, on the logical insight that any individual act might well be one that triggers a perceptible harm for some. It turns on the fact that there is simply no way to tell exactly which out of numerous individual acts will be the one that actually makes harmful a set of individually harmless acts (due to the aggregate effect brought about by the crossing of some threshold). As such, individual acts have some non-negligible probability of being trig-

---

[174] The NESS condition is a specific type of the larger INUS condition, proposed by Mackie, which identifies an "insufficient but non-redundant part of an unnecessary but sufficient condition" (Mackie 1974) Cf. also Honoré (2010).

gers leading to the crossing of a threshold. Since one cannot know that one will *not* make this difference, the overall *expected* outcome of my act will turn out to be negative. The expected outcome is also negative in cases where I do not actually trigger a negative consequence, and hence when my act ultimately turns out not to have made any difference. It is the risk that my act might be the one which brings about harm for others that is sufficient for this version of (act) consequentialism to morally condemn the act and to morally demand that the agent refrain from doing it.

Contrary to Parfit, Kagan does not rely on imperceptible harms, but on a threshold model, where the likelihood that the individual minuscule act will bring about harm suffices to justify the verdict that it is wrong. Kagan also presents thought experiments to illustrate his claims. His main example involves imagining buying chicken in a store in which the owner will order more chicken once a certain number of them has been sold. (Raising, distressing and slaughtering chicken for human consumption is considered to be the moral harm in question here.) Once 25 chicken have been sold the store keeper orders another crate of 25 chicken, which will then be raised, slaughtered and brought to the store. Kagan's point is that since there are already 25 chicken in the store, the purchasing acts of the first 24 buyers do not make any difference, since no more chicken suffer being slaughtered as a result of the buyers' decisions to purchase an already slaughtered chicken; it is the 25th buyer whose act makes all the moral difference, since it triggers the order for more chicken, leading to harm for another 25.

Here, as in Parfit's cases, it is the problem of sets of actions that raises consequentialism's concern, despite individual acts seeming generally not to make any moral difference. With the threshold approach, however, Kagan claims to show how the expected utility of an act will be negative, regardless of its actual utility. This allows him, in the end, to answer the title question of his essay *Do I make a difference?* with a determinate "I might" (Kagan 2011, 141).

Is this a plausible model for understanding the problem of minuscule contributions to large scale injustices like climate change? Much will depend on the plausibility of drawing a parallel between the threshold in the chicken case and potential thresholds with regard to large scale global challenges like global warming. At first sight, it may be utterly implausible to assume that such a parallel can be drawn, at all. What would be the threshold that needs to be crossed to actually trigger the climate to change (or, to reach the next, irreversible step in a cascade of events of a changing climate)? Is it not rather unreasonable to assume that any individual act (even the individual decision to build a new coal plant) will trigger or prevent tangible changes to the climate? Kagan himself rejects this objection and offers a way of modeling his example to fit to different cases: What matters to him is only that the *expected utility* of the act in question is negative. In the case of chicken raised and slaughtered in batches of 25, this is easily grasped: my act may trigger the death of another 25 chicken. This will certainly be a moral wrong, assuming one agrees with Kagan about the wrongness of factory animal farming, though not so huge a wrong as it would be to trigger irreversible climate change. But even if my individual act will be much less likely to trigger climate change, the moral wrong of it would be huge. Even if the probability of the negative impact of my single act is, say 1/100.000.000.000, this minuscule probability must be weighed against the huge detrimental impact for many people in case the negative event is triggered. So, even though the probability is minuscule, the potential damage is of such a huge magnitude that the expected utility of my act remains in the negative. The conclusion that it is wrong to act in this way is thus justified.[175]

Of course, it remains questionable whether climate change is analogous and amenable to analysis based on threshold notions. Logically, it seems very dubious that there will (or can) be only one such threshold, prior to which all earlier polluting of the atmosphere had no adverse effect. Fortunately, Kagan's model allows for a multitude of thresholds, each of which will lead to a small but morally significant, problematic step towards a worse climate. Increasing the number of morally relevant thresholds decreases the negative utility of each of these harms, but the probability that my act will be the one that leads to crossing one of these thresholds increases proportionally (for there are many more such thresholds), such that the net negative utility of my act proportionally remains the same.

Plausible as this may seem at first, Kagan's account faces the following serious problem: it deals only with ex ante assessments of acts. It is the epistemological difficulty of determining the actual outcome of my act that makes the expected utility of my act negative.[176] Yet, in many cases at least, we will in fact be

---

175 Parallel cases occur in the context of technological impact assessment, and particularly with the now familiar though still vexing problem of how to assess the minimal probabilities of major failures (with huge detrimental outcomes) at nuclear power plants.

176 The fact that Kagan mentions in his thought experiment with the chicken that some kind of light (green indicating that the order of a new crate of chicken is not imminent, yellow indicating that with the purchase of the next chicken a new order will go out) is somewhat misleading, because it suggests one could *know* in advance what would be the consequences of one's act. This, however, is not the point Kagan wants to make. It is for the uncertainty of the consequences that we have to deal with *expected* not *known* consequences. Rightly, he indicates that the chicken vendor will most likely have no such light indicating the state of the stocks of chicken (Kagan 2011, 123). This saves the plausibility of his thought experiment for the actual challenge of individual contributions to climate change.

able to make ex post judgements about what actually happened. (The epistemological challenges for such ex post judgements may be equally severe, but for the sake of the argument let us assume they are more readily available.) But if I might be empirically able to show that my act *did not* trigger any negative consequence, how can I escape the conclusion that it was in hindsight morally acceptable to pollute? The appropriate description then would be that the agent took a gamble and, through moral luck, did not cause any harm. Yet, taking such gambles with significant risks for others might in itself be morally dubious and not in line with how one should act (cf. also Munthe 2011).[177]

3 The most good you can do?

The preceding section analysed an example, where the outcomes of one's acts—both as possible parts of the problem and as possible parts of its solution—were difficult to identify and evaluate. In other cases, however, we might not be able to make, through personal action, any difference for the overall problem; but our acts might be able to make all of the difference for some part of the problem. A paradigmatic example of this is not climate change or the global economy, but poverty and acts to contribute to poverty relief. An influential debate was triggered, half a century ago, by Peter Singer through his seminal paper *Famine, Affluence, and Morality* (1972). In it, Singer puts forward a compelling account of the moral demands of individuals in the face of the massively unequal conditions under which human beings live and die on this planet. Deeply affected by the extreme famine in East Bengal in the early 1970s, Singer relentlessly sets about demolishing the many standard assumptions governing the every day behaviour of affluent people everywhere, who are, quite undeniably, hardly at all affected by the suffering of people elsewhere. Spelling out the massive scale of preventable human suffering and death in non-affluent regions, and contrasting that with the amount of money spent on private luxury, and national projects such as supersonic jets and weaponry, Singer concludes that the standard way in which money is spent in Western societies lacks moral justification. He argues that "the whole way we look at moral issues—our moral conceptual scheme—needs to be altered, and with it, the way of life that has come to be taken for granted in our society" (Singer 1972, 230). The straightforward argu-

---

[177] Pinkert has discussed the question *What if I cannot make a difference (and I know it)?* further and convincingly argues for adding an element of virtue ethic to the act-consequentialist theory in order to secure that people act rightly and do so for the right reasons (Pinkert 2015).

ment Singer has developed has, to this day, not lost any of its bite and the "vise that Singer has clamped on us still binds tightly" (Arneson 2009, 290).

Singer's argument involves several steps, leading from a rather uncontroversial axiological assumption of a—seemingly uncontroversial but ultimately extremely challenging general principle. The basic axiological assumption is that "suffering and death from lack of food, shelter, and medical care are bad" (Singer 1972, 231). Indeed, who would want to deny this claim, given the importance of food, shelter and medical care for all human beings? The fact that in some societies there is no system of medical care to speak of, and the fact that some people choose to live unsheltered outdoors, or to temporarily fast on health or religious pretexts, are not objections to the claim that suffering and death caused by involuntary lack of food, shelter and medical care are a bad thing. It is important to realise that Singer doesn't claim that suffering or death are always unquestionably morally bad things; but they are so when they are involuntary and avoidable.

Singer's next step is to stipulate the principle that "if it is in our power to prevent something bad from happening, without thereby sacrificing anything of comparable moral importance, we ought, morally, to do it" (Singer 1972, 231).[178] It is important to see that by focusing on the acts an agent could engage in, Singer establishes a connection between the bad and the agent; a connection that exists on the grounds that the agent could act and address the moral wrong in question. In the face of such a possibility, choosing not to act of course is still an option; an option, however, that does not end the connection between the agent and the moral wrong in question.

At the core of this principle lies, again, the consequentialist assumption that the outcomes of an agent's actions determine their moral quality. Morality demands the reduction of what is bad and the promotion of what is good.[179] If I can help even a single starving person to survive and live, possibly even live well, if I can prevent the death of a child from an easily treatable disease, then I am tilting the balance between good and bad in the right direction—even if this should require that I renounce spending the money needed for this intervention on my own entertainment. Ultimately, all our decisions and

---

[178] In the revised and moderated form, Singer's principle goes: "if it is in our power to prevent something *very* bad from happening, without thereby sacrificing *anything morally significant*, we ought, morally, to do it" [emphasis added] (Singer 1972, 231). My discussion applies to both forms of the principle.

[179] The good and the bad can, of course, be determined in more fine-grained metrics than simple pleasure or pain, such as the fulfilment of informed and considered preferences etc. These important debates, however, are secondary in the present context.

acts should be seen and assessed in the light of their moral outcomes, which are importantly also determined by the opportunity costs: My entertainment comes at a price which I assign to someone else: If I spend money on champagne, I cannot spend it on famine relief. If I spend a lot of money on a luxury car, I cannot spend it on educational programmes in low-income countries.

While only very few would want to explicitly make the claim that their own car is more important than the survival of several people, or that it might be worth, to put it bluntly, sacrificing the lives of several people for one's car, Singer's argument establishes this very connection between the seemingly unconnected (or intentionally separated?) events or states of affairs. It challenges us with the question of whether we are not, at least implicitly, making the judgement that our own enjoyment, or the well-being of those near and dear to us, are worth the preventable misery of others. Our acts matter morally and they could make all the difference for some. This question arises whenever we spend money on going to the movies instead of donating it to a charity, or whenever we buy unnecessary things for our friends or children, instead of supporting those in dire need. The option to choose what would be morally better is available; the judgement that survival and famine-relief is morally more important than having the latest smartphone is widely shared; and yet—most agents most of the time do not act in a way that respects the Singer principle.

From the perspective of *cosmopolitan responsibility*, Singer's is a powerful and important voice.[180] His diagnosis is absolutely convincing, that the standard decisions people in the affluent countries make are, in the light of global inequalities and world poverty, morally tainted. His call to reconsider one's personal use and distribution of resources is urgently needed. And yet, a narrow act-consequentialist moral discussion of individual acts that address problems like world poverty etc. seems to be both implausibly ambitious on the one hand and insufficiently demanding on the other. That is why a consequentialist reasoning along these lines, I contend, can only be one element in a comprehensive assessment of the role and responsibility of individual agents in the face of global injustice.

The consequentialist reasoning appears to be implausibly ambitious insofar as the demand to get involved and donate according to the Singer principle puts

---

[180] The provocation of Singer's argument persists and has stirred an extensive debate (cf. Jamieson 1999, Schaler 2009), in recent years reinvigorated through the "Effective Altruism" movement (MacAskill 2015, Singer 2015) that has attempted to influence particularly well-off citizens to commit to donating larger amounts of their available resources to highly effective charities in order to produce the best possible outcomes. For a critical discussion, cf. Srinivasan (2015) and Gabriel (2017).

the call for impartial consideration of all as equals above all other moral demands; a call for action that will be difficult to silence. While impartiality in the assessment of people's basic needs, as I will argue in the following chapter in more detail, *always matters* and generates weighty demands, it is *not all that matters:* other severe moral problems besides poverty matter morally too (global warming for example), and so do our relationships with those we directly interact with, including those particularly near and dear to us. Pointing out these competing moral demands does in no way reduce the weight of the urgent demands that result from extreme poverty where it could be addressed. But it points out that in the multifaceted moral environment of an agent such poverty is not all that can legitimately call for moral attention. In this way Singer's account seems to be too narrow and its demands, in consequence, turn out to be implausibly ambitious.

How is Singer's principle with its focus on the outcomes of individual actions actually insufficiently demanding? In some cases, such as helping people in need of food etc., enough individual action might actually even be able to secure that all have enough; but doing so neglects what would ultimately be needed to change the structures that have caused deprivation in the first place. Addressing the severe symptoms directly then comes at the expense of targeting the root causes of the problem. It is not enough to alleviate poverty by handing out bread to all in need; it is necessary that all are in a situation where dire poverty does not exist as a danger. On the side of individual agents, the problem lies not only with their unwillingness to act or the ineffectiveness of their acts. It lies, more fundamentally, with their ignorance and apathy, and the lack of perceiving massive global injustices as problems that directly regards them. When looking at individual agency, the relevant effects of personal action are thus not only the direct effects on the symptoms (actual hunger and need) of a deeper problem (global structural injustice). They include also the different ways of contributing to addressing the root causes of the problem, e.g. through socially and structurally relevant interventions: individuals, through what they say and do, can inform *others*, influence their dispositions (for examply by helping others to overcome ignorance and apathy) and actions and thus support collective and structural change. As has been pointed out repeatedly (e.g. by Kuper 2002), placing so much direct responsibility on the individual agent simply tends to ignore the distinctively structural and institutional nature of the problems at hand. Particularly the 'effective altruists' seem to reconceptualise the task of addressing poverty as a task for private initiative; a reconceptualisation that seems to result, at least partly, from the conviction that public engagement and governmental or institutional action is inevitably ineffective and wasteful anyways; a conviction I do not share. While direct individual engagement clearly is welcome and needed, also on my account, the ultimate aspiration cannot be that some capable, affluent and benevolent people decide how to tackle some selected urgent problems effectively and then do so with direct, private intervention. This would only perpetuate existing power-imbalances where some people enjoy the additional advantage of making choices about the fate of others by directing resources, without sufficient public accountability, to projects they deem fit. Any lasting solution will have to respect the equal moral status of all as members of a community of equals; not put some in a position of dependency on others.

This discussion has shown that individual acts can make *different* differences. They can positively and dramatically change the fate of some, e.g. by saving lives; even though the overall, structural problem will persist. Importantly, however, individual acts can also contribute to social effects on other *agents*. Here again, my individual act alone will not cause the system to change. But I can become part of what can eventually lead to the solution of a large and severe problem.[181]

4 Making a difference in social structures

The best available understanding of the role and responsibility of individual agents thus will look at what people do *not only with regard to the direct effects they have on the overall and often oversize problem*. While direct effects and outcomes of individual behaviour clearly matter, they matter only partially (particularly as it will be, under current conditions of global structural injustice, impossible to fully avoid being implicated in the problematic structures). The *indirect* effects on other agents and the *call* for structural reform (by developing ideas, talking about the need for reform; underlined by a sufficient degree of credible action) must not be underestimated, when it comes to understanding the role and responsibility of indvdiual agents in the context of global injustice. Here, again, the work of Young offers important insights about how individual acts do matter in contexts of global injustice.[182]

The core idea of Young's "social connection model" is to address the role and responsibility of individual agents as elements in a complex and far ranging web of relations and interactions. She has made her case with the specific example of consumer-involvement in sweat shop labour; but her views apply to other

---

[181] In the concluding chapter, I will distinguish direct or 'vertical' effects from indirect or 'horizontal' effects of individual action.
[182] Young 2003, Young 2006b, Young 2011. Cf. also Neuhäuser 2014, Beck 2016, Parekh 2017.

frameworks of interactions, as well, such as climate change and poverty. And as an expansion of Young's view that "obligations of justice arise between persons by virtue of the social processes that connect them" (Young 2006b, 102), my own understanding of the relevant social processes includes *knowing* and *the sheer ability to intervene* as factors capable to establish a relevant connection.

Within a shared global sphere of social cooperation and interaction, where people's lives are connected in one way or another, "each of us expects justice toward ourselves, and others can legitimately make claims on us. Responsibility in relation to injustice thus derives not from living under a common constitution, but rather from participation in the diverse institutional processes that produce structural injustice." (Young 2006b, 119).

As indicated already, Young's work focuses on individual moral agents irrespective of whether these individuals are living in a shared institutional frame (such as a global equivalent of the nation state).[183] Instead, she contends that "political institutions are the response to these obligations rather than their basis" (Young 2006b, 102). Thus, individuals and the (actual and possible) interactions between individuals are constitutive for the existence of relations of responsibility and justice, and institutional arrangements are to be created to secure that these relations of responsibility among equals are honoured.

As long as such institutions that would secure the fair and just interaction between all do not (yet) exist, agents are often involved in causing harm by being part of unjust structures. Yet, blaming individual agents for wrongdoing under conditions of structural injustice is, according to Young, not the right way forward to identify a solution. In this regard, the involvement of ordinary citizens in global inequality, economic injustice and environmental pollution is different from standard wrongdoing. To explain this difference, Young distinguishes two different ways of linking individuals to a case of injustice, a "liability model" and a "responsibility model". Young is critical of the former because it is unable to fully capture the specific wrong of structural injustices, and suggests giving priority to the latter.[184]

Liability denotes the legal responsibility for some harm, a special form of responsibility that establishes the validity of certain sanctions: those found to be causally responsible for the harm in question are liable, should admit their

---

[183] While Nagel (2005) argues that some shared institutional framework is a precondition for legitimate claims of justice, others argue that the relevant "conditions" for legitimate claims fo justice are already met (Van Parijs 2007).

[184] However, she does not want to "reject or replace" the liability model. Instead, she points out its limited field of applicability, mostly in legal discourse (Young 2011, 100).

blameworthiness and be punished, and must be made to make restitution for the harm caused.

In the case of exploitative working conditions in sweat shops it may be possible to identify people or institutions that are indeed liable in the legal sense, as for example, the owner of a factory who orders her employees to be physically intimidated, or the supervisors who carry out such orders with brutality, or even government agencies or officials who pass laws or grant waivers permitting (even encouraging) the establishment of exploitative sweat shops in which basic human rights are systematically disrespected. Yet, as indispensable and appropriate as it is to single out such wrongdoing and point to legally liable individual or institutional agents, direct individual or institutional legal liability is certainly just one part of a much larger moral picture in cases of structural injustice. After all, both the sweat shop supervisor and the owner may themselves be under extreme duress to increase output and/or cut costs. Such pressure does not, of course, excuse them from acting brutally (or otherwise violating basic human rights), but it does give some context that helps explain (at least to some degree) why they may choose to act in such ways. Similarly, developing countries' governments that created special export zones may have been under extreme international pressure to do so, in order to generate much needed revenues, and/or because international trade agreements left them with no choice but to allow the installation of such zones.

This, of course, does not excuse in any way that a government allows systematic human rights violations on its territory (and, of course, it says nothing about how bribery and other forms of corruption shape government policy), but it does show that liability is too narrow a concept to capture the complexity of the task of assigning moral responsibility in cases of where it is widely dispersed. Suing factory owners, charging supervisors with assault, or attempting to make governments liable for the human rights violations committed in sweat shop on their territories—all this still only captures aspects of a structural problem, since the cause of human rights violations is not limited only to these agents. As Young and others have made clear, many more agents are involved in an entire system upholding the interactions and mechanisms that constitute the relevant injustice, if only indirectly. The legal liability model, however, cannot capture this involvement of multiple agents, since it is a characteristic of liability that only specific individual or institutional agents can be found liable. Moreover, liability seems also to simultaneously concentrate too much responsibility on specific agents, for the effect of, for example, sending a sweat shop supervisor to prison for having beaten workers (of assigning liability to a specific person) seems to shift all the blame onto that person—while relieving all others of any. So, the liability model falls short when it comes to understanding how complex mechanisms and structures also function to encourage the wrong kinds of individual decision-making (like a supervisor's decision to flog workers).

Instead of addressing structural injustices through a backward-looking perspective by trying to establish legal liability, Young proposes using her account of forward-looking responsibility based on social connection. This model assigns responsibility for carrying out activities in a more morally appropriate way to *all* agents actually and possibly involved in those activities. Responsibility here comes as a function of participation in the processes that produce structural injustice, since morally better structures (that is, structures in which basic human rights are fully respected) could and should be brought about instead. Responsibility thus "trickles down" through all the instances of a complex chain or system of connections, such that all those part of it—in one way or another—also bear (some still to be determined degree of) responsibility for the entire process, as well as for the harms or benefits it generates. With regard to sweat shops, again, this responsibility trickles down to the end consumers who buy (or who are able to buy[185]) products manufactured under sweat shop conditions, because there is a clear chain of connections—if admittedly complex and consisting of many links—between the privilege (of being able) to purchase some goods and the morally unacceptable exploitative conditions under which the goods have been produced. Young specifies:

> All the persons who participate by their actions in the ongoing schemes of cooperation that constitute these structures are responsible for them, in the sense that they are part of the process that causes them. They are not responsible, however, in the sense of having directed the process or intended its outcomes. (Young 2006b, 114).[186]

---

[185] This is in line with my own understanding of relations and connections that is wider than that of Young: Even a possibility to connect constitutes already a relation, particularly in cases where that possibility to connect should be actualised for moral reasons. For this, cf. above chapter two, section five.

[186] Cf. also Young (2011, 105): "Individuals bear responsibility for structural injustice because they contribute by their actions to the processes that produce unjust outcomes. Our responsibility derives from belonging together with others in a system of interdependent processes of cooperation and competition through which we seek benefits and aim to realise projects. Within these processes, each of us expects justice towards ourselves, and others can legitimately make claims of justice on us. All who dwell within the structures must take responsibility for remedying injustices they cause, though none is specifically liable for the harm in a legal sense. Responsibility in relation to injustice thus derives not from living under a common constitution, but rather from participating in the diverse institutional processes that produce structural injustice. [...] in today's world many of these structural processes extend beyond nation-state boundaries to include globally dispersed persons."

It is important to see that Young's assignment of responsibility does not rely on affirming the actual causation of harm by the agent deemed responsible.[187] She explains: "Even though we cannot trace the outcome we may regret to our own particular actions in a direct causal chain, we bear responsibility because we are part of the process." (Young 2006b, 119) In the case of the end consumer, for example, it does not matter whether the purchase of the t-shirt "makes a difference" for someone, or to anyone. The purchase, even the ability to purchase, constitutes a relevant social connection because consumers are part of the morally questionable overall social and economic process.[188]

Young's social connection model of responsibility is thus characterised by five main features, each of which has been implicitly referred to in the foregoing. First, the model does not isolate or single out only one or few agents to bear responsibility for some injustice. Many more individuals and groups can stand in a relation of social connection to one another, establishing mutual responsibility. Unlike the liability model which concludes from the assignment of responsibility to one agent (individual or institutional) that other agents are thus free from responsibility, Young's model contends that having identified someone as particularly responsible does not absolve others.

Second, the social connection model seeks to morally assess—and ultimately change—the structures and background conditions that shape decisions to act, in addition to individual acts themselves. If the injustice in question is structural, if it is deeply ingrained in the standard patterns of interaction and behaviour of numerous agents, it may be the case that even if many strive to act morally, others will continue to be systematically exploited. Single decisions against participating in structural injustice will in themselves be insufficient to stop the injustice from continuing. And often enough, those contributing to structural injustice do so unwillingly (a factory owner has to produce at "competitive" prices, otherwise he would have to shut down the factory; a poorer person in an affluent country cannot purchase expensive fair trade clothing). All involved often can only take small steps, limited by one's contingent capacities and one's often rather small sphere of influence. But, within the structural and other constraints, we, as agents, can decide between being more part of the problem and being more part of its solution.

---

[187] Consequently, Young does not have to discuss whether this difference is imperceptible, as Parfit did, or whether there is a likelihood that I *may* make a difference, as Kagan argued.
[188] On this inclusive account, it may very well be that being a citizen of an affluent country of the Global North establishes is already sufficient for establishing a general, morally relevant social connection to the countries of the Global South. For this, cf. also Lessenich on "externalising societies" (Lessenich 2016).

A third characteristic of Young's approach is that it seeks to establish responsibility by looking not primarily to the past, but by looking forward. Young is less interested in assigning blame for harm already caused than she is in identifying what would be necessary to end the ongoing structural injustice. Assigning liability or blame alone is insufficient. Yet it would be a misunderstanding to assume that Young is uninterested in the causal processes bringing injustice into the world, even if she is critical of the often overly backward-centred approach to identifying culprits. Starting from the existing social connections through which also ordinary individuals find themselves linked to structural injustice are the central way of establishing such forward-looking responsibility in Young's account.

Fourth, responsibility, for Young, is both personal and shared, not collective. Collective responsibility, in her understanding, would assume a collective agent as responsible for the necessary forward-looking action to contribute to overcoming structural injustice. This view would assign responsibility to, say, corporations, governments and states, and international organisations. Without denying the responsibility of such agents, Young's own account stresses the shared and personal responsibility of all those who are connected in one way or another with the injustice at hand: Individual ordinary consumers are personally called upon to acknowledge their role and responsibility in the shared system of cooperation and interaction that is shaped by structural injustice.

While responsibility is personal, the only way to appropriately and effectively discharge one's responsibility is through joint action. This is the fifth characteristic of Young's responsibility model. No single agent, responsible as she may be, can change the system alone, yet everyone personally bears a share of responsibility to work towards changing the institutions and processes underlying structural injustice. Seen in this light, Young's conception of responsibility is, ultimately, political: taking action to spread one's moral commitments, to credibly inform others, to coordinate and seek collective and structural reform is needed (Kahn 2016). And, importantly, this approach does not focus exclusively on the advantaged agents or those who benefit from injustice (i.e. those who are also at the centre of my analysis of cosmopolitan responsibility); it will assign responsibility also to those who are connected to injustice by suffering from its negative outcomes (Jugov/Ypi 2019). *All* connected are morally obliged to take action to bring about change; all bear a share of forward-looking responsibility to improve the situation.

So, how would Young determine the *content* of the responsibility of individuals in this context? Does she stipulate concrete duties for securing the rights of others? Does she demand agents sacrifice personal resources—which? up to which degree?—to ease the burden of those in need? Does she require we become activists in the fight for political reform? And does she claim that, in doing any of the acts possibly demanded, we can be sure to make a difference in the sense I have been discussing in this chapter? Young's writings do not reach a level of concreteness that would list particular actions as morally demanded, but she offers some guidance to individual agents to "reason about their action in relation to structural injustice along parameters of power, privilege, interest, and collective ability." (Young 2006b, 127).[189] While such a lack of concreteness may dissatisfy some, the vagueness of these parameters should rather be seen as an advantage. As I will explain in the concluding chapter of this book, the pervasive character of the numerous co-existing instances of global structural injustice makes it implausible to point to concrete and directly applicable demands that are placed on individual agents. Instead, responsibility should consist first and foremost in the form of general responsiveness that leads to some action that needs to be determined for everyone differently by taking into account the concrete circumstances of the agent. For this purpose, the parameters of reasoning function as a helpful guide.

Agents are advised by Young to consider their own situation with regard to the question where they can, through their individual contributions, generate most effects. The first parameter, *power*, thus acknowledges the fact that individuals are usually not entangled in a single form of structural injustice alone. The plurality of problems that stand in need of being addressed thus allow an agent discretion, as long as she considers where her inevitably limited resources can be put to some good, and effective use. Importantly, Young thus does not suggest assigning priority for one particular form of injustice over another. The apparently consequentialist reasoning about effects does not lead her to argue for the claim one should only do what would be maximally effective. Ultimately, say, both climate change and world poverty command our attention. And while it is clear that agents should respond to each of them, making choices is inevitable and acceptable for her. The first parameter demands that people make choices while taking into account their social position and their potential to generate impact.

The second parameter, *privilege*, points to the fact that in contexts of structural injustice some people or groups of people enjoy particular advantages. Such additional and possibly unfair advantages—maybe in the form of material goods, consumer choices, security, political influence etc.—increase the respon-

---

[189] Young not only *wrote* about the concept of responsibility, but she *lived* it as well. The anecdotical narratives about her own political and activist engagement should thus be considered as an exemplary illustration of how the responsibility of individuals can translate into concrete practice. Cf. Young 2000, 1–4; Nussbaum 2011b, Ferguson and Nagel 2009, 3–5.

sibility of individuals to act in order to address the injustice in question. Already the sheer ability to act on some form of structural injustice, the fact that one has an option to even consider doing something to address a massive wrong without having to fear repression, tangibly indicates that one is living under privileged circumstances, since these options are denied to many of those who suffer from the negative outcomes of injustice. Privilege thus obliges—irrespective of the question whether one has actually caused or contributed to a problem.

Privilege, I contend, should be understood in comparative, not in absolute terms. It is in no way a precondition for an agent to have responsibility that she is absolutely or in all possible regards privileged. On a comparative understanding, relative privilege is only one additional factor that can increase the degree of responsibility, also insofar as it opens options for action that are unavailable to, or much more costly for, those who are more disadvantaged.

As a third parameter of reasoning in the attempt to determine individual responsibility, Young mentions the *interest* of persons to overcome the injustice in question. But often enough, those benefitting from structural injustice have little or no interest in changing it. After all they enjoy the additional privileges, even if in a morally unjustifiable way. Doesn't this parameter then primarily oblige those who are suffering personally from the injustice in question, shifting responsibility to the victims of injustice? This parameter certainly has the effect that also those who are suffering from structural injustice are called upon to take up their share of responsibility (Jugov/Ypi 2019). As such, the parameter should be read as empowering (as far as possible) the disadvantaged groups: they have a strong interest in changing the state of affairs and they should also be doing what they can to bring about change. Yet, this does not relieve other individuals from their share of responsibility, which can, also on the side of those contributing to the injustice, be based on interest. Generally, everyone should have an interest in bringing about a better and more just world; and personally, all should have an interest not to be the reason for which others suffer avoidably. Triggering and increasing this form of interest, however, is one of the most important challenges ahead. Given the fact that many privileged people do not even see the connections or the injustices involved in their apparently morally acceptable life style, there is still a long way to go.

The fourth parameter of reasoning is *collective ability*. Here, Young points out that the relative ease with which some people could join forces in order to address an injustice more effectively should count as a factor increasing responsibility to take action. Such collective ability can again be found on the side of those benefitting from and on the side of those suffering from structural injustice. Yet, here again, using the dormant collective abilities often proves difficult and the question how individuals should proceed to effectively wake them is not easily answered.

Young's account, based on the concrete social connections within which agents find themselves, is a powerful tool to discuss how individual acts do matter in addressing global injustice. It integrates the concept of rights, insofar as rights violations are an important indicator of injustice, it obliges individuals as holders of rights-corresponding duties, it takes into account the limited, but existing effects of individual agency, that can be reinforced through repeated and coordinated action. It sees individual agency ultimately as a political responsibility, as an important driver of change where institutional agents still fail to move or to deliver. Underlying her arguments are the ideas that all are of equal moral standing and that people are connected, even across long distances, through actual interaction, but also through the sheer ability to interact. In my understanding, the ideal of relational equality implicitly underlies her reasoning, making her views particularly valuable for my account of cosmopolitan responsibility.

5 The responsibility to make a difference

The discussion of the question *how do individual acts matter in the context of global injustice* has lead to different ways of responding to the challenge that individual acts do not make any difference at all. Of course, one has to admit, that any single person's acts alone will never be enough to actually 'solve' climate change, end world poverty, or introduce fair global trade interactions. The massive mismatch between oversize problems on the one hand and the smallest type of agency on the other, individual agency, persists. Yet, generally, in each of their actions, agents decide whether they are more part of the problem or more part of its possible solution—and this holds true even if the direct effects of one's acts are imperceptible or make 'no difference' to the overall problem. Furthermore, individual acts might cause, in some cases, a big difference, when they function as the straw that breaks the camel's back by triggering a cascade of events. And, even if one's acts cause only imperceptible (if any) effects on the overall problem, they can make all of the difference for some individuals that suffer from the overall problem.[190] Once one extends the scope of moral concern and starts to see and acknowledge the multiple relations and connections that shape our current world, a theory of *cosmopolitan responsibility* places a significant

---

[190] These interim conclusions will be taken up and expanded in the concluding chapter below.

moral burden on the shoulders of individual agents. The feeling of being burdened, however, might be nothing but a particularly clear indicator of the fact that we know that we, as individuals, actually make a difference; and that we should see to it that we make the right kind of difference.

Chapter 5
Impartiality. The fragmentation of morality

1 The puzzle of partiality

We may very well conceive of ourselves as "citizens of the world" with universal obligations to respect and treat all others impartially as moral equals; but what about the special obligations we have towards those particularly near or particularly dear to us? This is the second major challenge for a theory of *cosmopolitan responsibility*.

When considering the role and responsibility of individual agents in the face of inequality and injustice from a cosmopolitan perspective, the concept of moral impartiality deserves special attention. After all, the universalist and egalitarian commitment, that every person is of equal moral importance, lies at the heart of cosmopolitanism and seems to oblige moral agents to assess their options and actions from an impartial point of view: From this perspective it is very clear that no one is more important than anyone else (Nagel 1991, 14) and that all persons are equally deserving of well-being and respect (Wolf 1992, 245). Thus, any partial assessment, biased towards the interests of some particular person or group, would seem to conflict with cosmopolitanism's universalist and egalitarian commitment.

This connection between equality and impartiality is challenging, because at least some degree of partial preference for some special people or groups of people is widely accepted not only as morally permissible, but even as morally praiseworthy or as a moral obligation. After all, interactions and special relations between friends and family members, maybe also the special relationships we have towards ourselves and towards our compatriots, are perceived as meaningful and valuable by most, including many who endorse a cosmopolitan worldview. And such special relationships generally come along with special responsibilities, that is a requirement to treat these people differently from random strangers. Both lines of reasoning resonate with most people and both have strong argumentative backing; yet, they stand in tension with one another so that it is difficult to see how both can be integrated into a coherent normative framework. This difficulty has been called the 'puzzle of partiality' (Keller 2013, 5), a puzzle with particular relevance for an account of cosmopolitan responsibility.

To illustrate: Human lives are multi-dimensional. Obviously, being embedded in social structures, and nurturing and being nurtured by caring relationships, is an integral and essential element of human well-being and flourishing lives. Special concern and care from parents (or those assuming such a role) are particularly crucial for early childhood development, for example. Similarly, close social contacts and activities, whether with partners, lifelong friends, or family are essential for a good life (Scheffler 2010). If some people choose not to engage in friendships or not to care about their family, they seem to forego important sources of experiencing meaning and realising value. Furthermore, special relationships between individuals are often seen not only as bringing meaning and value to life, but also as paradigmatic instances for moral behaviour: a parent caring for a child, a friend looking after another in distress, someone dedicating himself to a worthy social cause in his vicinity, all of these people and acts appear to be morally exemplary. From this perspective, the abstract ideal of moral impartiality may even appear remote, detached from life, "an idealist fiction" (Young 1990, 104).

But how do these intuitions about the importance of special relationships and the social contextualisation of a human life sit with the view that all human beings matter equally and should be considered and treated as equals by all? That all are, because of their equal moral worth, equally deserving of (at least the minimal) conditions to live a decent life? Doesn't it appear problematic if, under conditions of massive inequality, those who are well-off provide much more than the necessary minimum of relevant goods and advantages to their own children; while other children are suffering and dying, and that individual's decision to redirect resources could prevent at least some of this from happening by means of a more egalitarian distribution of resources? Or, how can the romantic distress of a friend be—morally speaking—more important than massive human rights violations or famines elsewhere? Can a call for political engagement to address such abhorrent problems be overridden by the demand to provide, for example, post-break-up support? How can the demands of impartiality, so urgently triggered by the unmet needs of some, be weighed against the demands of partiality emerging within already rather privileged lives of others? Obviously, not everyone perceives such questions as pointing to a moral puzzle or problem, particularly since even privileged lives have their own challenges, problems and unpleasantness that call for attention and generate demands and obligations. Also, the prevalent norms and values in our societies do not demand that moral agents take such a general, cosmopolitan standpoint: human misery that occurs elsewhere and is not a direct result of one's own wrongdoing does not command the same level of attention and concern as the more immediate context does.

The present chapter takes up this very challenge and focuses on different candidates for legitimate partiality, that is relations that might be able to override the universal and impartial obligations that seem to follow directly from a cosmopolitan perspective. I will discuss the special relationships and the corresponding special permissions and obligations one may have towards oneself, towards those particularly close to oneself, particularly one's children or, important in the context of cosmopolitanism, towards one's compatriots. It will become obvious that both a strict and exclusive impartialist and a strict and exclusive partialist view are no convincing options to provide moral guidance to human agents. Humans are not neutral machines that only execute what would be best according to a fully impartialist analysis. On the other hand, the partialist extremes—egoism, nepotism, nationalism, racism etc.—so clearly ignore the interests and legitimate claims of others that they do not even merit further consideration from a cosmopolitan perspective. Instead, human agents live in networks of relations and interactions that matter—personally and also morally—and give meaning to their lives. These relations extend, on my understanding of relations and what I have called frameworks of interaction, beyond the immediate interactions we have with those near and dear to us and can also include those with whom no direct interaction takes place: people living far away who produce goods for the global market or who could be helped in their situation of deprivation through political and financial support from others, not to mention future generations who will have to deal with the lasting effects of current greenhouse gas emissions.

Ultimately, I will defend the view that in all these contexts and relationships *impartiality always matters morally, but impartiality is not all that matters morally.* Yet, a unanimous solution for the perceived tension between partialist and impartialist moral reasons, or a middle way that accommodates both partialist and impartialist concern, might not be available. Given the quite different and independent sources of moral reasoning that appear from the impartial and general point of view on the one hand, and the personal partial point of view on the other, a convincing method of navigating these competing types of demands has not yet been found. Thus, morality does not present itself as a coherent whole, but instead shows its competing and incompatible sources and consequently appears to be not only plural, but fragmented.[191]

This is clearly unsatisfactory for those seeking guidance and a way to navigate the waters of conflicting demands of impartiality and the value and demands of special relationships: I will be unable to offer a 'clean' solution that would make preferential treatment towards those already well off morally acceptable, because both demands of partiality and those of impartiality can be justified, cannot be eliminated and thus inevitably clash. Thus, in order to

---

[191] Nagel has also argued that an integrative account cannot be found (1986, 1991).

have options for action *at all*, one must consider also those options that are not unambiguously morally acceptable. Although irritating, I think this conclusion is correct: Preferential treatment towards those already well off inevitably becomes morally tainted by the background conditions. Yet, this conclusion should not so much be considered as a flaw in theorising (with the hope that better thinking will eventually provide a solution to this theoretical tension) but as a practical flaw in the real conditions of our current, massively unequal world. In a better, just world, within which all would have secure access to the conditions necessary to live decent or flourishing lives, much more room for legitimate preferential treatment—untainted by the weighty moral demands that result from the background conditions—would exist. Thus, the diagnosis of a fragmented morality with competing and contradictory demands, should motivate agents to seek to improve the conditions of the real world.

2 Preference for oneself

A first question to be considered is whether we as individual persons are allowed to, or even obliged to assign preference to issues and goods that primarily or exclusively regard ourselves. Are we permitted to rank our own interests higher than those of others, and are we permitted to dedicate special concern to our own preferences? To discuss these questions, the present section starts with a critical engagement with arguments from Cottingham, a prominent and ardent proponent of qualified partiality, who argues for the permissibility of pursuing one's own projects and of giving preference to obligations towards oneself, even if these preferences include securing a rich life which is far above any threshold of minimal subsistence and well-being and which takes place in a world where such minimal subsistence is not secured for a large number of people.

In a paper on *Impartiality and Ethical Formation*, Cottingham defends the claim that partial obligations, in this case the particular obligations individuals may have towards *themselves*, are justified and can trump impartial moral reasons (Cottingham 2010). For him, impartialism plays a role only in rare and specific circumstances, such as when agents occupy professional roles like being a judge that oblige them to act impartially.

At the heart of Cottingham's argument lies the assumption that morality can be divided into two dimensions, one dealing primarily with what we do to others (an inter-personal dimension), the other dealing primarily with what we do to ourselves (an intra-personal dimension). The inter-personal approach to ethics has dominated in the modern era, while the intra-personal figured prominently in ancient and early-modern periods; or so Cottingham argues, with the intention of reinvigorating the classical tradition. With this intention, Cottingham defends an "*auto-tamieutic* perspective," that is, the idea of responsible stewardship for one's own life and development (Cottingham 2010, 69). Such stewardship is primarily concerned with "intra-personal ethical formation—with the individual's journey towards self-knowledge, self-development, and harmonious living" (Cottingham 2010, 65). According to this approach, the project of morality embraces the goals of self-understanding and self-improvement, but this is seen simultaneously, although only as an indirect consequence, as conducive to better inter-personal relations (Cottingham 2010, 68). Cottingham stresses that this focus on "the self" is not a selfish one. Instead, he stipulates an *ethical* centrality of the self. The self-stewarding that applies to the self includes in particular a special responsibility for developing one's own character and talents. Along with this particular responsibility comes an "automatically implied pre-assignment of time and energies to meet my duty of self-discovery and self-perfectioning" (Cottingham 2010, 71).

Cottingham's neo-Aristotelian argument rests on an account of basic goods that are based in our human nature and that include the mentioned goods of self-discovery, self-perfection, and a harmonious life. All human agents are supposed to seek realisation of these goods, the intrinsic human *telos*, in their own lives. I do not want to challenge here Cottingham's assumption of objective values that exist for all humans irrespective of their actual preferences or choices, but want to focus on Cottingham's idea that the possibility of realising such complex values in one's own life allows an agent to seek to do so, even if other people are condemned to lives in which there is little or no hope of realising these same goods for themselves.

This view clearly conflicts with an egalitarian commitment that assigns everyone equal moral importance. Here is my argument. First, I agree that the goods in people's lives include self-understanding and self-perfection. These, however are higher order goods that presuppose that some basic goods are already secured: If subsistence is not secured and one is dying of hunger, the ability to self-improve in the way envisaged by Cottingham is severely impeded because the capacities for agency are dominated by attempts to secure basic material need and cannot be directed to the goal of self-perfection, as valuable as it may be. Second, from an egalitarian perspective that does assign equal moral importance to all, the ability of some to achieve high levels of objective goods must not trump the urgent need of others who are unable to achieve even minimally sufficient levels of objective goods. In other words, as long as so many people are unable to reach a certain level of sufficiency in important goods, priority has to be directed to securing sufficiency for all over seeking perfection for some. Third, I admit that my talk of a threshold of sufficiency is in need of specification in at least two ways: with regard to both a *lower* limit of what counts as enough, but also with regard to an *upper* limit of what would exceed the legitimate realm of having more than enough. There is legitimate dissent about how ambitious the lower threshold of sufficiency should be set—generally I would defend a threshold along the lines of basic human rights as a good and rather uncontroversial starting point. However, in order to connect such a sufficiency threshold with the egalitarian commitment, it is imperative to also set a limit to inequalities in goods *above* the threshold, as well; and this upper limit is conspicuously absent in Cottingham's account. Instead, he accepts potentially unlimited melioristic standards such as self-perfection and self-discovery as objective goods that justify individuals to seek these goods, even if the resources needed to realise these goods could instead be employed to secure a much more minimal level of sufficiency for others. The necessary specifications of what counts as enough and of what counts as legitimate goods to be realised also in one's own life will thus have to take the shape of a 'corridor':[192] on the one side it is determined by what is needed to have *enough*; on the other it is determined by what counts as having *too much* under conditions of inequality where so many do not even have enough. The two sides can open a space of legitimate inequality that, however, must respect the egalitarian condition—in my account concretely: the global relational egalitarian condition—that all are still able to relate to one another as equals. Forth, if global relational equality serves as the standard to assess legitimate inequalities, such a corridor is not fixed but can, and should, evolve: Once sufficiency is secured for all, the lower threshold can in turn become more and more ambitious; and with this moving the lower threshold the upper threshold can move as well to include more goods that are, perhaps, more costly to realise.

Against this admittedly brief sketch of a moving corridor of legitimate inequality, Cottingham's suggested solution to balance impartial and partial reasoning by stressing the objective value of goods like self-improvement is unsatisfying. His suggestion that partial and impartial concern can be integrated since they "relate to interconnected rather than to conflicting goals" (Cottingham 2010, 80) and because "the realisation by each human being of his or her individual goals cannot be conceived in isolation from the realisation by others of their goals" (Cottingham 2010, 81) is questionable. Reality shows that the quest for self-centred self-improvement, self-discovery and a harmonious life is, alas,

---

[192] Cf. chapter two above.

for some very much possible under conditions where the dire fate of many others is ignored or even aggravated.

Certainly humans do not flourish in isolation, and interaction with others, whose well-being is essential to that ongoing interaction, is generally understood to be crucial to leading a good life. Also, the neo-Aristotelian focus on the character and the virtues of an agent, as well as the importance of defining and promoting conditions for flourishing lives, are generally welcome if they lead to an extension of moral concern beyond the overly narrow assessment of specific acts alone. But in face of the situation today—radical global inequalities and a huge amount of preventable suffering on this planet—Cottingham's account seems narrow-minded, unconvincingly undercomplex and overly optimistic. The assumed "reciprocal network" that would link *everyone's* well-being (Cottingham 2010, 81), so that the well-being of some trickles down and improves the well-being of others, simply does not exist (at least not yet). Furthermore, any connection between the conditions of capable, well-off individuals in affluent countries, on the one hand, and those living in dire poverty elsewhere, on the other, is denied by Cottingham's claims that "the poor's" suffering does not create an overriding or at least stringent restriction for "the affluent's" pursuit of well-being. With this, he ignores the multiple ways that indeed relate and connect people. Instead, Cottingham's theory, with his stipulation of some automatically implied pre-assignment of time and energies for meeting one's duties of self-discovery and self-perfectioning, actually provides cover for "the affluent" to be not particularly bothered by "the poor's" situation. The assumption of a fundamental prerogative to seek one's own well-being, and the attempt to realise the intrinsically valuable *teloi* in one's life, leads Cottingham to take the problem of global injustice insufficiently seriously, to say the least. Indeed, he only pays lip service to it when he says that "for us today, who have both the knowledge and the means to help, it *does* make sense [to assume]: the wider our power and knowledge extend, the greater the scope of our responsibility" (Cottingham 2010, 82).

I can now come back to the questions raised at the beginning of this section: is preference for oneself morally acceptable? My answer is that it is perfectly acceptable to care for oneself and to invest resources to secure one's own well-being so that one lives above a certain lower threshold of sufficiency. It is also permissible to seek self-perfection, self-knowledge etc., but the resources invested to realise these goals have to be limited by an upper threshold: Money, time and environmental resources employed to secure these goals must not exceed a certain upper limit of legitimate investment: One cannot justify an extremely costly (in terms of money and environmental damage) intrusion into a protected ecosystem for vacationing in order to reach higher levels of personal insight—

when the monetary resources spent on leisure travel could save lives elsewhere, e. g. by purchasing vaccines. Having access to additional resources is a privilege which one would wish for everyone; and having such access and resources is in itself not yet problematic.[193] However, using such access only for one's own benefit—above the upper limit of the egalitarian corridor—is morally problematic. With regard to the resources people control, *cosmopolitan responsibility* thus demands moral action in the form of *self-limitation:* agents morally ought to assign their time, their money etc. in ways that bring more people, who were initially excluded, into what I called the egalitarian corridor. Once one finds oneself within it, it is luckily often possible to pursue goals like self-improvement in ways that do not require the expense of resources that ought better to be used to make others enter the corridor in the first place.

My reasoning thus allows some partial preference for oneself, but on egalitarian grounds and within egalitarian limits that are influenced by the actual circumstances one finds oneself in. Under the catastrophic circumstances of global inequality and injustice, however, the legitimate egalitarian 'corridor' cannot be expected to include costly material goods; but it will certainly include what is necessary to function as an equal member of society.

3 Relationships and integrity

Partiality towards oneself is one possible instance of partiality. Another, particularly important case is the partial, preferential treatment agents may want to extend to those near and dear to them, such as their partners and friends to whom they are connected through a special, personal relationship. Does the existence of such a special relationship provide sound ground for treating some better than others?[194] A prominent line of argument has been initiated by Williams, who argues that *not* displaying preferential treatment towards some would come with the risk that individual agents perceive themselves no longer as *persons* with an individual character and personal "integrity," but rather as "utility maximisers".

---

193 Of course, it could be problematic, if the unequal distributions result from injustice. But the major moral problem I am focussing here from the perspective of the individual agent is not so much the fact of *having* resources, but it is *keeping them* and spending them only for oneself.
194 Below, I will discuss the cases of children and compatriots; here I focus on relationships between two persons.

At the centre of Williams's argument is a now famous example: A man finds himself in a tragic situation in which he can save only one of two drowning persons, one of them being his wife.[195] He can choose either to save his wife or the other person, though he could also flip a coin and thereby "randomly" choose to save one of them. How should the man, and the rest of us, think about the particular challenge in which partial considerations generate strong biases for an agent to act in a way that favours a beloved or a friend? Is saving one's partner in a similar situation to be considered obligatory (required from a moral point of view), permissible (neither demanded nor prohibited), or prohibited?

Williams asks whether it could be shown that "*this* is a justification on behalf of the rescuer, that the person he chose to rescue was his wife?" and calls for a specification:

> It depends on how much weight is carried by 'justification': the consideration that it was his wife is certainly, for instance, an explanation which should silence comment. But something more ambitious than this is usually intended, essentially involving the idea that moral principle can legitimate his preference, yielding the conclusion that in situations of this kind it is at least all right (morally permissible) to save one's wife. [...] But this construction provides the agent with one thought too many: it might have been hoped by some (for instance, by his wife) that his motivating thought, fully spelled out, would be the thought that it was his wife, not that it was his wife and that in situations of this kind it is permissible to save one's wife. (Williams 1981, 18)

So, can a general justification of this behaviour—not just an explanation—be provided?[196] Williams seems to think so, but, as often with his critical writing, it is difficult to pin him down to a clear statement of his positive views. The man's moral reason and justification for saving his wife seems to be simply

---

[195] Cf. Williams (1981, 17, first published in 1976) and Fried (1970, 227), who both take up Godwin's classical example (1793).

[196] Here it is helpful to remember the context in which discussion of this example takes place. Williams is critical of utilitarianism for its disrespect of the separateness of persons, and the reduction of moral agents to "impersonal utility-maximisers" (Williams 1981, 14). Being sympathetic but not uncritical towards a deontological approach, he asks "whether the honourable instincts of Kantianism to defend the individuality of individuals against the agglomerative indifference of Utilitarianism can in fact be effective granted the impoverished and abstract character of persons as moral agents which the Kantian view seems to impose." This question, if affirmatively answered, may lead the way out of the dilemma wherein "Kantianism abstracts in moral thought from the identity of persons, Utilitarianism strikingly abstracts from their separateness." (Williams 1981, 4). The example of the drowning wife is hence an *experimentum crucis* for a Kantian ethics, insofar as it aims to show how Kantianism allows for some personal relationships to have genuine moral weight, which in consequence, allows for a less impoverished concept of moral agency.

the fact that she is his wife to whom he has a very special relationship. A stronger form of justification is apparently not needed—and adding the thought that "in situations of this kind it is permissible to save one's wife" would be "one thought too many" (Williams 1981, 18). The moral justification for partial preference thus lies in the particular relationship between husband and wife and this fact is, for the agent, the only fact that matters, in Williams' account.[197] Impartial reasons thus have to step back in this situation.

Allowing that special relationships justify special obligations and preferential treatment is important in Williams account because it allows him to conceive of moral agents as persons with "integrity," and with their own character that motivates them to act morally. Personal relationships are not contradictory to moral reasoning and acting; rather they have genuine moral weight that cannot be outweighed by impartial reasoning and obligations.

In *A critique of utilitarianism* Williams defends the inevitability and justifiability of a first-personal approach to actions, as well (Williams 1973a). His "integrity objection" holds that any action is inevitably *someone's* action. The assumption that the individuality of any action could be eliminated and replaced by a fully impartial or neutral concept of agency would, if true, eliminate the entire person and eventually hinder all action. Williams writes:

> The point is that he [scil. the agent] is identified with his actions as flowing from projects and attitudes which in some cases he takes seriously at the deepest level, as what his life is about (or in some cases, this section of his life—seriousness is not necessarily the same as persistence). It is absurd to demand of such a man, when the sums come in from the utility network which the projects of others have in part determined, that he should just step aside from his own project and decision and acknowledge the decision which utilitarian calculation requires. It is to alienate him in a real sense from his actions and the source of his action in his own convictions. It is to make him into a channel between the input of everyone's projects, including his own, and an output of optimific decision; but this is to neglect the extent to which his actions and his decisions have to be seen as the actions and decisions which flow from the projects and attitudes with which he is most closely

---

[197] Williams supports his view with the possible objection the wife might raise if her husband would justify his act of saving her by saying "I saved you because you are my wife and in situations of this kind it is permissible to save one's wife". But, as Derek Parfit has pointed out, the wife might also object to a justification which excludes Williams's thought too many as still including one thought too many: "It's odd that Williams gives, as the thought that the person's wife might hope he was having, that he is saving her because she is *his wife*. She might have hoped that he saved her because she was *Mary*, or *Jane*, or whatever. That she is his wife seems one thought too many" (Parfit in personal communication to Liam Murphy, cf. Murphy (2000, 140, fn. 36)).

identified. It is thus, in the most literal sense, an attack on his integrity. (Williams 1973a, 116–117)

By "integrity" Williams does not mean the honesty, purity or praiseworthiness of a person, but his or her being a person with projects, intentions and concerns that make him or her able to act at all. It is the connection of moral actions to such individual "ground projects" that generates motivating reasons to act in the first place. Being under the exclusive authority of an impartial morality would ultimately undermine any motivation for acting at all. We are not "agents of the universal satisfaction system", nor "primarily janitors of any system of values, even our own" (Williams 1973a, 118), which any radically impartial moral theory would possibly insist upon.[198] In Williams' view, in some situation *all that matters* from a moral point of view is the personal relationship to another person. Thus, according to Williams, morality must neither condemn the particular attachments, preferences and affections we have towards some, nor the actions that result from them. In this case morality would misconceive what a human agent is and also lose its strength to motivate people to act morally.

Williams clearly advances strong arguments here. A life within which persons were not allowed to act out of the special attachments and feelings they have developed towards some people who are really special to them would be massively impoverished; it would also deligitimise many actions that are understood to have not only genuine but special moral value, such as the special concern friends are willing to extend to one another. If agents exclusively aspire to advance the amount of good in the world, without taking into account their own personal positions nor any of their individual features, human agency would degenerate into a machine-like execution of a single (albeit morally beneficial) task. Yet, here again, a cosmopolitan perspective will not give a free pass to all such preferential treatment towards some under all circumstances, but aspire to embed partiality into a fundamentally impartial framework that respects the equal moral value of all. As humane and as understandable partial action towards those who are special to us may be, the context within which people live and act must never be ignored when it comes to comprehensive moral assessments: *all* have fundamentally an equal entitlement to being well, having

---

[198] It is important to acknowledge that Williams endorses a form of internalism about the motivational power of moral reasons: moral reasoning is not intrinsically motivating; only by linking moral reasons to already pre-existing personal "ground projects," does morality take on motivating power. This view is not without alternatives; externalists stipulate the independent and genuinely motivating power of moral reasons. The question of motivation will be taken up again in chapter six.

their basic needs, interests and rights respected etc. Under current, non-ideal circumstances all preferential treatment towards those whose basic needs etc. are already respected will have to be weighed against this very fact. The case of the drowning spouse illustrates a situation of emergency where the life of two persons is endangered. In such cases, preferential treatment for those we love can be explained and appears to be justified, even demanded, from the perspective of the agent who perceives the relationship to this person as particularly valuable and generating genuine reasons for moral action. From the impartialist perspective, however, flipping a coin about whom to save would be morally demanded, because only such a randomisation would establish equal chances for all in need to be saved. This option, however, is not appealing to those who feel compelled to save their beloved one. In conclusion, a tension between the two perspectives persists and saving a beloved person cannot be considered an unambiguously or perfectly moral act: after all, one does clearly *not* ascribe equal moral value to the life of *each* person in need. Taking the perfectly impartialist perspective and flipping a coin about saving one's spouse or not, on the other hand, seems to neglect the special importance and value that exists in intimate relationships that come with particular ways of special concern for the lot of the other. Acting in a perfectly impartial way thus also seems to miss out on something of great moral importance.

The upshot of the discussion of the case of preferential treatment for oneself and for one's intimates so far is that the two perspectives cannot be integrated into a coherent whole. Consequently: even what appears to be moral from one of the two perspectives appears to be flawed from the other, so that a perfectly moral act seems not to be available.

4 Parental partiality

To illustrate this claim further, I want to discuss another field of human agency in which partial treatment is often seen as particularly valuable but in which claims of partiality and impartiality clash, namely the family.[199] Often, the family is seen as a place where some of the most valuable human goods are realised (Cottingham 1983) and not many are inclined to hold the family—with loving parental-filial-relationships—to be morally problematic. Quite to the contrary, flour-

---

[199] I understand a family not in the narrow sense of a hetero-sexual couple and their biological children. Many other constellations that I do not specify here can count as families (cf. Golombok 2015).

ishing family relationships are seen as morally exemplary and admirable insofar as they result from altruistic and benevolent motives, instantiate loving relationships, and generate well-being and security for those involved. Indeed, it may even seem rather strange to scrutinise and challenge the apparent moral innocence of close and caring relationships that characterise flourishing families, even if commitments within families may conflict with other obligations. Yet, this scrutiny is important.

Here is the impartialist concern: Given that families have a significant impact on the lives led by children, and given that the advantages that are distributed within families are accessible only to those living in such beneficial family-relations (an arbitrary fact fully beyond a child's control), morally relevant questions about access to and the distribution of goods arise. These questions appear even if no one doubts that relationships within a family can and often do realise important moral values and hence clearly have moral value from some perspective. The question is, however, how parental partiality in well-off families is to be assessed from a moral point of view, given that the social background conditions are shaped by massive inequality and structural injustice.

In this section I will (1) introduce the moral challenge that comes along with the existence of unequal types of familial environments, (2) present and discuss Brighouse's and Swift's view of legitimate parental partiality and (3) locate this view of legitimate parental partiality within the context of *cosmopolitan responsibility*. My general worry is that justifications of familial partiality insufficiently acknowledge the realities of the larger social and potentially global context. Taking this broader view generates and justifies at least some universal demands, based on an impartial consideration of the equal moral value of all. This generates the question if, and if yes how, the two perspectives—some degree of partial preference for those near and dear and an infinite moral concern for the lot of all—can be integrated into a morally coherent way of life.

(1) *Families as a moral challenge.* The widely accepted challenge posed by parental partiality is that the goods that are realised in a well-working family structure, "familial relationship goods", are goods pertinent to questions of distributive justice (Brighouse and Swift 2009). The value of a family is hence analysed and explained instrumentally in terms of the specific goods realised by it.

What now are these goods that are realised or distributed within a family? Different options are available. One could conceive of them—following the established metrics of justice—as subjective states of happiness or well-being, or objectively as resources, or as opportunities for well-being. Clearly it is intrinsically rewarding and hence conducive to individual well-being to enjoy loving relationships among children or parents. Reading bed-time stories, playing, and cuddling can be a source of joy and satisfaction for all involved. Taking responsibility for the development of a human being feels intrinsically rewarding, as is the feeling of being cared for. Furthermore, concrete material resources may be distributed in familial relationships, for example by bequest, among them money, lodgings, access to jobs, etc. In short, growing up in a supportive and advantaged familial environment helps children to develop, and provides them with opportunities, that they would be unlikely to enjoy outside of such a functioning family or family-like environment. Having—as a result of a successful education and loving upbringing—the basic conviction that life is meaningful, that one's own decisions matter, that other people can be trusted, and having developed a stable self-confidence or an attitude of whatever traits are socially desirable, will certainly further facilitate one's future life as a member of a society. This, ultimately, comes along with an increased number of opportunities and higher abilities to realise one's own projects and to fare well later in life.

But these goods—desirable states, resources, and opportunities—are distributed in a morally arbitrary way. No one choses his or her family. And thus even seemingly innocent, even morally praiseworthy actions, like reading bedtime stories, can contribute to the perpetuation of social inequality. The more a child is exposed to words and reading is correlated with (and possibly causally related to) how well that child develops certain key skills—like paying attention, being able to understand other people's intentions—that will "cash out" in their adult lives. Given the massive differences between the possible familial environments—within a single country, and even more so globally—it is clear that some children will benefit a lot from their familial setting, while others will be severely harmed and set back by it. The type of family within which a child grows up, however, falls to brute luck, and is fully beyond the control of the child. Individual flourishing or failing is determined to a large degree by the family one grows up in. But if everyone matters equally, irrespective of the social background, it seems morally unjustifiable to accept that the existing social inequalities in a society are perpetuated through leaving parental partiality unconstrained.

If one shares the (luck-) egalitarian concern that distribution and access to such goods should not depend on facts beyond one's control, and if one shares the (relational) egalitarian concern that circumstances should be such that people can interact with one another on a footing of equality, the unequal distribution of the goods of the family clearly is a matter of justice. Consequently, agents —both institutional and individual agents—are obliged to justify their actions that affect the realm of the family.

The moral challenge which presents itself in a particularly striking sense from the perspective of *cosmopolitan responsibility*, consists in determining whether, or which form of, parental partiality is fair and can be justified, given that it may contradict with various global egalitarian standards. From an impartial and egalitarian point of view, one that does not favour any specific individuals (or families, or social backgrounds) over any others, no child should have significantly diminished or increased life prospects simply because of the arbitrary fact who her parents are.

This particular clash between partial and impartial concern is theoretically interesting because the choice it requires is not only between sacrificing something of *no* or *less* moral value in order to secure something else of moral value.[200] With regard to familial partiality, it may be the case that something which indeed has moral value (familial relationship goods) is morally tainted and may even have to be reduced or "sacrificed" to some degree in order to realise a higher degree of justice, or in order to avoid moral wrongdoing. Before turning to the question if and how the potentially incommensurable demands of partiality and impartiality can be weighed against one another in the context of the family, I want to discuss Brighouse's and Swift's attempt to morally justify certain forms of parental partiality.

(2) *A defence of parental partiality.* Brighouse and Swift present an elaborate account of familial relationship goods, and they attempt to determine up to what degree parental partiality is legitimate (Brighouse and Swift 2009). They focus on the adverse impact of family relationships on fair equality of opportunity.[201] Their argument departs from the assumption that families, and the goods families realise, are of such important moral value that their existence trumps (at least some) social inequality. A world in which fair equality of opportunity would obtain perfectly, but at the expense of families entirely, appears less desirable to them than a world with significant inequalities of opportunity, but in which people continue to grow up within loving families. As they have it: "We share the common view that familial relationships are valuable enough to make society A, in which people enjoy Rawlsian fair equality of opportunity but lack familial relationships, worse than society B, where there is a good deal of inequality of opportunity but plentiful family life" (Brighouse and Swift 2009, 50).

Obviously, this position turns on determining of just how much a "good deal of inequality" is, and why that is still regarded as permissible. All but the strict-

---

[200] This is the case in the famous Singer scenario (1972), discussed in chapter four, section three.
[201] Rawls defines fair equality of opportunity in the following way: "supposing there is a distribution of native endowments, those who have the same level of talent and ability and the same willingness to use these gifts should have the same prospects of success regardless of their social class of origin, the class in which they are born and develop until the age of reason" (Rawls 2001, 44).

est telic egalitarians allow for *some* distributive inequality: But how much of it is morally acceptable?

That families appear so desirable, and that their value is potentially able to trump concern about fair equality of opportunity, is based on the finding that those involved in a family or its surroundings tend to have a strong and legitimate *interest* to preserve it (Brighouse and Swift 2009, 50). Children have an interest in being raised in secure conditions which will allow them to develop the skills they will later need to fare well during their lives. Parents have an interest in the family, because having a family (or at least having the possibility of having a family), as well as developing meaningful relationships with its members, and being able to realise some mutual aims, will impact on how well they will judge their own lives to be. Additionally, third parties also have an interest in families because of the positive externalities they generate; it is beneficial for society as such that children are raised well, such that they become "potential economic and civic contributors to social life" (Brighouse and Swift 2009, 52). For Brighouse and Swift, there seems to exist no alternatives to the family, at least when it comes to securing the interests just enumerated: "Family life, appropriately arranged, makes available to its participants [scil. including third parties] distinctive goods, goods for which nothing else can be an adequate substitute" (Brighouse and Swift 2009, 52).[202]

Yet, Brighouse and Swift do not grant full discretion to parents: Only forms of parental partiality that are *necessary* for realising the core familial relationship goods are legitimate; those that can be replaced by alternatives that are less averse to fair equality of opportunity, they contend, are not. Concretely, Brighouse and Swift conclude that it is morally acceptable to be partial towards one's children in reading bed-time stories to them (and not to random other children) or accompanying them to religious and other activities that are valued within the family. This can be legitimate even if it corresponds with a general parental motivation to further the child's interests. Bequeathing large amounts of money, however, is morally not legitimate because an alternative that would increase fair equality of opportunity without putting anyone in a dire situation can be easily imagined (e. g. through taxation and redistribution).

(3) *Challenging parental partiality.* A defence of parental partiality faces several objections. In the following, I will engage with five of them. First: Is "the family" indeed entirely without alternative when it comes to realising the

---

[202] This claim can be plausibly disputed, of course, since it is very much possible that another institution, similar to the family in the important respects, would be able to realise such goods. Yet, such an objection is of no relevance here, since some form of partiality would presumably still figure among the characteristics of this substitute institution.

goods that Brighouse and Swift have called familial relationship goods? This, of course, is an empirical question, and one about which philosophical analysis is ill-equipped to provide empirical arguments. But the mere fact that the understanding of what counts as a "family" is vague (and may include many different forms of living together that deviate from the Western ideal of a nuclear family with mother, father and two biological children) seems on its own to show that what matters more than a fixed definition of a single form of "family" is a certain pattern of certain relationships: If people of different ages live together and, as a joint undertaking, attempt to raise the younger ones well, I do not see why one should assume that *only* those structures that are families in any narrower sense should be able to successfully do so. People live in very different settings, and what matters is stable loving relationships. Obviously, families in the conventional sense can provide these, and since they are the dominant standard in Western societies, it may be difficult for some to imagine viable alternatives. Yet, there is no reason to assume that other forms of relationships besides families should not be able to realise the values at stake. And, of course, families can and, alas, often enough do fail to do so. Even state-run child-rearing institutions (the bogeyman evoked by Brighouse and Swift) can—if they are run well and if the people working there really engage with the children they are in charge of—do the job of realising the core relationship goods stipulated by Brighouse and Swift.

Second: Brighouse and Swift accept the distributive objection, that burdens and benefits are conferred in an unfair way, as a central challenge to their view (Brighouse and Swift 2009, 44 et passim). They refer to Scheffler's formulation of it, who introduces it as "an objection on behalf of those individuals who are not participants in the groups and relationships that are thought to give rise to associative duties. The distributive objection sees such duties, not as imposing unreasonable burdens on the participants in special relationships, but rather as supplying them with benefits that may be unreasonable" (Scheffler 2001, 56). Scheffler elaborates: "The objection turns on the observation that special responsibilities give the participants in rewarding groups and relationships increased claims to one another's assistance, while weakening the claims that other people have on them. In this way, it asserts, such responsibilities provide the participants with significant advantages while working to the disadvantage of non-participants" (Scheffler 2001, 99).

The quotes make the structure of the objection clear. It includes two elements in the structure of groups to which access is limited or arbitrary (like a family) namely that the benefit for group members is increased in an unreasonable way while the burdens for those who are excluded are increased, to their unjustified disadvantage. Those who are most excluded are thus most entitled to raise this objection, but since the distribution of advantages to the members of the in-group is unjustified (albeit favourable), they themselves should also speak up against such undeserved privilege, or at the very least acknowledge an unsolved moral problem.

Indeed, the distributive objection seems to be the decisive counterargument against parental partiality that perpetuates inequality. For which arguments could be convincing to legitimise perpetuating substantial inequalities in happiness, resources, opportunities, etc.? If these inequalities persist at least in part *because of parental partiality* (and they do), and if there are alternative patterns for raising and educating children, then this speaks strongly against the moral legitimacy of partial actions by parents in favour of their children. Denying the legitimacy of these acts does not necessarily entail denying the moral quality of these acts that can become visible from a certain perspective: of course, there is something morally good in reading bed-time stories to children and in being read such stories. Yet, this is only an agreement about which *distribuenda* are indeed goods worth caring about, but this agreement makes their unequal distribution ever more problematic.

The moral legitimacy of parental partiality increases, the closer circumstances are to being perfectly just—which is to say that it is of questionable legitimacy under the current circumstances of vast global inequality where apparently even the best acts of parental concern and partiality (directed at their own children) remain in some sense "tainted," since the children benefitting from this concern are already well above the threshold of sufficiency, while so many other children are not. It thus seems difficult, perhaps even impossible, to do what is morally right under circumstances that are, morally speaking, just plain wrong.

Admitting such a distributive challenge obliges partial agents—if not to withdraw concern from their family members—to at least extend concern also to those excluded from their group and to take action in the light of this widened scope of moral concern. As Young explains (albeit in a different context): "When structurally privileged people attend to one another's claims and needs, they often contribute to the maintenance of their structural positions. Recognizing this fact does not constitute a reason to begin ignoring or withdrawing attention from structurally similar people whom one encounters. It is reason, however, to be aware of the dynamics of the reproduction of privilege and oppression and to take self-conscious action." (Young 2011, 164). Such acknowledgement and awareness are an essential first step towards addressing the wrong in question in an appropriate way.

Third: Brighouse and Swift argue that a society with fair equality of opportunity and without familial relationships would be morally inferior than another society in which familial relationship goods are realised but fair equality of opportunity is impaired (Brighouse and Swift 2009, 50).[203] A general challenge with regard to this thesis is whether fair equality of opportunity should indeed be the pertinent account of justice in the first place. Is equality of opportunity really what one should be concerned about most when thinking about inequalities in a society, as well as how familial structures contribute to such? Is it of *prior* importance that all are able to compete on equal terms in the race for individual benefits? While equality of opportunity is certainly relevant, this seems not to be the most urgent issue at hand: indeed, more basic for an account of justice—particularly so under the immensely unjust circumstances that currently characterise so many societies and the injustices of the dysfunctional global order—is status equality and subsequently relational equality. On this alternative understanding of the ideal of justice, efforts need to be made first and foremost to secure the equal standing of all, in a functioning society, by securing for each a certain threshold of sufficiency or of adequacy enabling them to be respected equal members of their society—even if some contingent factors impede perfectly fair equality of opportunity. From the perspective of relational equality, it appears problematic to begin by stipulating fair equality of opportunity, since the opportunities in question include mostly the competition for questionable, even illegitimate pay-offs: If, even under conditions of fair equality of opportunity in a society without relational equality among all, the more successful are still disproportionately able to secure positions of superiority, then the entire point of fair equality of opportunity appears to be misguided. Concern should primarily be directed, both through institutional reform and individual behaviour, to realise a society in which the equal moral status of all is fully respected and in which all have enough of the relevant goods so that all can and do interact with each other on a footing of equality. But as long as we remain so far from establishing such circumstances, fair equality of opportunity does not appear to be an appropriate first concern for justice.

Fourth: Brighouse and Swift distinguish between core familial relationship goods, and goods that are "parasitic" on such goods. While the general parental motivation to further the interests and well-being of their children is a legitimate

---

[203] Comparing societies with more or less familial relationships and correspondingly less or more fair equality of opportunity would have been preferable to Brighouse's and Swift's comparison between a society A, "in which people enjoy Rawlsian fair equality of opportunity but *lack* familial relationships" (my italics) and society B, "where there is a good deal of inequality of opportunity but plentiful family life" (Brighouse and Swift 2009, 50). After all, *abolishing* the family would be a quite drastic measure and more moderate interventions such as reducing the impact of familial relationships should be analysed first.

form of parental partiality (because it realises the central familial relationship goods), it can nevertheless often be close to, or may contain some problematic forms of favouritism. To prefer one's children beyond what is necessary to realise the core familial relationship goods, and to do so at an unacceptably high cost to the basic well-being of others, renders some forms of partiality illegitimate, and their respective goods "parasitic". This is why parents must actually take into account the (opportunity) costs related to their actions that are imposed on others. In their moral consideration of how to act, parents must thus include not only the intended consequences of their actions on their own family, but also the foreseeable side-effects, even if they are unintended. Even though reading bed-time stories clearly constitutes a case of favouring one's children (and probably also a case of giving them a competitive advantage in society), this form of parental partiality remains legitimate because it is intended to realise familial relationship goods, and not intended to give children a competitive advantage. Also, as Brighouse and Swift claim, this is done at merely a moderate cost to others.[204] On the other hand, as they argue, bequeathing large amounts of money, or real estate, or paying for children to attend elite schools *in order to* enhance their competitiveness on the employment market (and not out of a more acceptable wish that children perpetuate the family tradition of going to the best schools), are forms of *illegitimate* parental partiality. Here the intended consequences are morally problematic, even if the respective actions to realise these problematic intentions could alternatively be justified by reference to the morally acceptable aim of realising familial relationship goods, such as educating the children in the valued tradition of a family. In this case, goods like competitive advantage are "parasitical" on the core familial goods of perpetuating a family tradition.

Brighouse and Swift accept that parents should not have *full* freedom to promote their children's interests, yet the criteria which they suggest to identify illegitimate forms of partiality appear to be misguided on one hand, and too vague and ambiguous on the other. They are *misguided*, at least from the theory of justice I endorse, because—as argued above (iii)—fair equality of opportunity is not the appropriate standard to be applied under non-ideal circumstances in a society shaped by structural injustice. They are *vague* because, even on their account of fair equality of opportunity, they are unable to offer a specific threshold to distinguish acceptable from unacceptable costs imposed on others. And they are *ambiguous* because the distinction between intended and merely foreseeable

---

[204] It is, however, unclear whether the actual relative *dis*advantages of those who are not being read bedtime stories constitutes only a "moderate cost" to them.

but unintended consequences will be—for psychological and empirical reasons —hard to make in real cases.

Fifth: Even if one is willing to accept much of Brighouse's and Swift's theory about legitimate forms of parental partiality—namely that it is morally acceptable for parents to read bed-time stories to their children, as well as encourage them to follow certain valued traditions etc. as a way of developing their skills and personalities—the global context of "ongoing disaster" quite definitively alters the picture, and well beyond the degree that follows from the typical inequalities seen within a single affluent society. Brighouse and Swift see this challenge themselves, when they write tentatively:

> Perhaps, in a world where some lack what they need for mere survival, much of the time and energy spent by affluent parents on promoting the interests of their children is illegitimate self-indulgence. Perhaps, in a world of that kind, much of the provision, for oneself and one's children, of those very familial relationship goods that our account holds crucial to human well-being similarly exceeds the bounds of legitimate partiality. (Brighouse/Swift 2009, 50)

Here is a question: Why "perhaps"? Isn't it obvious that, in a world in which available resources could go toward providing minimal medical care for children dying from diarrhea or malnutrition, spending money for more and more toys, or the fiftieth bed time book, constitutes a moral problem? Can any explicit justification be provided for choosing another book or toy for a child with many already over, say, a life-saving vaccine for another child elsewhere (justification that would be acceptable to those who are in need of the vaccine)? Considerable psychological efforts seem to be necessary to suppress moral concern once one starts to think about such questions, efforts that, however, are facilitated by a widespread collective practice of ignoring and suppressing. Given that the background conditions of our moral considerations are simultaneously both catastrophic and considered to be quite normal some may regard it as daring merely to suggest that "perhaps" such efforts and such practices lack moral legitimacy.

But even at their most daring, the authors only suspect "much of the time and energy" of parental partiality to be morally problematic. In light of the huge dimensions of the problem at hand, it might more plausibly be the case that very nearly *all* time and energy spent providing yet more advantages to children living already well above the standard of adequacy may turn out to be morally tainted, since a plausible justification that would seem acceptable to *all* sides involved—the rich family on the one side and the poor one on the other —is out of reach.

I do not undertake to spell out the appropriate standard of adequacy here, but I do want to mention one problem with attempting to do so. If the standard of adequacy is set *high*—in a way that would include the possession of many toys, fresh organic food, etc.—this would indeed allow the justification of many forms of partiality. Dozens of expensive high-quality toys or nice clothing would then be included in what counts as necessary for living an adequate life. However, this would come along with two counterintuitive consequences. First, we would have to admit that only a truly minuscule percentage of the world's children reach adequate standards of living; and second, that access to certain goods currently considered to be luxury items, e.g. organic or expensive food, is a matter of justice.

If the standard of adequacy is set *lower*—for example by stipulating the conditions for a minimally decent life in a secure, healthy and supportive environment—most parental partiality, at least in the developed countries, would still appear excessive and unjust, because it goes beyond the stipulated basic standard of adequacy. The problem now is that it seems generally desirable to set the standard of adequacy as high as possible, in order to encourage and eventually secure the best possible lives for all. Adequacy, however, in contrast to a more minimalistic demand for sufficiency, is certainly more ambitious than the conditions for bare survival. What would be needed, hence, is to spell out the standard of adequacy in a way that really guarantees the conditions for a decent human life without including luxurious elements that can be realised only at a high cost. Thus, again, a 'corridor' is needed providing both a lower and an upper limit of acceptable inequality.

If moral reason includes impartial reasoning, then parental partiality becomes, under current conditions, morally problematic if it is directed at children who are already well off. The assumption that parental partiality per se is morally legitimate thus has to be rejected, no matter how widely spread and deeply anchored this idea may be in a society. Everything valuable in loving and successful familial relationships in families that are already well off is realised at great cost; a cost that has to be paid by others who don't benefit from the partial actions. Not only are some excluded from ever accessing a family setting in which such familial relationship goods could be realised; furthermore, the goods realised in these settings constitute an additional competitive disadvantage for those who are exluded.

Yet, understanding these social dynamics does not necessarily mean that parents must treat all children in exactly the same way or that any kind of special treatment for one's children should end. But *extending concern* beyond one's own family and increasing and integrating awareness for existing social and global inequalities into one's considerations and actions is imperative. From this perspective, the price for partial action, generally paid by those who are excluded from it, will be taken into account. Absent official regulation, individuals who are morally concerned about inequalities have to self-regulate and accept an upper limit on how many goods they realise and keep for themselves and for their children. The hope would be that, eventually, a corridor of morally acceptable inequality can be reached for all within which preferential treatment for one's children is not tainted by the high opportunity costs born by others. Under current, catastrophic global conditions, however, even a quite reduced and moderate familial lifestyle in the affluent countries cannot be considered as perfectly morally innocent and any form of partiality towards those who are already well off has a morally dubious aspect to it.

5 Preference for compatriots

Cottingham, Williams, and Brighouse/Swift have focussed on what can be called *relationship*-dependent reasons. The relationships in question hold between the agent and specific individuals, (e.g., herself, a beloved person, her family members), and the relationship-dependent reasons are held to justify partial preference for these particular individuals. There are, according to a classification suggested by Scheffler (e.g. Scheffler 2010), two other types of reasons that can justify partiality, namely *project*-dependent reasons and *membership*-dependent reasons. Here, I will neglect the project-dependent ones, because I am mainly interested in interpersonal conduct and the responsibilities that exist between persons.[205] Instead, I will discuss the case of preferential treatment among compatriots in which membership-dependent reasons are advanced to justify legitimate partiality. Alas, the borders between the different types of reasons are blurry: particular obligations and permissions to act partially towards one's family members can be discussed either as relationship-dependent (as it has been the strategy of Brighouse and Swift), or as group membership-dependent (in this case with the family as group), or as both simultaneously. Other groups in which members may feel permitted or obliged to act partially are, for example, religious communities, clubs, or nations. However, when considering partiality towards compatriots, it is important to keep in mind that the nation-state is a very specific kind of group. Analogising from what may be legitimate or not in a club or in a family may not have much argumentative force when determining what is legitimate in a nation-state. Each type of group needs to be considered

---

[205] Project-dependent reasons, however, may also relate to Cottingham's justification of dedicating particular concern to one's own life, including to the specific projects one is pursuing as meaningful. They also figure in Williams' concern for personal integrity.

individually and independently. Even if, in the end, one were to find similarities between membership-dependent reasons that pertain to different types of groups, each case requires an independent argument.

The debate about reasonable and legitimate partiality for compatriots, and about national responsibility, has been proliferating for many years (cf. e.g. Cohen 2002, Miller 2007). Given the huge inequalities between countries, and given the growing interconnectedness of countries, it is easy to see why the question about legitimate partiality towards compatriots matters: extending preferential treatment to those already well off needs a special justification in a world in which so many others are systematically excluded from accessing the multiple advantages that can result from cooperation and interaction and that are provided by nation-states.[206] This question has, again, both an institutional and an interactional side to it. Laws, policies and public institutions express and mirror an underlying normative commitment that becomes tangible for example in the way resources are allocated, migration is regulated and emergency help is extended; also individual behaviour corresponds with normative commitments, be it in voting, in arguing, or in taking action such as supporting others in need. In the following, I will use Miller's influential defence of national responsibility and partiality for one's compatriots to structure my discussion. While I do not doubt that membership in a community, also a national community, can have value for some involved, I point to several difficulties with justifying compatriot partiality that underline the importance of limiting such membership-dependent preferential treatment by installing universalist and impartial constraints.

In numerous publications, Miller has elaborated a sophisticated account of moderate statism, or liberal nationalism in which "reasonable" partiality, and some special obligations towards one's compatriots, are defended (e.g. Miller 1988, Miller 2005, Miller 2007, Miller 2016).[207] Miller stipulates three core condi-

---

[206] Such preferential treatment of those already well off is in line with the primary interest of the present book, namely to analyse the role and responsibility of the advantaged citizens in the affluent countries. However, partial treatment among members of an oppressed state, for example in order to advance the project of emancipation, will fall into another category. For this, cf. Bascara, who has argued not to "comprehensively reject compatriot partiality. We can justify compatriot partiality on the same grounds that liberation movements and affirmative action have been justified. Hence, given cosmopolitan demands of justice, special consideration for the economic well-being of your nation as a whole is justified if and only if the country it identifies is an oppressed developing nation in an unjust global order." (Bascara 2016, 27).

[207] My interest in this section is directed to the fundamental justification Miller provides for permitting partiality towards compatriots in the first place. I discuss in this chapter neither the concrete obligations towards compatriots Miller deduces from his partialist account about

tions under which shared nationality justifies the existence of special obligations and thus calls for preferential treatment of compatriots.[208] Such reasonable, justified partiality will then have to be weighed against the demands that are based on universal human rights in his account of global justice. With this, Miller defends what he calls a "split level" view: the need to weigh the possibly conflicting global duties towards all with the special duties towards some. The three conditions for reasonable and legitimate compatriot partiality are: that the relevant relationship is intrinsically valuable, and does not simply have instrumental value to those engaged in it; that the particular forms of partiality in question are an integral part of that relationship (which is to say that the very relationship would be different if it were not for the forms of partiality that are justified by it); and, that the relationships that may be at the origin of special obligations are not in themselves unjust. I will critically review these conditions in turn.

(1) Miller's first condition for legitimate partiality within a community of compatriots is that its members find and experience intrinsic value in communicating and understanding one another, in sharing and enjoying joint practices, in jointly pursuing projects, in offering and receiving mutual support etc. Such intrinsic value goes beyond the privileges membership in a particular state can confer to its citizens, such as strong passports, access to social welfare etc. I agree with Miller that such intrinsic value can, under favourable circumstances, be realised not only in small communities such as circles of friends, but also in large communities, such as nation-states. People then do not only instrumentally enjoy certain advantages of being joint members in a state, but perceive their joint membership as meaningful.[209]

However, tying these intrinsic values in any particular sense to nation-states —or to culturally homogeneous communities—seems arbitrary and too narrow when they are meant to morally justify special obligations that come at the ex-

---

"national responsibility," nor his qualifications of the demands of global justice (Miller 2007). For a critical discussion of these, cf. Brock (2009, 261–264).

208 Miller finds these conditions fulfilled in other relationships, as well, where they also justify reasonable forms of partiality.

209 Some may enjoy "the opportunity to place their individual lives in the context of a collective project that has been handed down from generation to generation" (Miller 2005, 68) leading to what Walzer called "communities of character", i.e. "historically stable, ongoing associations of men and women with some special commitment to one another and some special sense of their common life" (Walzer 1983, 62).—However, as already indicated above, I doubt that it is possible to draw meaningful insights about large communities such as nation-states and about the legitimate partiality among compatriots from an analysis of friendships. Being co-citizens or friends is too different, most importantly with regard to the number of friends a person has and the personal and individual character of relationships among friends.

pense of others. After all, finding intrinsic value is contingent upon factors that are not necessarily realised, neither in the context of nation-states nor in the context of "communities of character" (Walzer 1983, 62). Most importantly, not only the instrumental value, but also the experience of intrinsic value depends on generally favourable factual conditions: failed states, autocratic states, states comprised of conflicting populations, even if culturally homogeneous, often do not realise the rather rosy conditions mentioned by Miller[210]: Neither does an existing sense of community necessarily correspond with the borders of states; nor does shared nationality necessarily inspire a sense of community. This indicates that shared nationality is an unsuitable even arbitrary proxy for the conditions that have to be fulfilled so that there is inherent value in joint membership in a community.

Yet, if one generally thinks that a shared sense of community (accompanied by an experience of intrinsic value that supports a tendency to display particular concern) is possible in the case of large and quite heterogeneous populations— for example in a country as large and diverse as China—, then it should also be possible to allow for the very same possibility on a global level, within a global community of all humans. If 1.5 billion Chinese can form a community of intrinsic value, scaling up to 8 billion humans on planet Earth does not make any categorical difference. In both cases, a significant degree of inter-group and inter-individual variety will exist, that should not count as an insurmountable obstacle to fostering a sense of community, neither in the case of China, nor in the global case. After all, the existing differences between, say, Chinese and German culture, pale in comparison with the differences between, say, human and chimpanzee culture (or also, most certainly, between human and extraterrestrial culture, should there be any). An inclination to foster concern and engage in preferential treatment, based on the experience of intrinsic value in a community, thus can also apply on the global level.[211]

---

[210] "[C]ompatriots must first believe that their association is valuable for its own sake, and be committed to preserving it over time, in order to be able to reap the other benefits that national solidarity brings with it. [...] a political association that was entered into and supported purely for instrumental reasons could not work in the way that a national community does. And in fact the way that most people think about their nationality reveals that its value for them is indeed intrinsic. They would, for instance, profoundly regret the loss of their distinct national identity, even if they were guaranteed the other goods that nationality makes possible, stable democracy, social justice and so forth." (Miller 2005, 67).

[211] I do not believe that it is necessary for such universal concern and benevolence to determine an out-group that is excluded from this concern; but should it be necessary, other species or alien life forms could fulfill this function.

(2) Miller further contends, second, that preferential treatment must be an integral part of the relationships within which such preferential treatment should also count as legitimate. His paradigmatic examples are friends or spouses taking special care of one another. And indeed, without any such special concern and treatment it would be impossible to distinguish friends from non-friends, spouses from non-spouses etc. But the relations between spouses and those between compatriots are of a very different nature so that pointing to such personal relationships is not yet illuminating regarding the relationships between compatriots.

An important difference is that the preferential treatment among spouses or friends is direct, while any 'preferential treatment' between compatriots is indirect, that is it is mediated by public institutions. True, through taxation and institutions compatriots exercise solidarity towards another that becomes visible, for example, when the French embassy extends special protection to French citizens who are in danger abroad; but if I, a German citizen, find myself in Japan where I could save through personal engagement either a Japanese or a German citizen (both unknown and unmarried to me), making a case for me to save the German citizen, because he is German and not Japanese, should not be considered to be the expression of a justified special obligation between compatriots but as outright nationalist or possibly racist. Thus, pointing to the parallel that some (albeit quite different) preferential treatment is de facto realised in (and an integral part of) both marriages and national institutions, does not support a general moral justification for the legitimacy of preferential treatment among compatriots. More analysis is needed.

Furthermore, one must not forget that also within special relations among friends or spouses limits for preferential treatment pertain: nepotistic favoritism among friends and uncritical loyalty between partners indicate the need for further moral scrutiny of any form of preferential treatment before it can possibly count as morally justified. Helping a friend in need is generally morally good, few would object here; but helping her cover up past misbehaviour is morally problematic. Also, preferring one's romantic partner by offering considerately chosen presents to him is morally good and maybe an integral part of having such a relationship; but one should, morally, neither expect to receive very expensive gifts nor give disproportionate gifts. Here again, setting an upper limit for any preferential treatment—determined also by the opportunity costs paid by those who are not preferred—seems to be the most sensible way forward.[212]

---

[212] To challenge Miller's account further, I also want to point out that the special treatment among people in special relations frequently is particularly demanding, not particularly lenient

(3) Miller's third criterion for legitimate partiality towards compatriots requires that inherently unjust communities or associations are excluded from the possibility to provide a basis for legitimate partiality among its members. This criterion is included with the intention of refuting a frequently made objection, namely that a group of, say, racists could also feel and display inherently valuable preferential treatment as an integral part of their relationship. I do not want to put membership in a racist party and membership in a nation state on the same level, but pointing out differences between both types of association (nationality is usually not chosen, nationality is not inherently supremacist etc.) does not in itself exculpate nationhood and compatriotism from any possible charge of injustice. In groups where membership has massive implications for access to advantage and where access is arbitrary and tightly regulated by the members of the in-group, injustice exists. The random and arbitrary inclusion and exclusion of people in the context of citizenship through birth have made some draw a parallel between citizenship and the medieval feudal system (Carens 2013). The tight regulation of migration and access to citizenship (fortified borders; occasionally the possibility to 'buy' passports through investments into countries; etc.) which can be determined by in-group members without consultation with those who are excluded makes the concept of citizenship with its massive impact on the distribution of advantages and disadvantages generally morally dubious, if not—under current world conditions—inherently unjust.[213]

My critical discussion of the three criteria for legitimate partiality among compatriots proposed by Miller is, obviously, committed to a cosmopolitan perspective that takes the idea of the equal moral worth of all individuals seriously and suggests, on these grounds, always including an impartial and universalist perspective when considering the role and responsibilities of individuals and also when considering (domestic and international) institutional design and reform. Miller does not in any way deny the existence and the importance of such a global justice perspective. Instead, he proposes a "split level" view that acknowledges the existence of both universal and special obligations and invites a weighing of both. My disagreement with Miller does not lie here: I agree with him that there are different sources of moral reasons and that both universal

---

or generous. On moral terms, people with particular moral standards will often impose these moral expectations on their friends or partners, even if they do not expect everyone else to meet these expectation; that is they will be even stricter, in moral terms, with their intimates than they would be with those they are not friends with.

213 This judgement can hold even if genuine malevolent intend to harm others is absent when children are born and raised into particular societies. Securing one's own unjustified privileges where they are way above a reasonable threshold of sufficient well-being is structurally unjust.

and particular considerations do generate moral claims. However, I strongly disagree with Miller regarding the possibility that the personal preferences and the experience of value of those who live well-off in functioning communities under conditions of security, and even luxury, can so easily trump concern for the lives of those who are so far away from even minimally decent living conditions. Pointing to the intrinsic value of being part of a valued cultural tradition to justify inaction towards those in extreme distress, does not place equal weight on the lives of all. Pointing to the need to preserve cultural purity in order to justify the systematic exclusion of others whose basic rights are systematically violated gets the moral priorities wrong. My argument thus neither denies the value of being part of a tradition, nor the value of cultures, nor the value of being well-off; instead, it invites a more *self-critical attitude* towards the unjustified privileges that are an often unquestioned condition for experiencing these values. Taking the lives of all seriously will thus invite those better off to question the legitimacy of their own advantages and consequently to *limit*—not to give up—preferential treatment for those near and dear. A moral justification for preferential treatment of compatriots (simply because they happen to be members of the same nation or culture) cannot be given. This, however, does not exclude the general possibility of justifying preferential treatment on pragmatic, or organisational grounds: Local groups, or nations, are not wrong to tackle their problems in the context they find themselves in. And, say, Mexicans are well advised to try to build a health care system in Mexico, not in, say, Japan. Such a organisation and division of labour, however, does not need a (dubious) moral argument that the Mexicans have a moral duty to be concerned only or primarily with the well-being of Mexicans. Since it is not necessary to make this argument, it should be better left out.

It is time to conclude my critical discussion of several attempts to justify partial and preferential treatment of some in the light of a generally impartial morality. All the proposals I have reviewed have been shown to rely on intuitive plausibility, and thus point to the importance of being careful not to fall prey to the factual fallacy: It does not suffice *that* some practices and intuitions exist and are widely accepted in order to consider them morally legitimate. Moral philosophy as a critical enterprise should scrutinise all views, even those that are widely accepted. In discussing special relationships between individuals, within families and among compatriots, I have put a particular emphasis on the "distributive objection," which highlights the point that a distribution of advantages within special relationships/groups generally occurs to the disadvantage of those who are excluded from those groups/relationships. Often, as I have repeatedly mentioned, the reason for unequal distributions lies in the unequal relationships between individuals, and in the social structures which assign people unequal moral importance, weight or standing. This problem, I argue, persists even if one is willing to see the—perhaps even intrinsic moral—values that are realised in special relationships and calls for institutional reform and behavioural change.

Generally, I have shown that *relationship*-dependent reasons justify and thus permit some preferential treatment (within limits) towards oneself or one's intimates. *Membership*-dependent reasons for preferential treatment, however, have been shown to lack moral strength: membership in communities to which not all have equal access is an insufficient moral justification for preferential treatment of the in-groups at the expense of those excluded from these groups.

6 Two standpoints and the fragmentation of morality

This chapter has discussed the challenge of integrating partialist reasoning into a generally impartialist normative framework. This challenge was important for the purpose of the present inquiry, because the cosmopolitan commitment to the equal moral value and importance of every person seems to commit cosmopolitans to a fundamentally impartialist point of view when it comes to weighing and assessing peoples options and actions—possibly leaving little or no room for the different special relationships to some special people that give so much meaning to human lives. My discussion has covered the questions of legitimate preferential treatment for oneself, for one's intimates, particularly one's children, and for one's co-nationals. Even though special relationships realise moral values and thus seem able to provide a moral justification for special, preferential treatment of some, these reasons were shown to be unable to eliminate or trump the impartialist reasons that demand equal respect and concern for all as moral equals. Relationship-dependent reasons were shown to be able to justify some degree of preferential treatment, but within limitations. Membership-dependent reasons, on the other hand, were shown to have less moral force, because the special relations in groups (such as clubs, nations etc.) are not directly interpersonal but mediated through institutions. Where agents prefer co-members (from their club or their nation) in matters of moral importance, such as whom to help in dire need etc., preferential treatment lacks moral justification.

But one can and should, also from an impartialist point of view, acknowledge that genuine moral values are often realised within special interpersonal relations; values that, when absent or made impossible by a perfectly impartial way of life, would significantly impoverish human lives. In consequence, morality was seen to include conflicting perspectives—an individual and partial point of view on the one hand and an objective and impartial one on the other; perspectives that could not be integrated into a coherent whole.²¹⁴

Altogether, I have argued that a cosmopolitan analysis will call for more scrutiny for the preferential treatment for some, even if it realises and secures important moral values: Much of what many people tend to consider as perfectly morally acceptable preference exercised towards themselves, their friends, their family members or their compatriots, appears to be morally problematic and dubious and might be morally unjustifiable—particularly under conditions of a massively unjust world. I have doubted that these special relationships are able to generate special *duties* for preferential treatment. But it would definitely be *permissible* to exercise preferential treatment towards those we stand in an intimate relationship with; preferential treatment that will be a condition for realising goods of unique value and thus should even be encouraged. Placing some material constraints to such emotionally close relationships will do them not harm. I have voiced doubts that the considerations that could justify a qualified permission to preferential treatment towards oneself and individuals near and dear can be transferred to the group of compatriots. Preferential treatment to this group thus is morally more problematic than the interpersonal preference exercised in special, personal relations.²¹⁵

---

214 Nagel has analysed the existence of two standpoints not only in practical philosophy, but across different philosophical disciplines (Nagel 1986). The general problem he addresses is "how to combine the perspective of a particular person inside the world with an objective view of that same world, the person and his viewpoint included. It is a problem that faces every creature with the impulse and the capacity to transcend its particular point of view and to conceive of the world as a whole" (Nagel 1986, 3). The difficulty of combining the subjective and the objective into one comprehensive view arises in the shape of many of the most puzzling philosophical topics: the freedom of the will, the nature of reality and knowledge, the meaning of life—but also in both of the dimensions of practical philosophy, the political and the moral. Nagel's point is that the objective dimension inevitably has to leave out the subjective dimension, which is unaccessible for it. But also the subjective perspective is incapable of fully accessing and mastering objective reality. What would be desirable is what he calls a "world view," a single, grand, overarching, unifying theory: "If one could say how the internal and external standpoints are related, how each of them can be developed and modified in order to take the other into account, and how in conjunction they are to govern the thought and action of each person, it would amount to a world view" (Nagel 1986, 3). Nagel admits that he has not found such a comprehensive view. Both standpoints appear to be irreconcilable and resist such integration and also those able and willing to take the impersonal standpoint in addition to their personal standpoint find in themselves a "division of the self" (Nagel 1991, 14).
215 If special preferential treatment of compatriots cannot be justified on moral grounds, it might, however, be possible to justify it on pragmatic or organisational grounds.

To conclude, both types of perspectives—the impartial and the partial—generate moral reasons of genuine weight that cannot be ignored. In consequence, all possibly permissible degrees of preferential treatment need to be placed within limits that are determined by taking into account what would count as justifiable from an impartialist perspective. Preferring some people way beyond what is necessary for a good human life clearly cannot be morally justified in an unequal world. This raises two questions, one more conceptual and theoretical, the other more practical. First: Can those who live well-off in affluent countries live a fully moral life at all; a life untainted by moral imperfection, flaws, even failure? And second: What then are the moral responsibililites of the globally advantaged; how should they respond to the background conditions of global inequality and injustice? The remaining chapter of part II and the concluding chapter of the book take up these questions in turn.

Chapter 6
Imperfection. Overdemandingness and the inevitability of moral failure

1 Cosmopolitan demands and the danger of moral failure

Cosmopolitan thinking generates numerous and stringent obligations for individual agents. Can one actually meet them? Or is moral imperfection, even failure, inevitable if one endorses a cosmopolitan perspective in a massively unjust world?

Prior chapters have outlined the role and responsibility of individual agents in the face of global structural injustice by analysing normative concepts such as equality, rights and impartiality and their implications for individual behaviour as citizens of the world. The present chapter addresses the third challenge for my account of *cosmopolitan responsibility* that results from accepting these normative concepts as sources of moral demands incumbent upon individual moral agents. If the preceding reasoning is sound, the relatively privileged individuals will be—under current conditions of global structural injustice, gross inequality and in the face of massive amounts of preventable suffering and deprivation—subject to a large number of entirely well-justified but also very demanding obligations to act. Moral agents are morally obliged not to harm others, they must avoid being part of harmful structures that so negatively impact on the lives of others, they are required to contribute to changing such unjust structures and they are also morally required to directly help those in dire need.

Simultaneously, agents face a number of already demanding moral requirements from close range that also urgently call for moral attention, concern, and action: Agents are not only citizens of the world, but also children or parents, friends or spouses, colleagues or officials. Given that all of these roles generate requirements of genuine moral weight and given that one kind of demand cannot silence or eliminate the others, some moral requirements of genuine moral weight will necessarily remain unmet—even in generally willing and capable moral agents. The well-justified demands that result from cosmopolitan reasoning thus exceed what agents can actually do; and this problem of excessive moral demands is only aggravated by the numerous other demands that result from our embeddedness in concrete social contexts at close hand. In light of this uncomfortable situation, the following questions appear: Does this situation of impossible demands entail reducing the moral requirements to what is actually feasible? Or does the cosmopolitan commitment to the equal moral worth of

---

OpenAccess. © 2020 Jan-Christoph Heilinger, published by De Gruyter. [CC BY-NC-ND] This work is licensed under the Creative Commons Attribution-NonCommercial-NoDerivatives 4.0 License.
https://doi.org/10.1515/9783110612271-008

all support upholding such ambitious moral requirements, even if they are impossible to fulfill? The present chapter takes up these questions.

The charge of excessive or impossible demands is important in the present context, since it will arguably bear significantly on the plausibility and appeal of my account of *cosmopolitan responsibility*.[216] If the cosmopolitan ethos is understood as comprising a set of values, norms, and rules that are also meant to guide individual conduct, the certainty that agents embracing it will inevitably fail to live up to what is morally demanded seems to undermine the entire project.

I do not share this view. Instead, I will argue that a credible theory must prove first and foremost that it is *sufficiently* demanding; where sufficient demands are determined in the light of the normative commitments (equal moral worth of all, morally relevant community of all) and in the face of the identified problems that need to be addressed (global inequality and structural injustice). Thus, the primary danger, in my view, does not so much consist in demanding too much (which would mistakenly direct concern primarily to the privileged individuals who could be bearers of responsibility to address the problem), but in demanding not enough (which directs primary concern rightly to the disadvantaged). In other words, curtailing legitimate demands of the disadvantaged in order to save the advantaged from excessive demands is worse than confronting the privileged with what can be called impossible requirements that would have to be met to end lasting disadvantage and deprivation.

In a radically unequal and structurally unjust world, taking the moral value of everyone seriously has two controversial implications: First, it generates apparently excessive demands for the privileged, even if these demands are actually impossible to fulfill; and, second, it inevitably taints the lives of the privileged by debunking the illusion of moral innocence and perfection by pointing out their inevitable moral shortcomings, even failure. Such inevitable moral failure, however, should be understood primarily as a flaw of the current state of the world—not as a flaw of cosmopolitan theorising, nor of well-intended individual agents that cannot avoid being part of harmful structures.

Importantly, the account offered here will still permit a distinction between differing degrees of moral failure and of relative achievement, and does not condemn all to fail equally. Responsible agents will also have to assess and decide for themselves how much they remain part of the problem of global structural injustice—or how much they will be part of its solution. In assessing the

---

[216] For a discussion of moral overdemandingness in the context of socio-economic human rights, cf. Heilinger (2012).

moral merits of a person from a cosmopolitan perspective, it is important to disentangle a sober *objective* diagnosis of inevitable moral imperfection as a result of sound but unmet moral demands and failure under conditions of global structural injustice from both a *subjective* and an *intersubjective* attitudinal response to this diagnosis in terms of personal feelings and inter-personal reactive attitudes. Distinguishing these dimensions will help to specify the role of inevitable moral failure in my theory of *cosmopolitan responsibility:* I do not want to invite or inspire self-loathing or sour feelings of bitterness or deficiency, but I think that —at least from a philosophical perspective—a clear-eyed assessment of the current catastrophic injustices will show that a fully innocent or completely moral life, unaffected by background injustices, is impossible for the globally advantaged, as hard as they may try. If agents value the possibility of leading an innocent life, they should feel motivated to contribute to systemic change in the structural background conditions that currently make such innocence impossible.

My argument in this chapter is presented in several steps. The following section two critically reviews different strategies to limit moral requirements in order to avoid excessive demands. Section three answers the question of whether cosmopolitan demands can actually be met in the negative. In section four, I spell out the implications of this view by distinguishing an objective, from a subjective and an intersubjective dimension of such inescapable moral wrongdoing. Section five concludes.

2 Demanding too much vs. demanding enough

It is understandable that moral theories seek to restrict their demands on individual agents lest they appear to be unreasonably excessive to those whose action the theory aspires to guide. Several arguments speak in favour of such limitations, as I will show below. Overall, however, I argue that concern should be directed not towards securing that a normative theory does not demand too much, but primarily towards securing that the theory is demanding enough; i.e. *sufficiently* demanding to take the equal moral standing of all adequately into account. It seems to be a flaw of much theorising, I argue, that it is too quick in reducing the demands to which moral agents are subject, or too forgiving when it comes to accepting morally problematic behaviour, out of fear that excessive demands will fail to guide and trigger corresponding action. While assessing and guiding human action is uncontroversially a central task of ethical reasoning, it is not its sole task. Analysing and understanding the web of existing, morally relevant, relations and obligations, irrespective of their direct action-guiding potential, is another, maybe prior and more fundamental task of ethical reasoning. If circumstances are such that the moral requirements following from such an analysis exceed what actually can be done, or exceed what seems acceptable to those living comfortably, this should not count as a flaw of the theory, but as a flaw of the circumstances. The latter, not the former, then are in need of changing: *One should not aspire to make moral theories fit immoral circumstances; instead, one should aspire to improve immoral circumstances in the light of sound moral reasoning.* For this task, priority will have to be assigned to the basic needs, interests and rights of all and to the question what can and should be done to secure them; not to concern about possibly extreme demands for those whose basic needs, interests and rights are already comfortably secured. If the price for this is that some of the justified moral requirements will remain inevitably unmet, paying this price seems preferable to me than limiting genuine rights or reducing demands in order to develop a theory that corresponds with what people can actually do. I argue that any *sufficiently demanding* theory will, if one acknowledges the current catastrophic levels of deprivation and global inequality, inevitably generate what some see as *excessively demanding*. Any theory that does not put such demands on agents is not taking the equal moral value of all sufficiently seriously and consequently lets those who are subject to those demands off the hook too quickly.

Discussing the so-called "moral demandingness objection" has a long tradition and is an important part of the scholarly debate in ethics.[217] The objection, roughly, claims that a moral theory that places excessive demands on moral agents is flawed and stands in need of correction in order to regain plausibility. This objection is understood as a morally neutral, meta-theoretical principle that assesses the soundness of a moral theory, but does not make any substantive moral claims itself. It has been made most often against consequentialist ethics,[218] but other normative theories including contractualist approaches, rights-based theories, and virtue ethics can also be criticised for being unreasonably demanding (Ashford 2003, Cullity 2004, O'Neill 2009, Tessman 2015). The present focus is on the question of how the moral demandingness objection applies to individual moral agents under circumstances of cosmopolitanism. The global scope and the idea of a morally relevant connection between all human beings, which lies at the centre of my account of *cosmopolitan responsibility*, can easily be seen as generating a plethora of demands which stand, in the eyes of some at least, urgently in need of limitation.

---

[217] For an overview cf. e.g. Chappell (2009) or McElwee (2016).
[218] The demandingness objection most often focusses on maximising act consequentialism, as defended in the already discussed contribution by Singer (1972) or by Kagan (1989).

Two main strategies can be distinguished that are employed to limit moral requirements resulting from a cosmopolitan and egalitarian ethics for individual moral agents.[219] The first attempts to constrain cosmopolitan morality to only some areas of human activity, while excluding others: it confines the scope or the *pervasiveness* of cosmopolitanism. This approach, if successful, relies on an argument that certain limits (external to moral cosmopolitanism) apply such that cosmopolitan morality does not rule *all* human interactions and does not pervade the human life *entirely*. A second strategy for limiting the demands of a cosmopolitan morality admits the pervasiveness of moral demands but attempts to limit their *stringency*. This approach, if successful, relies on an argument that certain limits (internal to moral cosmopolitanism) apply such that cosmopolitan morality does not oblige moral agents to meet excessive demands. My assessment of these strategies will conclude that both strategies do not succeed in limiting the demands of cosmopolitanism.

2.1 Confining the moral space

I start with addressing, first, the *pervasiveness* of morality: Is every single human action a proper subject of moral evaluation? Is morality pertinent to everything we do, and must we consider everything we do also in the light of (cosmopolitan) moral demands? Or are there at least some *types* of actions and/or some *domains* of action that are exempt from moral assessment, such that morality does not pervade the entirety of human life, and we are free to act, at least sometimes, as we want, without this being disrespectful of any moral demands?

It seems implausible to assume that some types of actions are generally excluded from moral assessment, because even the most innocent and trivial actions can, depending on the context, be morally relevant. One example would be purchasing a T-shirt which, in some circumstances, might be morally problematic. The money used to pay for it could have been stolen from someone, or the T-shirt may have been produced under exploitative conditions so that an apparently innocent purchase links the consumer to human rights-violations.[220] And also innocent, even morally praiseworthy actions like reading bedtime stories to one's children can be subjected to moral critique, as I have argued above, insofar as they contribute to perpetuating social inequalities.[221] Even triv-

---

219 For an overview about the different views on the limits of morality's demands, cf. Scheffler (1992, 17–28).
220 Cf. chapter four, section four above.
221 Cf. chapter five, section four above.

ia like having dinner can be, under specific circumstances, morally wrong: think of a captain of a sinking ship who chooses to finish dinner instead of helping with the evacuation of his ship. These examples are meant to show that no *type* of intentional human action can be *generally* exempted from moral evaluation. It all depends on the context and seemingly innocent actions can very well be morally problematic and wrong.

But are there certain domains of human existence in which morality simply ceases to make demands of agents (at least if they otherwise act morally)? Is it for example morally permitted to relax and drink a glass of wine—or engage in another morally "neutral" activity—after a hard day's work? Or does morality relentlessly raise its demanding voice, here as everywhere, and demand action to fight world poverty in every moment? Again, it seems implausible to assume that some domains of intentional human activity can generally avoid moral evaluation and prescription: something morally questionable always remains about spending 100 Euros for a fancy meal and an opera ticket in a world where that money could have been donated to famine relief, to help people whose most fundamental needs are not being met. This line of reasoning can still be justified, even if the moral agent in question did decide the week before to donate instead of going to the opera. Insisting on the fact that each single action is subject to a moral assessment, however, does not speak against a simultaneous broadening of the scope of moral evaluation to include assessing people's *habits* and *patterns* of behaviour, as well.[222] The focus on one time actions in a single, specific setting seems overly limited when it comes to an assessment of a person's actions and to spelling out the requirements of *cosmopolitan responsibility*.

So, a general moral exemption, either of some types or of some domains of human action, seems implausible. Morality, I contend, does indeed pervade our entire life, insofar as it is always possible to evaluate every single intentional human action from a moral point of view.

Let us address now, second, the *stringency* of morality: If morality indeed pervades all of human life, does morality—with its ambition to be of genuine and irreducible importance—leave any room for anything but moral actions? Are there at least *internal* limits to moral demands that guarantee that the obligations agents are confronted with do not exceed a "reasonable" degree? Two variants of such internal limits to moral demands can be distinguished, the first can be phrased in terms of the "ought implies can"-principle of deontic logic, the second as a cost-argument that takes into account the normative principle of fairness.

---

[222] Cf. chapter three, section three above, and the concluding chapter below.

2.2 Does 'ought' imply 'can'?

A moral demand can be said to be excessive and overdemanding in different ways. An often invoked principle to identify and subsequently limit excessive demands is the "ought implies can"-principle of deontic logic. It stipulates that any sound obligation is matched by the addressed agent's capacities for action. If someone is morally required to do something, it must be possible for her to actually do it.[223] The "ought implies can"-principle introduces a particular upper limit to what morality can legitimately demand of agents; a limit that, however, can be very high.

The following section distinguishes four different understandings of moral overdemandingness. They can all be advanced as objections against a cosmopolitan theory that seems to place excessive moral requirements on agents, requirements that agents cannot meet. The first type of possible overdemandingness relates to what is generally physically possible, the second to what is possible in dilemmatic situations, the third to what is psychologically possible, and the fourth to what is epistemically possible. Generally, such reasoning is put forward to limit moral requirements to what is considered to be practically feasible for moral agents. In my brief overview, however, I want to raise doubts about these different strategies, and defend the view that a more ambitious account of (cosmopolitan) moral requirements is possible and justified. Such an account would not, from the outset, focus on what those bearing responsibility might be able or unable to actually do. Instead, it would direct attention and concern first and foremost to what is required in order to secure that the equal moral value of all is respected. Thus, I will critically engage with the four variants of the overdemandingness objection against cosmopolitan moral demands and show how they fail to curtail cosmopolitan demands.

(a) Moral requirements can be impossible to fulfill if they conflict with the nature of human agency. A possible obligation to, say, single-handedly save the world, simply does not make sense and in the case of such incommensurate demands the "ought implies can"-principle calls for giving up unintelligible demands (cf. Kramer 2005, 308). Such overly general and incommensurate demands can at best count as general goals of human moral action, but not as concrete requirements for individual action. Yet, such general demands can often be specified insofar as an individual can very well *contribute to* saving the world in the form of, say, contributing to fighting world poverty (even if no single person

---

[223] Cf. Zimmerman (1996) and Haji (2002) for a defense of this principle. For a discussion cf. Kühler (2013).

alone will be able to end it). Such a reformulation and specification of the requirement respects the nature of human agency and the general and sound way in which an "ought" indeed presupposes or implies a "can". This reasoning, however, only excludes irrational demands that do not match with what people can possibly do. It is not particularly helpful to avoid situations where there is more than one morally demanded action and where the different competing moral requirements are individually feasible but mutually exclusive.

From the perspective of cosmopolitanism, this kind of presumed violation of the "ought implies can"-principle can be accommodated rather easily. Incomprehensible or incommensurate demands simply have to be broken down into requirements that fall within the range of what agents can possibly do.

(b) Here is the second attempt to limit demands. In some situations, more than one action is demanded, and to an equally strong degree, but the different actions mutually exclude one another. In such situations, an agent can only perform one of two (or of several) demanded actions, but not both (or all). These are cases of moral dilemmas. Some doubt that moral dilemmas exist at all, for example Kant, who stipulated that obligations simply do not conflict ("obligationes non colliduntur," Kant 1797, 224), or Hare, who similarly defended the view that if "you have conflicting duties, one of them isn't your duty" (Hare 1981, 26). On this account, conflicting demands can be put in a hierarchical order so that only one demand, and one that can actually be met, remains as a genuine moral obligation. With this aim in mind, others, such as Ross, have introduced a distinction between *prima facie* duties and *pro tanto* duties in order to solve potentially dilemmatic situations. The former are understood to appear as duties only at first sight, but stand in need of being weighed against other duties an agent may have. As a result of such a weighing process, a conclusion is reached whereby only one feasible option remains, which is considered to be the one—pro tanto—duty one should (and can) actually follow (Ross 1930, 19–20, 28–29).[224]

Yet, some situations of mutually exclusive but equally important moral demands impressively indicate that such clean solutions are at least sometimes un-

---

[224] Kagan, in *The Limits of Morality*, criticises Ross's distinction between prima facie and pro tanto duties and comes to a conclusion similar to mine, explained below. He argues that "prima facie" only indicates an "epistemological qualification" and that what Ross calls prima facie duties should be understood as a "reason [that] has genuine weight, but nonetheless may be outweighed by other considerations". He specifies: "although the reason to promote the good may be overridden, it does not disappear: it is a *pro tanto* reason" (Kagan 1989, 17).—For a thorough criticism of Ross's idea of prima facie duties and the resulting claim of moral failure, see also Mallock (1967).

available. A prominent example is "Sophie's choice": the horrible situation of a mother of two, who was forced by a Nazi guard upon arrival at the Auschwitz concentration camp to choose which of her two children, Eva or Jan, would be sent to immediate death, lest both of them would be killed (Greenspan 1995). Here, it is implausible to assume that, once Sophie had made a choice, she had done all that could be morally required from her. After all *both* Eva and Jan, not *either* Eva or Jan could demand to be saved by her mother. Of course, Sophie is not to blame for the moral wrong in this situation which is caused by the Nazi regime and its supporters. Yet, analysing this constellation illustrates how agents can find themselves, through no fault of their own, in tragic situations where, no matter what they choose, important and weighty demands—like that of a child to be saved by her or his mother—will inevitably remain unmet. This will generate in Sophie residual feelings of remorse and regret, indicative of a sound yet unmet moral requirement (Williams 1973b). Denying the possibility and reality of such scenarios of inescapable moral wrongdoing by suggesting that any sound 'ought' is always matched by an actual 'can' fails to capture this significant aspect of moral reality. (It will also provide no relief but rather appear cynical to Sophie and others who find themselves in such situations of impossible demands.) The fact that such impossible oughts that generate some form of inevitable moral failure exist, however, has no bearing on the legitimacy of the children's claims towards their mother nor on the weight of the mother's obligation to save them.

This reasoning is important for the present analysis of the role and responsibilites of individuals from a cosmopolitan perspective. Cosmopolitanism will, I contend, generate numerous and conflicting moral demands, at least under the current conditions of massive inequality and injustice. These requirements, if they are morally sound and generally respect the limits of human agency, equally cannot be reduced to the status of only *prima facie* duties; nor are there other ways to silence them or lessen their moral importance. Instead, they should be considered as obligations with genuine moral weight, despite the fact that they so obviously conflict with other requirements (some of a cosmopolitan nature, others possibly generated in the immediate surroundings of an agent) and thus often cannot lead to corresponding action. Morality, at least in an imperfect world like ours, seems to demand more than we can actually do.

(c) Next, moral requirements may be impossible to fulfill for psychological reasons, insofar as they exceed the psychological or motivational capacities of an agent, even if she is willing and capable to an above average degree. Williams has famously defended such a limit to individual motivation when he argued that excessive moral demands resulting from an impartial moral assessment of a situation may endanger the personal integrity of an agent ("integrity objection"[225]). If one were to subject oneself to such stringent, impersonal moral demands that are imposed upon the agent from an impartial, external point of view, all individuality, all authenticity and all motivation to act would eventually come to an end. For moral requirements to become effective they have to link to (and match with) some prior subjective set of motivations in the moral agent. This view has been called "internalism about reasons" (Williams 1981, Chappell 2007).

But should such considerations about the limited motivational resources of persons and about the negative psychological or motivational impact of excessive demands indeed be taken into account when it comes to determining legitimate moral demands themselves? An alternative view would hold that it is possible—and necessary—to deliberate about and to identify moral requirements *independent* of the prior existence of (and their compatibility with) an already given motivational set in the agents that are obliged by these requirements. This view can be called an "externalism about reasons", because it allows for moral requirements that do not yet connect internally with the subjective motivational setup of agents.

Against Williams, I think that it is also possible to follow such "external reasons" in one's actions, because understanding moral requirements and their justification can—but clearly not always does—motivate people to take corresponding action. As a consequence, the actual psychological or motivational capabilities or weaknesses of an agent have no effect on the moral soundness of the requirement itself, only on the probability with which the agent will meet this requirement. Determining requirements according to the somewhat arbitrarily existing subjective motivational setup of agents would seem to approach the problem from the wrong direction: Concern should lie primarily with the unmet needs and what should be done about them; and this concern should not be curtailed from the outset by contingent preferences and motivations of those who could be called upon to address these needs.[226]

(d) The fourth attempt to limit moral demands on the grounds of their presumed impossibility to be met is based on epistemological considerations. While an objective, comprehensive judgement about what an agent morally ought to do in a particular situation might exist, this judgement might not be available to the agent itself. Maybe it would require knowledge about a number of factors that is

---

225 Cf. also above, chapter five, section three above
226 Even if I endorse externalism about reasons that allows for moral requirements that are unconnected with one's subjective motivational setup, I do not doubt that connecting such external reasons with one's personal motivational setup will facilitate acting in accordance with these reasons and requirements.

difficult or impossible to obtain from the subjective perspective of the moral agent. But if a person cannot even know what is truly morally demanded from her (or if finding out would be extremely costly and time consuming), she cannot reasonably be required to act upon such an ideal but unknown demand.

Yet again, is it plausible to assume that contingent facts about epistemic states limit what an agent should morally be doing? Of course it makes sense to distinguish between subjective knowledge about obligations, and a more ideal, objective account of obligations.[227] And clearly, it does not make sense to expect agents to acquire full and accurate knowledge about all morally relevant facts about a situation before they make a choice and act. Instead, one would ask that agents invest a resonable but limited amount of energy in finding out about the relevant facts before coming to a decision. Yet, what ultimately matters is not that a person has done what would be considered the single perfect act (often enough, there might not be a single such action), but that a reasonably informed and good act has been realised. Existing epistemic difficulties can be acknowledged and possibly justify some discretion of moral agents when deciding how to act, as long as they do so in good faith. Epistemic difficulties must not, however, be used to reduce genuine moral demands or serve as a pre-emptive excuse for apathy and inaction.[228]

These four attempts to limit moral demands according to the capacities of moral agents are based on important insights about the nature of agency. There are indeed limits to what people can actually *do:* they cannot do what is physically impossible, they cannot perform several mutually exclusive actions simultaneously, they might be unable to get themselves to doing something if they are not personally convinced of its relevance or importances and thus lack motivation, and often they are unable to find out what exactly would be the right thing to do. However, as important and relevant as these considerations may be, they focus too much on the perspective of the *agent* who might be called upon to respond in some way to a moral problem, and in doing so, these considerations fail to assign appropriate weight to the *origins* of the demands, which lie in the unmet basic needs, neglected interests or violated basic rights of others. Thus, the four strategies *get their priorities wrong:* they are more concerned with

---

[227] A similar distinction, pointing out the difficulties to acquire knowledge to identify and justify specific obligations, appears also at the level of institutional agents (cf. Herzog 2012).

[228] A similar principle exists in many legal contexts: *ignorantia iuris non excusat* (ignorance of the law is no excuse). As should become clear below, I assume that some types of ignorance could provide "extenuating circumstances," and hence figure as an excuse in moral matters, but this has no impact on the prior fact that something is morally demanded in the first place, since the "time for excuses" comes after the act, not prior to it.

the difficulties of the privileged (who could and should contribute to remedying severe moral wrongs) than with the difficulties of the disadvantaged (who suffer such severe moral wrong). It would be morally appropriate instead to look first and foremost at the sources of moral demands and assess whether the resulting obligations are sound. Considering what people can actually do, and also understanding the limits of human action, then follows—but only as a second step; a step that, however, has no bearing on the soundness of the existing *demands*. It can only provide an explanation for not doing what is morally demanded, but it cannot reduce or eliminate what is morally demanded.

2.3 Fairness and interpersonal justification

Although the "moral demandingness objection" is often regarded as a normatively neutral, content-free meta-theoretical principle, it can also be read as substantive normative concern for fairness. A prominent attempt to limit the degree of moral demands by employing fairness considerations has been undertaken by Liam Murphy. He has defended the view that a moral agent is only morally demanded to contribute his *fair share* to fighting moral wrongs, where that fair share is determined by what would be necessary to do under conditions of full compliance of all. If it would, say, take 1000 units of action to solve a given moral problem, and there are 1000 able agents to tackle it, everyone is morally required to contribute one unit to the solution of the problem, and not more. Giving more would be considered beyond the call of moral duty, a supererogatory act (Murphy 2000). Murphy explains his "cooperative principle":

> Each agent is required to act optimally—to perform the action that makes the outcome best—except in situations of partial compliance with this principle. In situations of partial compliance it is permissible to act optimally, but the sacrifice each agent is required to make is limited to the level of sacrifice that would be optimal if the situation were one of full compliance. (Murphy 1993, 280)

The obvious advantage of this account is that it is sensitive to fairness and unfairness of distributing costly burdens within a group of agents. Alas, we have good reason to assume, under real world circumstances (and even if it would be possible to determine the exact share that each person would have to contribute in order to address problems of global injustice), that full compliance with moral demands will not occur. The consequence of Murphy's principle in such circumstances of less than full compliance is that moral demands are limited to what would be necessary under conditions of full compliance; consequently, his approach leaves it up to individual willingness to do more than one's fair share, to take up the slack, if any problem that needs collective action is ever to be solved. This is a major disadvantage of Murphy's theory (Arneson 2004, 35–39) and shows how inadequate it is to effectively address large scale moral wrongs. On a cosmopolitan account and in an imperfect world it does not make sense to free moral agents from a moral requirement to urgently address severe wrongs once they have done the rather small fraction that they would have to contribute in a perfect world. It is generally difficult to see how moral demands for action in the face of absolute deprivation (and other severe infringements of basic rights) could ever depend on the immoral behaviour of other capable agents who fail to do what would be right. Morality, in a way, does not care about the moral failure of others when it comes to assigning duties to an individual agent. And generally, a relevant cosmopolitan analysis of the role and responsibility of individuals should not direct attention primarily to the question what individuals would have to do in an ideally just world, but ask what individuals have to do in our unjust, real world.

The fairness-based argument for limiting the requirements for the well-off to the degree which would be necessary under conditions of full compliance hence does not adequately take into account the severity of the problem. Murphy's principle, if applied to world poverty, seems to get moral priorities wrong: it places fairness considerations among those who are well-off above considerations about the existential needs of those in states of absolute deprivation. Yet, while the former are clearly not without moral relevance, they are also clearly not as morally relevant as the latter. Phrased in terms of an argument about cost, it protects the well-off against cost that they might consider excessive while imposing a truly existential cost on those who are suffering from deprivation. Within a generally egalitarian framework, this is not an acceptable position.

Concern for fairness thus should not start with fairness among the well-off agents who are morally required to respond to problems but concern for fairness should instead focus on the justifiability of particular ways of behaviour towards those who suffer from the given severe moral wrongs. According to my relational understanding of the ideal of moral equality (cf. chapter two) and in line with the cosmopolitan call to integrate universalist and impartial demands into one's deliberation about what to do (cf. chapter five), I propose a variant of what Cohen has called an "interpersonal justification test" in order to identify sound moral requirements that are non-negotiable, even if they cannot be fulfilled.[229]

---

[229] Cohen has employed this test to challenge the soundness of the incentives argument (that the rich need the incentive of low taxation in order to work hard so that they generate goods that

Global relational egalitarianism asks not only from an external perspective what should be done, but also asks from the personal perspective (of concrete agents and of those who are affected by the acts of these agents) how the cosmopolitan commitments—of universality, moral equality, and the idea of a morally relevant global community within which all are supposed to be able to relate and interact as equals—are integrated and respected in one's behaviour and action. Concretely, the test involves imagining to give an explicit justification for one's behaviour directly to all those who are affected by it. For example, one could imagine someone having to justify one's action or inaction in the face of world poverty or climate change, in a personal conversation with those whose dire fate is caused by structures, the existence and persistence of which is partly caused by one's (in-)action. In such interpersonal relations and contexts of justification, one's concrete behaviour and one's normative commitments come under moral scrutiny from different perspectives: one's own but also the perspective of those affected by it.[230]

I propose Cohen's intersubjective justification to support the critique of the different strategies to limit the moral responsibility of the globally advantaged as undertaken in the preceding pages. Having to explain one's own apathy and inaction to those who are dying from hunger, working under human rights-violating exploitative circumstances, or suffering from a dramatically changing climate that destroys their livelihood will be an expression of blatant disrespect for the equal moral value of all.[231] It will also include an outright denial of relations and connections, and thus be repugnant to the idea of a morally relevant global community of all. Or can one imagine that pointing to some unfairness between the privileged or to the need to take more self-care and exercise yet more preferential treatment towards one's already well-off children can ever be accepted as a legitimate justification for *not* saving someone from dying from hunger, for *not* preventing that someone's livelihood will be destroyed etc.? All such exceptions might, at best, become morally justifiable when they are integrated into a way

---

will then lead to everyone, not only the rich, being better off). I propose to use it generally to challenge the soundness of moral requirements and of attempts to limit the demandingness of moral requirements in different contexts, including the global context.

230 This idea is also at the heart of Forst's *right to justification* when he writes that the "demand for justice is an emancipatory demand, which is described with terms like fairness, reciprocity, symmetry, equality, or balance; [...] its basis is the claim to be respected as an agent of justification, that is, in one's dignity as a being who can ask for and give justifications. The victim of injustice is not primarily the person who lacks certain goods, but the one who does not 'count' [...]." (Forst 2007, 2).

231 Nagel is right when he states: "to suffer from the unavoidable blows of fate is bad enough; to suffer because others do not accord one's life its true value is worse" (Nagel 1991, 19).

of living in which much concern and corresponding action already respond to the wrongs in question.

Of course, some are willing to deny the equal moral value of all, ignore connections and do not care about community. But for all those who generally buy into universalism and egalitarianism, imagining to have to justify one's behaviour to those who suffer from structural injustice, will, I contend, lay bare how much is going wrong—in the structures that are upheld also by our individual and ultimately unjustifiable behaviour.

Thus, the moral requirements—generated by human suffering and rights violations and addressed to the advantaged and capable agents—might very well ignore a fair distribution of duties among all capable agents, they might go way beyond what the better-off are likely to do and, if the situation is very bad, as it is, they might even go beyond what individuals actually can do. And yet, these demands cannot be rejected. They are non-negotiable because they are caused by fundamental needs and rights of some that are violated by structures upheld by the behaviour and contributions of many others. The essential question to be asked hence is *not whether we can do* all that is demanded. Under current circumstances we might not be able to live up to all such requirements. Instead, the essential questions are *what we should do* and how to integrate as much as possible of what we should do into *what we actually do*. The real danger here is hence twofold: First, morality might be *demanding not enough* and let agents too easily and too early off the hook; the interpersonal justification test is meant to prevent this from happening. The remainder of this chapter will spell out the implications of accepting non-negotiable but impossible moral requirements. Second, we might be *doing not enough*. The concluding chapter of this book will conclude with thoughts on how individuals should actually respond to the global wrong of structural injustice.

3 Can cosmopolitan moral requirements be met?

Against attempts to limit the duties generated by *cosmopolitan responsibility*, I argue that legitimate demands (e. g., to have one's basic needs secured) that correspondingly oblige potential agents (e. g., to secure the basic needs of all) are impossible to reject if one takes seriously the normative core content of the cosmopolitan ethos—namely those of equal moral status of all and of ubiquitous relationships of responsibility among all. In this section I will further defend the view that the fact that such cosmopolitan demands may turn out to be excessively demanding does not necessarily render them unsound. Quite to the contrary: Overdemandingness should not be seen as a flaw of the theory, but as a flaw of the circumstances of ongoing catastrophe which generate it. In this regard overdemandingness is, under current conditions, rather an indicator of the soundness of the moral theory said to be excessively demanding. The more convenient and feasible the demands of a normative theory are in an unjust world like ours, the more dubious the entire theory becomes for discounting the moral weight of the lives of some.

The first important step in this process of defending *cosmopolitan responsibility*, as we have already seen, is to determine who exactly holds a rights-corresponding duty. The bearers of responsibility for violations of basic rights are, on my cosmopolitan view, not only those who have directly caused rights infringements, but all those who are involved in doing so by some form of social connection; and particularly all those who would be able to do something about securing the basic rights and particularly those who benefit from structural injustices. This is a maximally inclusive view that takes seriously both distinctively cosmopolitan ideas, namely the idea of equal moral importance of all and the idea of ubiquitous relationships of responsibility. As a consequence, all those who are capable of doing something about the moral wrong in question are subject to a moral demand to do so.[232]

But can we, the well-off citizens in affluent societies, or all those who could do something to help those living under conditions of absolute deprivation indeed accept such excessive, positive moral obligations? Given the amount and the magnitude of human suffering on this globe, can we stand taking on the kind of moral responsibility required to fight this disaster?

It may help to specify what I call a moral requirement—or demand, obligation, or duty—rand to distinguish it from two further concepts: moral *reasons* on the one side, and executable and executed *action* on the other. Moral reasons are numerous, of different strength and can often be ranked. They result from the different sources of morality which I identified within my generally pluralist framework (cf. also above, chapter three). And, under certain conditions,

---

[232] To put it pointedly, with regard to the fundamental rights and basic interests of all, one could even stipulate a principle that "can implies ought": if an agent could at least in principle do something to prevent the violation of a basic right then he morally ought to do so. Luban, for example, explains this view in the context of basic rights with the following words: a "human right, then, will be a right whose beneficiaries are all humans and whose obligors are all humans in a position to effect the right." He continues: "Human rights are the demands of all of humanity on all of humanity. This distinguishes human rights from, for example, civil rights, where the beneficiaries and obligors are specified by law" (Luban 1980, 174). Ashford also defends a similar view, stating that we know who is responsible for fulfilling positive obligations in the context of world poverty: all those who can; that is normally every somewhat affluent individual (Ashford 2009, 198).

moral reasons can justify a moral demand, requirement or duty. Such a requirement is supported by sufficiently strong moral reasons that assign some responsibility to a moral agent, i.e. that they oblige the individual to respond. On the level of moral requirements it is clear that not all of them can be transformed into actual action. It is also possible, that some of these demands are negotiable. By this I mean that in some situations a moral requirement can indeed be rejected on the grounds of another requirement. Yet, in the class of such requirements are also some that are non-negotiable.[233] Such demands persist and keep their responsibility-constituting normative force no matter what, because they are based on the unique and intrinsic equal value of each person.[234] I contend that the class of requirements I am particularly interested in (cosmopolitan demands to individually respond to basic rights-violations or massive preventable suffering and deprivation) are non-negotiable. And because of this feature it is possible that there are many more and many overly demanding such moral requirements than any moral agent can actually fulfill. They call for responses, particularly through action[235], but it is impossible to act upon all moral requirements. That is why the class of such moral requirements has to be distinguished from the relevant corresponding action which would count as an adequate response. The latter class, even if smaller, does not lead to reducing the size of the former class. Moral requirements are justified through reasons and immune against attempts to undermine or limit them based on the domain of executable actions.

Now the question arises whether it is possible to fully discharge one's moral responsibilities and duties, as when, for example, a moral agent were to do her very best, and far more than her peers? Would that effort, that sacrifice, those actions taken together, be sufficient? Is it enough to dedicate one's life fully and solely to fighting world poverty (or other forms of suffering that follow the deprivation of basic rights elsewhere), should one choose to do so? Would such a person be entitled to claim that there are no remaining moral obligations to which she is subject?

My view is that it is humanly impossible to fully discharge all cosmopolitan obligations under the current conditions of structural injustice. Even if one were to do his best, there would always remain unmet moral obligations aplenty. Fur-

---

[233] For the terminological distinction between negotiable and non-negotiable moral demands, cf. Tessman. For her, a requirement is non-negotiable if it is based on a unique and non-substitutable value and if the cost of violating the requirement generates "a cost that no one should have to bear" (Tessman 2015, 44).
[234] Cf. also Gowans (1994, ch. 6).
[235] More on the relevant forms of responses in the concluding chapter, below.

thermore, there will be unavoidable dilemmas, wherein agents face mutually incompatible obligations. Even in cases where it is possible to establish a hierarchy of demands, one cannot assume that the second or third obligation in the established hierarchy would, after the first demands are discharged, no longer be demanded.[236] Consequently there will, under current conditions, *never* be a moment in time, and *no* deontic space available for moral agents, where they can legitimately claim to be free from all moral obligation. Clearly, most of these moral demands will ultimately turn out to be necessarily "non-effective"; that is, they will not be able to trigger a corresponding action even in well-intentioned and skilled moral agents, simply because they are too numerous and/or too difficult to fulfill. However, this does not provide any reason for a cosmopolitan moral agent to deny the existence of such moral demands, or to deny that those demands are sound. In taking those who suffer from basic rights violations seriously, and in admitting that there is some form of universal community of all human beings, rejecting such demands (even if they may be necessarily non-effective) is no option. It would contradict the basic commitments of moral cosmopolitanism.

If such demands cannot be silenced, if they persist no matter what we do, cosmopolitan moral agents must embrace the fact that moral perfection is out of reach: agents have not, will not, and cannot ever fully meet the moral demands to which they are subject, no matter what they do. Endorsing cosmopolitanism means admitting not only moral imperfection, but even moral insufficiency or, to put it even more sharply, some form of personally felt moral failure—irrespective of how well one has tried and succeeded (or failed) in doing one's share. This view, as we saw above, has prompted manifold attempts to restrict the overdemandingness of moral obligations, but I have argued that these attempts all fail. It seems to me to be more truthful simply to admit that, in a world like ours, the moral demands placed upon moral agents are such that they are impossible to fulfil.

I am thus aligned with Young, who claimed that the moral demands under present circumstances *should* be extremely demanding. She writes, in response to the charge that her own cosmopolitan account would "overwhelm" those on whom it makes demands:

> that this is a truth we should pause at. In a world with significant and multiple structural injustices, people's responsibilities in relation to those injustices can and should appear to be too much to deal with. However, those who raise this fact as an objection to the theory of responsibility [...] are mistaken. While it is not uncommon for moral philosophers to appeal

---

236 See also the apt analysis of this setting by Mallock (Mallock 1967).

to intuitions about what kind of actions and costs can reasonably be expected from people, the intuitions appealed to usually suggest that individuals should not be asked to change their normal habits and practices or sacrifice a great deal of what reasonable people regard as their normal self-interest for the sake of furthering justice. In a very unjust world, such an attitude is overly conservative and allows most of us to tell ourselves complacently that we are doing what we can and all that can be expected of us to improve things. Philosophers who object to theories on the grounds that they overwhelm our feelings only serve this complacency. (Young 2011, 123–124)

According to Young, if a moral theory fails to generate extreme demands under extreme circumstances, that is all the worse for it. And those supporting such lenient theories make themselves complacent accomplices, providing a justification for inaction.[237]

What is the point of such a seemingly pessimistic and somewhat revisionary account of moral obligations leading to inevitable moral failure? What is the point of arguing, as I have, that this is the *only* way to take seriously the basic convictions of moral cosmopolitanism? The point is *not* to push all agents into pessimistic or apathetic states of mind or to make them just feel awful; but rather to make them acknowledge the magnitude of the chronic disaster that is going on, and to avoid silencing the voices of those who suffer. Attempts to rid oneself of the moral obligation to act, no matter what one has already done, are disrespectful towards those in states of absolute deprivation.[238] To suffer from structural injustice where those causing it are ignorant but not malevolent is bad enough; to continue to suffer from it because others do not accord one's life its true value is even worse.[239] If the consequences of inevitable moral failure are, for the advantaged, painful and difficult to bear, this should translate into a strong motivation to act for systemic change that would increasingly rid the world of such injustices and make it a place in which the conditions of chronic disaster—and the subsequent moral burden and failure—do not hold any more.

---

[237] Tessman has defended a similar view in her defense of non-negotiable moral requirements that contravene the "ought-implies-can"-principle in certain circumstances (Tessman 2015). Some moral requirements, particularly those based on basic needs, keep their binding force on the agent even if they are impossible to fulfill. Apprehending a moral requirement that one cannot meet one faces one's own inevitable failure to fulfill it.
[238] Applying the intersubjective justification test, as mentioned in the preceding section, would support this conclusion.
[239] Cf. Nagel (1991, 19).

4 Necessarily non-effective moral requirements

I have argued that cosmopolitans must, under conditions of global structural injustice, accept numerous and mutually exclusive moral demands as sound and as non-negotiable, even if most of these requirements will remain necessarily non-effective, insofar as only a relatively small number among them will be able to trigger a corresponding action. Following a terminological suggestion from Martin, one could also call the ideals of cosmopolitanism generating such necessarily non-effective moral requirements "infinite ideals," and the cosmopolitan ethos could be said to display an "infinite moral consciousness". Martin defines an infinite ideal as "a norm or demand that retains its authority over us even in the face of our conviction that the norm itself is impossible for us to fulfil" (Martin 2009, 103). Acknowledging human agential limitations while simultaneously accepting cosmopolitan infinite ideals will require accepting *impossible* moral demands and correspondingly some form of *inevitable* moral failure of agents. Such failure, however, has different dimensions and should be distinguished from moral failures that result from straightforward cases of wrongdoing. Admitting inevitable failure under conditions of global structural injustice has a subjective dimension, an objective dimension, and an intersubjective dimension. All these dimensions may impact on the motivation of a moral agent to act. I will go through them in turn.

4.1 Objective assessment

Even skilled and well-meaning agents have to make choices in a world in which legitimate moral claims abound; many place higher urgency on the needs of people with whom they have some form of relationship, and most also pursue non-moral projects in their lives; all have to rest, to sleep, and to eat. But, as the scholastics knew long ago, *omnis determinatio est negatio:* in choosing to act one way, agents exclude the possibility of acting in all other ways. So, it is simply impossible to always meet all moral demands, or even to always meet the most urgent among them, as sound as they may be. Given, as I have argued above, that moral demands have genuine weight, and cannot be silenced or rejected, some form of moral imperfection, even of moral failure, becomes inevitable for every agent, at least under the current conditions of our world.

From his distinctively consequentialist perspective, Kagan has phrased this insight in the following way, but his assessment pertains also to my pluralist account of *cosmopolitan responsibility:*

Ordinary morality judges our lives morally acceptable as long as we meet its fairly modest demands. It is not surprising that this view should be so widely—and uncritically—held: it is not pleasant to admit to our failure to live up to the demands of morality. But the truth remains that we are morally required to promote the good and yet we do not. Faced with this realization what we must do is change: change our beliefs, our actions, and our interests. What we must not do—is deny our failure. (Kagan 1989, 403)[240]

Moral failure on such objective terms—even though generally inevitable because many of the moral reasons that oblige agents are necessarily non-effective—still allows for comparative distinctions among agents, since they will differ in how far they try to meet and actually meet their moral obligations. Inevitable moral failure hence is a scalar concept which can be diagnosed comparatively and in *degrees*, and is usefully qualified in some cases as *partial* moral failure, enabling comparisons between different agents with regard to their moral failures and achievements. Note here that my claim is only that full moral achievement, i.e. moral perfection, is out of reach, and not that it is impossible to meet any moral demands, nor that it is impossible to act morally well. Yet, stressing the point that individual moral perfection is out of reach because so many others live under conditions of preventable suffering and deprivation justifies labelling this imperfection also as a failure. This pointed statement implies the acknowledgment that unmet moral requirements are of particular moral importance.

4.2 Subjective feelings

But what then is the appropriate *subjective* attitude towards this objective diagnosis of such inevitable, partial moral failure? Is it appropriate to regret one's inevitable moral shortcomings, to feel awful about them, or would this feeling express a fetishistic attitude towards moral perfection? Certainly there is a difference between how we should feel about direct and straightforward cases of wrongdoing, such as harming, hurting, exploiting others on the one hand, and the inevitable failure that comes through our involvement in structural injustice and the impossibility of fully avoiding it on the other. Reacting to both types of moral failure in a similar way appears to be inappropriate, indeed. After all, the fact that most of our cosmopolitan obligations are *necessarily* non-effective provides an explanation and thus extenuating circumstances—but no permis-

---

[240] Others agree, although on the grounds of different normative theories, among them Tessman (2015), Gowans (1994), and Stocker (1971).

sion or general excuse—for making such moral mistakes. However, even if inevitable, some wrongdoing is taking place and thus some kind of subjective emotional response to it is warranted.[241]

Williams has, in his analysis of moral dilemmas, analysed the existence of "residual moral feelings" of regret in cases where agents failed to meet some moral requirement, even if they have performed an action that seemed morally demanded, and even if they would not want to have acted differently (Williams 1973b). As a consequence of taking unfulfilled but sound moral obligations seriously, a specific internal and subjective attitude of regret is appropriate. The absence of such a response would be indicative of not having taken the grounds of the unmet obligation sufficiently seriously.

This understanding of inevitable moral failure makes clear that the feeling of regret in the present context is *not self-centred:* It is not about the agent who is obsessed with the impossibility of keeping her hands clean. Instead, feeling regret about not having done more or about not having been able to avoid one's implication in morally harmful forms of structural injustice is an *other-centred* indication of moral sincerity. Increasing awareness of the ongoing moral disasters worldwide implies taking the dire situation of others seriously—even if one's own practical and psychological limitations and shortcomings become painfully obvious. In the worse cases, such widening of the circle of moral concern and responsibility with the resulting feeling of overdemandingness and imperfection can promote pessimism and cynicism; in the better cases, however, experiencing the right amount of regret can foster and support a willingness to take action—or to take more action—to address the problems in questions directly or indirectly.

Yet, if the structures are such that even better or best behaviour would not have freed one fully from such moral shortcoming, does it make sense at all to permit such negative feelings about it? In my view, it would be a rather coldhearted strategy to reject such subjective feelings on the grounds of inevitability. First, most agents could—and should—certainly have done more and acted better in order to address the outrageous moral wrongs that shape our world. And second, even if one did what one could, one's limitations are obvious. And hardly anyone of those who is considered to have acted morally in an exemplary way reports having experienced a feeling of satisfaction. Most often, aid workers and others who commit their entire lives to promoting the good and advancing justice are only too aware of their own limitations and wish to be able to do more

---

[241] Besides this emotional reactive response, a forward-looking practical response is also appropriate. I discuss the former in this section and the latter in the concluding chapter of this book.

(MacFarquhar 2015). That is why I contend that even inevitable and foreseeable moral shortcomings should not count as a pre-emptive excuse that avoids any feeling of regret;[242] the time for explanations and possibly for excuses comes later, when the sincerity of one's acts can be taken into account.[243]

But, again, I do not want to argue for self-centred feelings of sourness and excessive bitterness about one's own imperfection. But a sober analysis of the state of affairs in the present world makes obvious that the privileged lives of the globally advantaged cannot be justified, because they come at the expense of so many others whose basic needs remain unmet. The fact that we cannot fully avoid being part of structural injustices and that we cannot fully avoid enjoying some of the privileges that come along with a privileged lifestyle (among them the privilege to decide about how many of the available advantages we use or not), should inspire a personal feeling of other-centred regret. This feeling is no invitation to passive brooding but a call to take action in order to overcome the conditions that are so massively unjust that not only the basic rights of many are violated, but that also the good lives of many others are morally tainted.

Belief in the possibility of moral perfection which is indicated by the absence of feelings of remorse and regret, then, misunderstands the urgency and the legitimacy of the moral claims of those living in dire circumstances: we are living in a world of ongoing disaster, where people suffer and die from preventable causes, and wherein moral perfection is impossible. Any and all claims of innocence or moral perfection thus reveal the claimant to hold a disrespectful, sometimes even outright cynical attitude towards those whose legitimate demands remain unheard and unmet. On egalitarian, cosmopolitan grounds, this is not acceptable.

---

242 The moral obligations that were non-effective with regard to initiating a corresponding action hence are not fully non-effective all things considered: they still induce, as a side-effect, a morally relevant subjective feeling of regret.

243 It may be helpful to distinguish two conceptually different perspectives on the evaluation of acts or omissions that can be illustrated by reference to time: The time for *excuses* (or for providing extenuating circumstances) comes after the act, and must not be confused with timeless or prior *justification* of certain acts. The latter would actually aim at diminishing the initial obligations, and clear the agent from the charge of failing. Providing excuses or pointing to extenuating circumstances ex post, by contrast, offers an explanation for why an agent has not done or could not do what she should have done. The moral demand hence remains intact, but the excuse provides a protection against exaggerated moral (self-) criticism (Cohen 2000, 157–158).

4.3 Intersubjective reactive attitudes

The third dimension of necessarily non-effective moral requirements regards the intersubjective reactive attitudes such as praise and blame with which people react to other people's behaviour. Generally, moral behaviour, for which agents bear moral responsibility, is met with praise; immoral behaviour is met with blame (Strawson 1962). If failing to meet the impossible cosmopolitan requirements is inevitable under current conditions, but if some subjective feeling of regret is warranted, is blame the appropriate intersubjective reactive attitude, as well? Standard blaming, as for some intentional wrongdoing, clearly seems not to be appropriate, for at least two reasons. First, the moral failure in question was inevitable and thus the agent can be held responsible for it only in a limited way; the agent may even have chosen to do something that was morally praiseworthy, but at the cost of not doing something else that was also urgently morally demanded. Second, anyone who could consider blaming the agent in question for that kind of inevitable moral failure would himself not be free from this very form of failure. In order to be in a position to call out the moral shortcomings of others one must not be subject to the same form of critique. Nevertheless, some kind of negative response also in intersubjective attitudes could still remain appropriate, but only in a specific and moderate form.

What I propose instead of actual interpersonal blame is an increased collective awareness for the distinctive wrong of structural injustice in which one's own advantages are connected with the unjustifiable disadvantages of others. This reactive attitude is not isolating, insofar as it does not single out any individual as bearing responsibility for the overall wrong in question, but it assigns responsibility to the collective that is part of causing and upholding the injustice. But since it also specifies that the individuals in this collective are inevitably part of the problem, an intersubjective attitude that I suggest calling "softened" blame is justified.[244] Agents who are willing to accept that form of blame display moral sincerity, because they acknowledge their own involvement in the problematic structures that so unequally distribute advantages and disadvantages. Yet, this form of 'softened' blame, again, is not meant as a final judgement that closes debate; instead, it should serve as an incentive to seek for a way out of this situation where collective blame also affects the lives of individual

---

[244] Goodin, in a discussion of the reactive attitudes that would be appropriate towards those who fail to act upon what could be considered excessively demanding supererogatory duties, writes that 'we would not want to blame them terribly' (Goodin 2007, 7). Even if the demands in question were truly excessive, not acting upon them in situations of urgency, also justifies some kind of critique or blame.

agents without malevolent intent. In a forward-looking way, the discomfort of blame, even if only 'softened', makes an urgent call for ending this situation by realising conditions, through systemic and structural reform, where no one is inevitably drawn into structures that distribute advantage and disadvantage in an unjust way.

This generalised attitude needs, of course, to be distinguished from the particular attitudes towards concrete instances of morally problematic behaviour. 'Softened' blame in the form of moral sincerity is the appropriate response for inevitable moral failures under conditions of structural injustice. Other forms of clearly avoidable moral failure in the context of global structural injustice—such as careless and excessive consumption, failure to respond to the needs of others at all etc.—still invite the regular forms of intersubjective blame: moral critique, sanctioning, invitations to correct past wrongdoing and to improve one's future behaviour.[245]

But does my theory of *cosmopolitan responsibility* then leave no room for appreciation, recognition, or praise? Does it remain limited to negative appraisal even towards those who, through what they say and do, clearly display personal commitment and considered effort to address global injustice? Do these persons also deserve intersubjective softened blame for their inevitable imperfection? Or can we express admiration towards those examplary individuals who bring about real good, even though their acts are, under current conditions, also inevitably imperfect?

I tie my answer to the self-evaluation of those who display exemplary behaviour. Would such moral role models ask for praise or admiration? Would they feel wronged if they received the form of *softened* blame as explained above? As already indicated, moral exemplars often report to have acted just out of duty, claim that others in their situation would probably have done the same, and are only too aware of their own limitations and frequently wish they would be able to do even more good (Urmson 1958, MacFarquhar 2015). Thus, I doubt that moral role models would *call for* admiration, because they themselves seem to foster no self-congratulatory inclinations and are not overly satisfied with what they did under conditions of massive injustice. But insofar as those who act morally do right (in spite of their inevitable imperfection), this clearly deserves to be recognised.

---

[245] I admit that the question of where *exactly* to draw the line between what can be expected from agents (so that full blame is appropriate when agents fail to act accordingly) on the one hand, and what should count as inevitable moral failure (so that only 'softened' blame is appropriate) may in concrete cases still be subject to debate. Yet, my aim was only to distinguish the two dimensions, not to define a clear line separating them.

Yet, praise and admiration from the outside might be problematic, insofar as they can come with the danger of establishing a distance between oneself and the admired person. Admiration must not obscure the fact that acting out of a cosmopolitan ethos is an option that is, in principle, available to everyone, not only to some moral exemplars. Insofar as admiration and praise distances the agent from the admired person, and insofar as it obscures the possibilities to act, from one's own contingent position, upon what is morally demanded, it is problematic. But insofar as it acknowledges that what the person did was the right thing to do (under given conditions and with all limitations and imperfections), recognition and "softened" praise are indeed appropriate.

4.4 A word about motivation

One obvious objection against this proposed account of inevitable moral failure comes to mind: Would objective statements of moral shortcomings, subjective attitudes of regret, and reactive attitudes of softened blame, if implemented in our everyday moral consciousness, not have a disastrous effect on the motivation of moral agents to even try to act morally at all?[246] If it is impossible to do what is really morally right, why should one even make any effort to do so? Answering this question partly requires an empirical discussion of the psychology of motivation and the actual triggers of behavioural change. I will not engage with the psychological literature to answer this question, but I want to point to the fact that the illusion of innocence—the belief that no moral wrongs are being committed if we continue our privileged lives without engaging into any directly harmful actions in our direct environment—obviously does not provide a great motivation to act better, either. Instead, willful ignorance and apathy often seem to come together.[247] Narrowing moral concern down to just one's immediate surroundings and adopting a corresponding indifference towards serious moral wrongs elsewhere that result from structural injustice is arguably a much bigger obstacle

---

[246] Gheaus (2013) has critically discussed the feasibility constraint in the context of *institutional* justice and argued that the clear identification of injustice, even if it cannot be fixed, can increase the "action-guiding potential" of a theory of justice. It does so by providing an "aspirational ideal" that *might* be, at some point, achieved through coordinated collective action. She concludes that "a conception of justice that drops the feasibility constraint is more generous in its prescriptive force than an understanding of justice restricted to honouring rights" (Gheaus 2013, 463). I agree that this kind of 'prescriptive generosity' is urgently needed, when determining both institutional and individual obligations of justice.
[247] Cf. again Young (2011, 123–124).

to realising behavioural change and moral progress than pointing out the problematic structures that connect advantages enjoyed by some with the disadvantages suffered by others. Increasing awareness and pointing out the role of individual agency in causing, but also in possibly addressing structural injustice can have a motivating effect simply by raising awareness for the voices of those who were not previously heard.

The argument about the impossibility of moral perfection, and the diagnosis of inevitable imperfection, can help to relieve agents both from an illusionary assumption of innocence and the misguided idea of living a morally untainted life. It will also indicate that genuine moral perfection is, under current conditions, out of reach for anyone. Here, the situation in ethics might show parallels to the situation in the arts: As Salvatore Dalì is said to have recommended aspiring artists: "Don't fear perfection, you will never reach it." Artistic perfection and moral perfection, on this understanding, may not be worthwhile goals. The resulting advice would thus be to seek avoiding severe forms of avoidable moral failure, and otherwise strive to realise as much good as possible. Or, in my strict language: try to fail as little as possible. On the basis of a gradually differentiated scale of moral achievement, distinguishing between better or worse moral agents will still be possible, and this fact may be sufficiently motivating to lead to actual moral acts and improvement in the world.

Even if my conjectures about the psychological and motivational impact of my theoretical account would prove to be empirically untrue, this must not be of major concern here, since the focus of the present work lies in moral philosophy rather than in motivational psychology. The task at hand is to understand, not to directly and effectively stimulate behavioural change: Moral philosophy and its subfield of political ethics strives to help us to understand the problems at hand, and sees such understanding as essential to the task of acting for the right reasons. An illusionary feeling of moral innocence is not to be wished for from the point of view of philosophy, even if it did turn out to be more effective in motivating agents to act well.[248]

---

248 Philosophically equally undesirable is the religious narrative of a hell in which moral sinners will burn eternally, even if this too might effectively motivate agents to behave more morally. But cf. the concluding chapter for some insights from social psychology about how to motivate agents to take action that corresponds with the values of the cosmopolitan ethos.

5 Cosmopolitan sincerity

The reasoning presented so far allows to meet the third major challenge for *cosmopolitan responsibility*, namely that it places unreasonably excessive demands on moral agents: Yes, *cosmopolitan responsibility* does indeed place—at least under current conditions of massive global injustice—excessive demands on moral agents, and this is the necessary consequence of taking all human beings seriously as ultimate units of moral concern. *Cosmopolitan responsibility*, in my understanding, thus embraces the overdemandingness objection, and uses it to debunk the assumption of moral perfection and the illusion of moral innocence. The idea that all moral demands have to be accomplishable in order to be sound, and the idea that there is a threshold, probably even a convenient threshold, of sound moral demands that depend on the capacities and dispositions of the agent instead of the state of affairs involving humans in the world, is rejected. There are, under conditions of global structural injustice, non-negotiable moral demands that uphold their binding force no matter what. Taking the needs and unmet basic rights of the disadvantaged seriously deserves priority over worrying about the moral innocence of the advantaged.

This understanding of moral requirements speaks in favour of introducing a scalar and gradual understanding of better and worse moral actions, with perfection remaining out of reach—at least under current conditions. The possibility of evaluating an agent's actions and comparing the moral qualities of different agents is of higher importance for moral cosmopolitanism than specifying the assumption of a sufficient threshold of accomplishable moral demands. With an abundance of moral requirements, increased also by the plural sources of morality, and with moral perfection out of reach, the spotlight of philosophical attention will include, next to specific acts, also the general moral attitudes and dispositions that inform and shape a person's way of life. Moral behaviour and the decision about which degree of moral failure seems permissible to an agent appear in this light also as a personal, existential choice about what kind of person one wants to be: Someone who sees the ongoing injustices as part of the context that places non-negotiable requirements on all those who could, at least in principle, do something about it; or someone who prefers to uphold a —morally deceptive—illusion of innocence which presupposes discounting the moral value of those suffering from disadvantage so that others can enjoy their advantages.

Conclusion
The ethos of cosmopolitan responsibility

1 Responding to global injustice

Individuals and their acts do matter morally; even in the face of large and complex global challenges which make individuals and their acts seem to look small and insignificant. This last chapter combines insights from preceding chapters to conclude the exploration of the role and responsibility of individual agents— with a focus on well-off, ordinary citizens in the countries of the Global North —in the face of global structural injustice. It recapitulates key features of a theory of *cosmopolitan responsibility*, which can be, in the form of a cosmopolitan ethos, personally endorsed by individuals and thus shape dispositions and behaviour. Such an ethos is based on a sense of belonging to a broader, morally relevant community of all humans as equals. It acknowledges the multiple political, economic, environmental, social, and cultural relations, interdependencies and interconnections that link the local, the regional, the national and the global levels with one another, making all humans morally equal citizens of the world.

My considerations may offer some guidance for individuals reflecting on what they should do concretely, but they will not identify precise tasks or specific duties. Given the size and the pervasiveness of structural injustice and its multiple appearances, such ambition would be misguided. Instead, in this book, I argue more generally that the suitable moral response of individuals to structural injustice should consist in developing and fostering an *egalitarian ethos of cosmopolitan responsibility* that, in overcoming indifference, permeates an agent's thinking and feeling, informs choices, leads to some action directly tackling injustice but also generates indirect effects on other agents in the community surrounding the agent. Such a cosmopolitan ethos of individuals links cognitive and rational normative *analysis*, with a socially embedded and emotionally charged *feeling* of relational equality in the global community, and a disposition to *act* according to the values of *cosmopolitan responsibility*.

Importantly, determining individual responsibility in terms of an ethos (instead of identifying concrete duties or tasks) has two main advantages: by avoiding atomistic assessments of single acts, the ethos, first, matches individual attitudes and patterns of behaviour (not single acts) with the distinctive wrong of injustice embedded in structures, and, second, it allows to stress the relational and social components of individual agency. Thus, *individual* responses are not only to be assessed in terms of their (accumulated) actual and direct ("vertical") effect on addressing need or increasing justice; they also matter with regard to their ("horizontal") effect on other agents, i.e. as contributions to the development of a *collective* ethos providing an important basis for collective action and, possibly, for successful institutional reform of unjust *structures*. This last chapter further spells out these claims.

2 Four features of global individual responsibility

My account of cosmopolitan, global individual responsibility is characterised by the following four features: it is inherently *personal, pluralist, forward-looking*, and *pragmatic*.

The essential feature of *cosmopolitan responsibility* is its *personal* nature. It contends that individuals are bearers not only of basic rights, but also of responsibilities which correspond to those rights. Several ways of linking individual agents to collective harms and instances of structural injustice have been discussed in the preceding chapters. The fundamental reason for establishing responsibility is—on universalist and egalitarian terms—the existence of *relations* between persons. Persons are understood as needy and vulnerable beings on the one hand, and as capable agents on the other. Furthermore, they are understood as common members of morally relevant communities within which they are connected through personal and structural interactions.[249] In a global community, individuals morally ought to become self-aware about their role and responsibility not only to avoid harm and to remedy harm already caused, but more generally to respect others and secure equality, also by helping to fight moral wrongs and by promoting and securing the rights and flourishing lives of all. The relevant point here is that *individuals* are called upon to engage in political action and, ideally, work towards structural solutions—even if effectively changing the structures far exceeds their particular capacities. But the impossibility of changing large-scale problems alone does not free anyone from a personal moral obligation to respond to them. Governmental politics and science alone will not fix the problems under discussion unless a sufficient number of persons acknowledge their urgency, call for change, accept some personal responsibility, make use of their capacities, and undertake efforts to address them in one way or another. People within and outside of institutions have to show personal commitment and demand change. Only then will institutional

---

249 This explicitly includes also *possible* connections where there is a moral case to be made for such connections, as well as connections to *future* generations where the impact of today's decisions will impact on their lives. Cf. chapter two, above, on the ideal of *relational* equality.

agents—such as corporations, governments or the international community—ultimately feel compelled to take action.

Thus, *cosmopolitan responsibility*, although distinctively individualistic, is certainly not atomistic and does not isolate individuals. On the contrary, it is based on the insight that persons are, as individuals, dependent on others; they live, interact, and flourish in exchange with others. It also acknowledges that the personal responsibility of individual agents may best be discharged by coordinating with others in order to collectively create adequate institutions. The fundamental point is that *individuals matter also as individuals*; their single acts, over which they have control, are relevant for flagging problems, for starting to address them collectively and for promoting structural reforms. Thus, individuals are—in spite of the limited direct impact their acts may have—personally called upon as bearers of responsibility for the larger structures they live in.

The moral relevance of such personal involvement with unjust structures can be explained in numerous ways, making the account of *cosmopolitan responsibility* inherently *pluralist*. This is its second characteristic. The preceding chapters discussed different forms of entanglement justifying personal responsibility: persons may bear responsibility for their past or ongoing contributions to injustices, they may have a general moral obligation to minimise harm and maximise the good for all, they may have an obligation to foster and develop their own character in a specific way, and they may be required to respect everyone as moral equals in all interactions, including indirect interactions with those temporally or spatially remote. I contend that all these different normative strategies have genuine moral weight, and one should not be forced to give exclusive preference to only one of them. Quite to the contrary, expanding one's view by acknowledging multiple sources of morality should be seen as an opportunity, not as a burden. Such a broader view not only avoids that one misses important moral dimensions of a problem; it also allows a better appreciation of the richness and complexities of the multiple dimensions of human life; it may also help, if deployed wisely, to mobilise a greater number of moral emotions, thus increasing motivation—in contrast to the somewhat impoverished focus of more narrow moral theories relying on a single, rational criterion alone.

However, pluralism has a price: it often comes along with less clear advice than straightforward adherence to a single principle would, particularly because an 'algorithm' to calculate and weigh the competing morally significant perspectives and considerations is unavailable. I also doubt that it will be possible to come up with such an algorithm, neatly integrating the different perspectives. Yet, the risks attached to the pursuit of unambiguous normative neatness are greater than those attached to living with plurality: The suggestion of clarity where it does not exist invites activity under the illusion of knowledge and impedes the pursuit of engaging further with the problems at hand instead of pursuing the search for adequate ways of engaging with them.[250] Thus, a pluralist account of responsibility will invite and welcome contributions and assessments from different normative perspectives and attempt to identify morally adequate responses in light of obligations, consequences, connections, etc. And in many cases, at least, significant convergence between different normative perspectives will appear: the general wrongs of global structural injustice can be acknowledged by deontic, consequentialist, virtue-based, contractualist, and other approaches alike.

A third feature of *cosmopolitan responsibility* is its temporal dimension: it assigns priority to the *present* and the *future*, not to the past; responding personally to a given global challenge here and now means to specify the general intuition that someone should be doing something about a problem by determining *what* can and should be done by *whom*. Here, initially *all* those who *can* address a significant moral wrong are included as possible bearers of moral responsibility. In this regard, *cosmopolitan responsibility* is extremely inclusive and 'generous' in assigning such initial, forward-looking responsibility. This is done to limit the possibly negative impact of obsessing about past events and activities and blame-shifting, which can undermine and complicate necessary responses to address a wrong (for example by assigning responsibility only to some while letting others too quickly off the hook).

Assigning priority to the forward-looking perspective, however, is not to be identified with exclusivity: Looking back also matters to some degree, particularly when it comes to distributing burdens among several capable agents in a fair way. Those who have done wrong, caused harms, or through doing so are enjoying particular advantages, bear, and should willingly accept, greater forward-looking responsibilities in acting to address a wrong. The fact that more powerful, privileged agents are frequently unwilling to acknowledge their harmful contributions and instead prefer to engage in blame-shifting, avoid costly remedial action or argue strategically for equal burden sharing is, of course, lamentable. However, it does not speak against the soundness of the normative judgement that past acts generate special responsibilities. But neither does it free *other* capable agents from their own, past-independent, forward-looking responsibility to address massive moral wrongs today (even if those bearing special responsibility fail to live up to it).

---

[250] To put it pointedly, as a variation of an important insight by Wittgenstein: An unbalanced diet, where one nourishes one's thinking with only one kind of normative reasons, is the main cause of philosophical disease (cf. Wittgenstein 1953, § 593).

The fourth characteristic of global individual responsibility is its pragmatic nature. By this I mean a combination of three features: *epistemic humility*, an optimistic belief in the *possibility of progress*, and *practical ambition*.

Pluralism, already mentioned above, makes a case not to strive for unambiguousness but instead to use the best available theoretical and practical tools to assess a given challenge and weigh adequate options of response. Acknowledging epistemic limitations—resulting from incomplete factual knowledge on the one hand and selective or narrow perspectives on the other—supports an attitude of modesty in making judgements and in prescribing specific actions. Epistemic modesty then demands a general willingness to hear other opinions, to listen to the voices of all affected, to engage with them on terms of good faith, and to pursue the task of identifying an adequate moral response to a given problem together. Modesty in this regard, however, must not be confounded with a weakened willingness to defend one's judgements: defending one's own, well-considered point of view by explaining it with the help of good arguments that are accessible to others, is an integral ingredient for successfully determining appropriate solutions.

The second pragmatic element is a general yet non-naive optimism, which asserts that progress towards a better future, in which current problems are increasingly being addressed and can eventually be solved, is possible. Taken together with the forward-looking perspective and the call for epistemic modesty, it calls for a wide and inclusive dialogue about what such a better future would entail and what would be necessary to bring it about. It seeks to articulate values and ideas, rights and responsibilities that promote progress by remedying relational inequalities and structural injustice, and by promoting circumstances for flourishing lives for all. And it also remembers past instances of successful progressive change to refute pessimistic or apathy-inducing voices.

Practical ambition, the disposition to transform one's attitudes, value judgements, and one's perception of connectedness in a morally relevant community into concrete acts, is a third element of the pragmatic nature of *cosmopolitan responsibility*. It deserves particular attention and thus will be taken up in the following section.

These four features—personal, pluralist, forward-looking, and pragmatic—characterise the normative outlook of *cosmopolitan responsibility* in general terms. Now, the task ahead is for each agent to respond personally by considering his or her role in the problematic structures at hand and by analysing and improving behaviour.

3 The cosmopolitan ethos

The primary philosophical ambition of this book was to defend the normative outlook of *cosmopolitan responsibility* by exploring norms, values, and ideals that shape our understanding of the roles and responsibilities of individual agents in a globalised, interconnected world. These normative considerations yield practical relevance when they shape the *ethos* of an agent; where the ethos is understood as an intra-personal 'institution' integrating normative values and considerations in one's motivational setup, influencing one's dispositions to act, and thus leading to tangible individual responses to global structural injustice. Importantly, such an ethos can spread beyond what an individual feels, thinks, says and does; it can inform others and invite dispositional and behavioural change in them, too.

To make sense of this claim and to explain the link between the theoretical, social and behavioural dimensions of moral action, the notion of an ethos required clarification.[251] An ethos was understood as a set of values, norms or principles that, held explicitly or implicitly, informs practice. It is an internalised endorsement of values underlying a person's or a group's way of perceiving and categorising different states of affairs, shaping both the conscious and unconscious responses to specific situations or stimuli, and determining the range of options and actions perceived as appropriate to choose from when confronting an issue. In other words, an ethos shapes people's ways of feeling and thinking, and their dispositions to communicate and to act about something. In this sense, an ethos is pervasive: it is embedded in the basic setup or character of a person and motivates corresponding action.[252] Importantly, however, this setup is neither static nor immune to change. Instead, it can be shaped and developed through such different practices as critical reflection and argumentation, seeing and copying what others do, and, not least, through education, both through factual information and emotional storytelling.[253] Inferences about the ethos of a

---

[251] Cf. Wolff (1998, 105), and above, chapter one, section 5.3.
[252] Cohen called it "a structure of response lodged in the motivations that inform everyday life" (Cohen 2000, 128).
[253] The United Nations's Sustainable Development Goals mention in target 4.7 the need for global citizenship *education* as a way to promote sustainable development also through increasing knowledge and inviting individual behavioural change. UNESCO's guiding document on topics and learning objectives of global citizenship education directly tackles this target, rightly pointing out the importance of the cognitive, the social, and the behavioural dimensions (UNESCO 2015). The practical importance of the "sentimental" aspects of promoting cosmopolitanism is highlighted also by Rorty (1998), Long (2009), and Woods (2012).

person are possible based on what someone says and does; such visible expressions of an ethos provide information and communicate normative commitments to others in the surrounding social community of an agent, thus generating "horizontal" effects on other agents. In this regard, the personal, i.e. one's internal commitments shaping observable behaviour, becomes inevitably public and political within a shared social space.

This description indicates how the ethos as an intra-personal 'institution' provides a possible link between the cognitive-rational side of persons, their often emotionally charged relations and social interactions, and their dispositional-behavioural setup, which shapes their actions. The point is that the cognitive dimension, the socio-emotional dimension, and the practical dimension of human lives are not separated from one another, but are closely connected and mutually influence each other. In order to promote lasting dispositional and behavioural change, all these dimensions need to be considered. The focus of philosophical ethics to engage first and foremost with the cognitive rational analysis of normative claims thus is but one part of the full story. Understanding how normativity can actually shape behaviour, and making good use of the psychological dynamics and mechanisms that help people shape and change their behaviour and embrace new, morally superior habits and conduct (both in individuals and in collectives) goes beyond philosophical analysis alone. Here, the analysis of the cognitive dimension should be enriched by paying attention to the social-emotional and dispositional-behavioural dimensions, as well.[254] The remaining pages of this book provide further thoughts on the *ethos* of persons in an attempt to do just this.

---

254 With this practical goal in mind, much can be learned from empirical studies in the social sciences and in social psychology about the creation and functioning of norms and the mechanisms of norm diffusion and effective norm change in individuals and social groups (cf. e.g. Elster 1991, Bicchieri 2016). For psychological research that can support the present philosophical project, cf. e.g. Buchan et al. (2011) and de Rivera and Carson (2015). The connection to the proposed focus on the "ethos" of persons and groups should be obvious, since social norms are understood as "socially shared and enforced attitudes specifying what to do and what not to do in a given situation" and norms "do not just specify what people ought and ought not to do; they also specify what people actually do, what they think, and how they feel." (Prentice 2012, 23–24). Humans are social beings very much influenced in their own dispositions to think, feel and act by what they think about what *others* think, how *others* feel and act.—In this philosophical study I am unable to give full justice to research in social sciences and psychology but others have started to take up the findings in these disciplines to discuss effective ways to communicate cosmopolitan norms so that they influence human behaviour (e.g. Brock and Atkinson 2008, Goodman, Jinks et al. 2012, Cameron 2017).

But why bother with apparently idle and idealistic talk about changing an ethos, when any reasonable person has to acknowledge that humans are persistently driven by selfish interests, neglect the legitimate and basic claims of others, and even knowingly accept the suffering and death of others and the deterioration of the environment simply to enjoy some, often rather trivial advantages? Why not give up hope altogether, in light of all the past, obviously unsuccessful attempts to realise a just world, and a current political climate in which populist, nationalist, isolationist and supremacist discourse seems to grow—employing denial, confusion, and blame-shifting strategies to legitimise the continuation of selfish practices and inaction—at the expense of internationalist and cosmopolitan discourse?

All this has to be seen and acknowledged. And yet: I do not see why it should be impossible that people and policies change, as they have done so often already in the past.[255] Things can change for better or for worse, *but change they can.* The sheer possibility of change—of both progress and deterioration—thus calls upon all morally sensible people to contribute their share; even if it is only small, and even if it faces a quite hostile political climate shaped by denial, parochialism, ineffectiveness, and outright passivity. To counter this, the very privileged are clearly called upon, as are those who occupy positions of influence. Activists leading the fight for change are urgently needed, too. But also ordinary citizens, if they are privileged enough to be able to inform themselves and engage in some form of action, are called upon to use their abilities. Apathy and inaction are simply not morally acceptable options in the face of the massive wrongs that shape our current world, and the impending threat that things will only get worse. Which, then, are the essential features of a cosmopolitan ethos?

Acknowledging problematic connections and relations. The original problem of structural injustice is, as we have seen above, that much of the current global inequalities and injustices are frequently *not* even perceived as being of concern to the privileged individuals living in the countries of the Global North. The manufacturing conditions of consumer products are at best briefly regretted but ultimately ignored; the pollution resulting from mobility is occasionally lamented but does not lead to sufficient behavioural change; the wealth and security within countries of the Global North is considered as unproblematic and generally

---

[255] The standard examples of change for the better include the abolition of slavery in many parts of the world, increasing equality between women and men, the decriminalisation of consensual sexual relations that were formerly labeled as deviant. Obviously, further steps still need to be made in all these fields, but this must not obscure the fact that significant achievements have been already made and that progressive change, that replaces old expectations of normalcy, is possible.

justified, so that others are either fully ignored or seen as undeserving or not entitled to equal standards of security and well-being. All this leads to a situation in which the suffering and deprivation of others are conveniently kept hidden from sight, often with the help of walls, fences and force. This set of dispositions is widely shared and can itself also be characterised as an ethos, although as one opposed to its *cosmopolitan* and *egalitarian* antithesis: an ethos endorsing a parochial view that insufficiently acknowledges, or even denies, both the existing connections and the equal moral standing of all.

The alternative cosmopolitan ethos acknowledges the existence of transnational, cosmopolitan relations and connections of all within a global community. These connections have both a *factual* basis, e.g. in the form of economic interactions, or the transnational effects of the global climate shaping our globalised and interconnected world, but also an *ideal* basis, i.e. the idea of a morally relevant community of morally equal global citizens who are willing to put themselves in the shoes of others and foster concern for how the lives of others go. In this scenario, indifference and inaction towards the fate of other fellow humans in need are understood as denial and rejection. From the perspective of a cosmopolitan ethos it is imperative to replace this indifference with explicit acknowledgment of a morally relevant relationship. The task ahead consists in seeking to develop that pre-existing, more parochial ethos with its insufficient acknowledgement of the equal moral status and relevance of all into a cosmopolitan ethos. This will move concern for the globally disadvantaged from the periphery more to the centre of people's concern, calling also for corresponding individual action.

Individual action in social context. Yet, ending the problems of global structural injustice through individual agency alone will be impossible, as anyone considering acting to address such large-scale challenges will immediately become aware of. Furthermore, when considering the number of important, morally urgent tasks, agents will realise, at least under current circumstances, the difficulties, even the impossibility of always acting in line with the pluralist demands of moral cosmopolitanism that assigns equal moral value to everyone and stipulates morally relevant relations between all within the mutual sphere of influence. So many of our everyday acts are morally tainted, as a critical reflection on consumer decisions, the everyday needs for mobility, or the preferential treatment extended to those near and dear to oneself, clearly indicate. Thus, seeking moral perfection is not a plausible goal. The task for individual agents hence cannot consist in obsessing about keeping one's hands perfectly clean or always attempting to do everything perfectly right; instead, it consists in making well-considered choices regarding how much one is willing to do, and about how many costs one is willing to accept to promote the good. It forces agents to place themselves on a spectrum of being more part of the problem or more part of the solution. Individual agents can always choose from numerous options, forcing upon themselves an inevitable decision about whether they want to start acting and how far they want to go. But importantly, they *can* start and improve, right away.

From the perspective of *cosmopolitan responsibility*, the sheer ability to choose from these diverse options—including the morally problematic option to remain inactive—is in itself a vivid indicator of privilege. Such undeserved privilege comes along with additional powers that often remain unappreciated and even undermine the motivation to expand the circle of concern for others. Awareness of this privilege, however, points out how relatively easy it would be, under conditions of security and abundance, to change behaviour and to ask for and promote political reforms. While the globally disadvantaged, if they have a chance to be heard at all, often have to accept immense risks when speaking up against exploitative employers, multinational companies, or oppressive regimes, the possible costs for endorsing a more egalitarian and cosmopolitan mindset as a globally privileged person are rather small, making it, I contend, a matter of simple decency to develop the egalitarian ethos and see to it that it translates into some concrete action.

The available options for action that individual agents may choose to realise in accordance with the normative outlook of *cosmopolitan responsibility* are numerous. The problems calling for cosmopolitan concern abound, as do the possibilities to address them, also from the perspective of individual agents. All responses are steps towards reducing the "passive injustice" that consists in inaction.[256] Options range from informing oneself and others about the problems to raise awareness; talking about them and taking a stance, both in private settings, such as the family, and in more public settings, for example at work; keeping ideas about alternatives to the current problematic situation ready, developing them further so that they are available at times when they could become effective; practically, agents can aspire to reduce their unintentional involvement in causing harm or upholding injustice; further options include the possibility of donating time or money to organisations actively addressing need and injustice, or even working in or for such organisations; to self-limit one's own wealth and use of resources and to make ethically considered consumer decisions; and, of course, for those who see this as a good fit for themselves, political, civic or activist engagement—e.g. in the form of inspiring creative, provocative or disrup-

---

[256] The notion of "passive injustice" has been coined by Shklar, albeit in a narrower sense than I use it here (Shklar 1990, 6).

tive, thought stimulating, symbolic action—is also an important option available to most citizens living in the affluent liberal democracies of the Global North (that may even invite and support such engagement).[257] Taking the perspective of *cosmopolitan responsibility* with its commitment to relational equality will encourage privileged citizens of the world to consider such actions and to engage in as many of them as reasonably possible. I do not offer a concrete minimal or a maximal set of obligations, because, in any case, it is impossible to avoid some degree of moral failure or to reach moral perfection (cf. chapter six). Because of the morally disastrous circumstances of structural injustice the privileged cannot hope to be doing enough; moral awareness and sincerity will not cease to demand more as long as others, living under conditions of preventable misery, can be helped. But it seems clear that, from the perspective of *cosmopolitan responsibility*, most, if not nearly all of the privileged citizens should move these concerns for structural injustice more to the centre of their own and the public attention and should be doing more to address them than they currently do.

Challenges to taking cosmopolitan action. Sure, endorsing a cosmopolitan ethos and displaying the corresponding behaviour frequently causes some friction with and irritation among those who do otherwise; such tensions increase with the consistency and costliness of the non-standard behaviour. Different kinds of counter-arguments and self-defense mechanisms are then advanced in order to justify continuing with the problematic, established patterns of behaviour. Blaming moral agents as naive "do-gooders" is one prominent strategy.[258] But—as long as no severe harassment, violence or abuse takes place—the costs incurred for moral decency are of rather limited weight compared to the costs suffered by those whose rights and plights are ignored, and who are often unable to make their voices heard, be it because they are struggling for survival or because they are dominated, threatened or silenced. Here, a general change in norms and in what is considered acceptable behaviour is needed; and there is no reason why such change should not, eventually, be possible—as many instances of progressive change in the past have shown. Each instance of such change started with some people moving first, others contributing, and

---

257 Further thought on the special role of academics can be found e.g. in Caney (2012) and Horton (2014); on civil disobedience that combines symbolic with confrontational ambition cf. e.g. Celikates (2016) and Delmas (2018). For an exemplary discussion of individual responsibility in the context of refugee and migrant integration, cf. the contributions to Kehoe/Alisic/Heilinger (2019), among them Grahle, Heilinger, and Phipps.
258 Attacking "do-gooders" is discussed e.g. in Sezgin (2017). For online attacks against academics speaking up for justice cf. e.g. Branford et al. (2019).

in doing so setting new trends, while initially also accepting criticism for their unusual behaviour.[259]

But how far will a cosmopolitan ethos actually shape agency? Can one ever do enough? Will agents, with the right ethos, have to dedicate their entire lives to addressing global structural injustices or other moral wrongs? Is it still permitted to assign (some) preference to those particularly near and dear to oneself? Clearly, doing more in order to promote the good is, from the moral point of view, always better than doing less, and engaged and committed activism is urgently required. But human lives have many facets and earning one's living, raising one's children, and taking care of oneself also matter and command attention. These circumstances may even explain (but not justify) why many people actually do not do more to address global injustice and thus fail to live up to cosmopolitan demands. However, moral concern in thinking about the problems at hand should not primarily be directed to the fate of the privileged individual agents and their concern about the ability to reach *moral perfection* (cf. chapter six). Instead, it should be primarily directed to the need of the disadvantaged and to the conditions of injustice. From this starting point it has to be asked whether and how it is possible to contribute to changing the circumstances that so negatively impact on so many people's lives.

It is one of the distressing truths of this world, that each act has opportunity costs. Thus, even apparently innocent acts, especially under circumstances in which an alternative to reduce injustice or secure rights would be available, have a price—a price born by those whose plight remains *un*heard, who are *not* helped. However, it is not my ambition to suggest that all should radically change their lives by suddenly ignore all special relationships and responsibilities and become concerned in a perfectly impartial way exclusively about the global problems at the centre of this book. Few would be impressed by such an argument, no one would follow it.

The importance of some people dedicating their lives primarily, even exclusively, to fighting injustice is undeniable. Moral progress and social change need such agents willing to incur high costs, take risks and expose themselves. But *cosmopolitan responsibility* is—on its more modest, realistic and practical side—an ideal accessible and relevant for many more people: everyone morally ought to contribute to the task of increasing justice by integrating awareness of the existing injustice in their everyday decisions and acts. And this demand

---

259 On the role of individual "trendsetters" in norm change, cf. Bicchieri (2016, ch. 5), on "norm entrepreneurs" who can start "norm bandwagons" and trigger "norm cascades", cf. Elster (1997, 35–37). In the context of climate change, Jamieson has made a case for the importance of developing virtues and of leading by example in responding to climate change (Jamieson 2005).

can be met even if one does not, or does only on occasion, take up the role of a committed activist.

The focus of the present book was, as indicated in the beginning, on 'ordinary' citizens. Their role must not be underestimated. It is crucial for promoting and securing global justice and equality, because some *general* concern for the problems at hand and a *general* commitment to addressing them needs to permeate society. To realise this goal, the outstanding acts of the few are important, but the commitment of *anyone* objecting to the current state of affairs will be imperative, too. And contributing to establishing a broad and sound basis for progress in addressing existing injustices is very well compatible with exercising other roles responsibly: It is possible to be a baker, teacher, bus-driver, parent, etc. *and* to display an egalitarian ethos that tangibly translates into feeling concern, acknowledging responsibility, talking about connections, and, of course, also taking action—as a political being and engaged citizen, as a consumer, as a friend—in ways that take background injustices into account and contribute to addressing them.

Individual impact. Focussing on the *ethos* of people and groups of people, and not prescribing specific acts, is particularly promising in the context of global *structural* injustice, where the moral wrong in question is itself not constituted by single instances of morally flawed action, but is pervasively embedded in the (global) social structures and the standard patterns of interaction and behaviour. Climate change, economic unfairness and world poverty are important examples. Here, a single instance of a good action (even if it is very much effective in saving or significantly improving the life of one or the lives of a few people) is insufficient to address the general, structural wrong—in the same way as single problematic acts are not at the origin of the structural wrong in question. Correspondingly, only a change in those structures and patterns of action and interaction, both in individual and in institutional agents, can adequately address such wrongs. And while ordinary individuals cannot directly change structures and institutions, they have an impact on the level of other individuals that constitute and shape them.

Thus, individual action is in no way futile. Two factors particularly increase the impact of individual behaviour. First, if people do not only act once in a certain way but change their dispositions, patterns and habits of action, this repetition will add up and increase the impact of their acts. Hence, the narrow scope, often dominant in ethics, to assess single acts must be widened so that individual behaviour over longer time-spans, potentially for the duration of an entire life, is taken into account. In this way, cumulative effects can be considered as well. On this account, the effects of individuals can really make a difference; even if unmeasurable on a global scale, they can make a significant difference for some. Second, as social beings, humans are attentive to the behaviour of others and perceive norm deviation—also new, morally improved behaviour—as an irritation that challenges the established patterns of behaviour. Such irritation, the moment in which standard behaviour becomes problematic, often is the beginning of inquiry (cf. above, chapter three, section three). Thus, every instance of it should be seen as a welcome trigger to start a collective reconsideration of current and insufficiently questioned practices, guided by the ambition to realise relational equality for all. Those taking action towards this goal thus influence other possible agents—through irritation, through information—and can contribute to establishing new, better standards of thinking and acting.

Of course, the call for accepting global connectedness and furthering cosmopolitan concern and responsibility seems to run against much of the current of our time. Maybe, in hindsight, the COP21 United Nations Climate Change Conference in 2015, which led to the Paris Agreement, will be considered as a peak of a globally interconnected human civilisation and of the international cooperation that began increasing after World War II. Six months later, the British voted for "Brexit"; five months later, Donald Trump was elected president of the USA; populist movements in many countries further gained in strength and, at the time of writing, an end to the rise of parochialism and nationalism does not appear to be in sight. In the light of such powerful current political developments and the spread of what could be called an anti-cosmopolitan ethos, calling for relational equality and *cosmopolitan responsibility* might appear irritatingly untimely and naively optimistic. Yet, the isolation of individuals and communities is not a viable option. No matter whether we like it or not, today we live in a global sphere of mutual influence, and mutual effects are inevitable; the circumstances of cosmopolitanism are an undeniable fact of our time. We are all in this together. This makes it imperative to develop and foster a rationally justified, emotionally felt, socially embedded and action-guiding cosmopolitan ethos of responsibility, no matter how bad the current odds stand. Every individual is thus faced with the existential choice of being part of the problem or part of the solution—acknowledging equality, connectedness, and responsibility in what one does.

4 Citizens of the world

It is time to conclude this book. I set out to analyse the dazzling link between large and complex global structural injustices on the one hand and the smallest unit of agency, the individual person on the other. I inquired into the moral roles and responsibilities of individuals, particularly the relatively well-off ordinary citizens in the affluent countries of the Global North. With my focus on individual behaviour, I have taken a bottom-up perspective to complement the important ongoing debates about global *institutional (in-) justice* by providing the outlines of a global political *ethics*, specifying *individual* responsibility through an account of a cosmopolitan ethos. This was defended in full awareness of the limited impact most of our individual actions will have. Yet, societies and institutions are set up by people, and they depend on individuals to shape them. Cosmopolitan reforms will take place only if they are demanded, and change thus can start where ultimate moral agency lies: with the individual agent demanding it and working towards it.

Based on the proposition defended above that individual moral agents matter—simultaneously as beings with legitimate needs and claims on the one hand, and as agents able to act according to normative convictions on the other—I have sought to develop the core elements of a cosmopolitan ethos that can and should inform how people respond to the challenge of living together in a global community. This ethos and its normative ideas yield practical relevance by being able to shape everyday habits and actions of individuals and groups. In particular, *equality* is neither a remote or theoretical ideal, nor a static state of affairs. On a relational account, equality is a practice. It is something agents can *do*.

It is my sense that the experience and acknowledgment of the joint co-existence and mutual influence of all on this planet can and ultimately must become transformative. The global sphere of citizenship, and a global civil society, increasingly materialises from rather abstract ideas into a felt reality. The random and arbitrary contingencies that assign everyone a place in the world will then, particularly for all those enjoying privileges and relative advantages, be re-envisioned as merely the position from which they contribute to the perennial moral project of acting responsibly as citizens of the world.

Bibliography

Abizadeh, Arash. 2007. "Cooperation, Pervasive Impact, and Coercion: On the Scope (not Site) of Distributive Justice." Philosophy & Public Affairs 35 (4): 318–358.
Alexander, Larry. 2010. "Deontology at the Threshold." San Diego Law Review 37: 893–912.
Ambedkar, Babasaheb. 1936. Annihilation of Caste. The Annotated Critical Edition. Edited by Sudhir Anand. Introduced with the Essay "The Doctor and the Saint" by Arundhati Roy. London/New York: Verso 2014.
Anderson, Elizabeth. 1999. "What Is the Point of Equality?" Ethics 109 (2): 287–337.
Anderson, Elizabeth. 2010a. "Dewey's Moral Philosophy." The Stanford Encyclopedia of Philosophy (Spring 2010 Edition).
Anderson, Elizabeth. 2010b. "The Fundamental Disagreement between Luck Egalitarians and Relational Egalitarians." Canadian Journal of Philosophy 40 (suppl. 1): 1–23.
Anderson, Elizabeth. 2010c. "Justifying the Capabilities Approach to Justice." In Measuring Justice. Primary Goods and Capabilities, edited by Harry Brighouse and Ingrid Robeyns. Cambridge: Cambridge University Press, 81–100.
Anderson, Elizabeth. 2012. "Equality." In The Oxford Handbook of Political Philosophy, edited by David Estlund. Oxford/New York: Oxford University Press, 40–57.
Appiah, Kwame Anthony. 2007. Cosmopolitanism. Ethics in a World of Strangers. New York: Norton.
Aristotle. The Nicomachean Ethics. Transl. by David Ross. Revised with an introduction and notes by Lesley Brown. Oxford: Oxford University Press 2009.
Armstrong, Chris. 2009. "Global Egalitarianism." Philosophy Compass 4 (1): 155–171.
Arneson, Richard J. 1989. "Equality and Equal Opportunity for Welfare." Philosophical Studies 56 (1): 77–93.
Arneson, Richard J. 2000. "Luck Egalitarianism and Prioritarianism." Ethics 110: 339–349.
Arneson, Richard J. 2004. "Moral Limits on the Demands of Beneficence?" In The Ethics of Assistance: Morality and the Distant Needy, edited by Deen K. Chatterjee, In Cambridge Studies in Philosophy an Public Policy. Cambridge: Cambridge University Press, 33–58.
Arneson, Richard J. 2009. "What do we Owe to Distant Needy Strangers?" In Peter Singer Under Fire: The Moral Iconoclast Faces His Critics, edited by Jeffrey A. Schaler. Chicago and LaSalle: Open Court, 267–293.
Arneson, Richard J. 2013. "Egalitarianism." The Stanford Encyclopedia of Philosophy (Summer 2013 Edition).
Arras, John. 2010. "Theory and Bioethics." The Stanford Encyclopedia of Philosophy (Summer 2010 Edition).
Ashford, Elizabeth. 2003. "The Demandingness of Scanlon's Contractualism." Ethics 113: 273–302.
Ashford, Elizabeth. 2007. "The Duties Imposed by the Human Right to Basic Necessities." In Freedom From Poverty as a Human Right. Who Owes What to the Very Poor?, edited by Thomas Pogge. Oxford/New York: Oxford University Press.
Ashford, Elizabeth. 2009. "Unsere Pflichten gegenüber Menschen in chronischer Armut." In Weltarmut und Ethik, edited by Barbara Bleisch and Peter Schaber. Paderborn: mentis, 195–211.
Banerjee, Amitava, Aidan Hollis, and Thomas Pogge. 2010. "The Health Impact Fund: Incentives for Improving Access to Medicines." The Lancet 375 (9709): 166–169.

Barry, Christian, and Kate Macdonald. 2016. "How Should we Conceive of Individual Consumer Responsibility to Address Labour Injustices?" In Global Justice and International Labour Rights, edited by Faina Milman-Sivan, Hanna Lerner and Yossi Dahan. Cambridge: Cambridge University Press, 53–91.

Bascara, Rachelle. 2016. "Compatriot Partiality and Cosmopolitan Justice: Can we Justify Compatriot Partiality Within the Cosmopolitan Framework?" Etikk i Praksis. Nordic Journal of Applied Ethics 2, 27–40.

Beck, Valentin. 2016. Eine Theorie der globalen Verantwortung: Was wir Menschen in extremer Armut schulden. Berlin: Suhrkamp.

Beitz, Charles. 1979. Political Theory and International Relations. Princeton: Princeton University Press.

Beitz, Charles. 2005. "Cosmopolitanism and Global Justice." The Journal of Ethics 9: 11–27.

Beitz, Charles. 2009. The Idea of Human Rights. Oxford: Oxford University Press.

Bhambra, Gurminder K. 2015. "On the Haitian Revolution and the Society of Equals." Theory, Culture & Society 32 (7–8): 267–274.

Bicchieri, Cristina. 2016. Norms in the Wild. How to Diagnose, Measure, and Change Social Norms. Oxford/New York: Oxford University Press.

Branford, Jason, André Grahle, Jan-Christoph Heilinger, Dennis Kalde, Max Muth, Eva Parisi, Paula-Irene Villa, and Verina Wild. 2019. "Cyberhate Against Academics." In Responsibility for Refugee and Migrant Integration, edited by S. Karly Kehoe, Eva Alisic and Jan-Christoph Heilinger. Berlin/Boston: de Gruyter, 205–225.

Bray, Daniel. 2011. Pragmatic Cosmopolitanism. Representation and Leadership in Transnational Democracy. Houndmills: Palgrave Macmillan.

Brighouse, Harry, and Adam Swift. 2009. "Legitimate Parental Partiality." Philosophy and Public Affairs 37 (1): 43–80.

Brock, Gillian. 2009. Global Justice. A Cosmopolitan Account. Oxford/New York: Oxford University Press.

Brock, Gillian. 2011. "How Does Equality Matter?" Journal of Social Philosophy 42 (1): 76–87.

Brock, Gillian, ed. 2013. Cosmopolitanism Versus Non-Cosmopolitanism. Oxford/New York: Oxford University Press.

Brock, Gillian, and Quentin D. Atkinson. 2008. "What can Examining the Psychology of Nationalism tell us About our Prospects for Aiming at the Cosmopolitan Vision?" Ethical Theory and Moral Practice 11: 165–179.

Brock, Gillian, and Darrel Moellendorf, eds. 2005. Current Debates in Global Justice. Dordrecht: Springer.

Brown, Alexander. 2005. "Luck Egalitarianism and Democratic Equality." Ethical Perspectives: Journal of the European Ethics Network 12: 293–339.

Brown, Garrett Wallace, and David Held, eds. 2010. The Cosmopolitanism Reader. Cambridge: Polity.

Buchan, Nancy R., Marilynn B. Brewer, Gianluca Grimalda, Rick K. Wilson, Enrique Fatas, and Margaret Foddy. 2011. "Global Social Identity and Global Cooperation." Psychological Science 22 (6): 821–828.

Buchanan, Allen. 2000. "Rawls's Law of Peoples: Rules for a Vanished Westphalian World." Ethics 110: 697–721.

Butt, Daniel. 2007. "On Benefiting from Injustice." Canadian Journal of Philosophy 37 (1): 129–152.

Cabrera, Luis, ed. 2018. Institutional Cosmopolitanism. Oxford/New York: Oxford University Press.
Calder, Todd. 2010. "Shared Responsibility, Global Structural Injustice, and Restitution." Social Theory and Practice 36 (2).
Cameron, John David. 2017. "Communicating Cosmopolitanism and Motivating Global Citizenship." Political Studies: 1–17.
Caney, Simon. 2001. "Cosmopolitan Justice and Equalizing Opportunities." Metaphilosophy 32 (1): 113–134.
Caney, Simon. 2005a. "Cosmopolitan Justice, Responsibility and Global Climate Change." Leiden Journal of International Law 18: 747–775.
Caney, Simon. 2005b. Justice Beyond Borders. Oxford/New York: Oxford University Press.
Caney, Simon. 2007. "Global Poverty and Human Rights: The Case for Positive Duties." In Freedom From Poverty as a Human Right. Who Owes What to the Very Poor?, edited by Thomas Pogge. Oxford/New York: Oxford University Press, 275–302.
Caney, Simon. 2012. "Addressing Poverty and Climate Change: The Varieties of Social Engagement." Ethics & International Affairs 26 (2): 191–216.
Carens, Joseph H. 1987. "Aliens and Citizens: The Case for Open Borders." The Review of Politics 49 (2).
Carens, Joseph H. 2000. Culture, Citizenship, and Community. A Contextual Exploration of Justice as Evenhandedness. Oxford/New York: Oxford University Press.
Carens, Joseph H. 2013. "The Case for Open Borders." In The Ethics of Immigration, by Joseph H. Carens. Oxford/New York: Oxford University Press, 225–254.
Celikates, Robin. 2016. "Democratizing Civil Disobedience." Philosophy & Social Criticism 42 (10): 982–994.
Chappell, Timothy. 2007. "Integrity and Demandingness." Ethical Theory and Moral Practice 10 (3): 255–265.
Chappell, Timothy, ed. 2009. The Problem of Moral Demandingness. New Philosophical Essays. Basingstoke: Palgrave Macmillan.
Cheneval, Francis. 2002. Philosophie in weltbürgerlicher Bedeutung. Über die Entstehung und die philosophischen Grundlagen des supranationalen und kosmopolitischen Denkens der Moderne. Basel: Schwabe.
Cicero. 1885. De Officiis. Edited by Johannes H. Parker. London: Oxford University Press.
Cicero. 1984. Tusculanae Disputationes. Edited by Michelangelo Giusta. Turin: Paravia.
Cloarec, Pierre. 2017. "Social Equality and the Global Society." Journal of Moral Philosophy 14 (5): 535–561.
Cochran, Molly. 1999. Normative Theory in International Relations. A Pragmatic Approach. Cambridge: Cambridge University Press.
Cochran, Molly. 2010. "Dewey as an International Thinker." In The Cambridge Companion to Dewey, edited by Molly Cochran, 309–336. Cambridge: Cambridge University Press.
Cohen, G. A. 1989. "On the Currency of Egalitarian Justice." Ethics 99 (4): 906–944.
Cohen, G. A. 1997. "Where the Action is: On the Site of Distributive Justice." Philosophy & Public Affairs 26 (1): 3–30.
Cohen, G. A. 2000. If You're an Egalitarian, How Come You're so Rich? Cambridge: Harvard University Press.
Cohen, G. A. 2008. Rescuing Justice and Equality. Cambridge: Harvard University Press.

Cohen, Joshua, ed. 2002. For Love of Country? Debating the Limits of Patriotism. Boston: Beacon Press.
Cottingham, John. 1983. "Ethics and Impartiality." Philosophical Studies: An International Journal for Philosophy in the Analytic Tradition 43 (1): 83–99.
Cottingham, John. 2010. "Impartiality and Ethical Formation." In Partiality and Impartiality. Morality, Special Relationships, and the Wider World, edited by Brian Feltham and John Cottingham. Oxford/New York: Oxford University Press, 65–83.
Cullity, Garrett. 2004. The Moral Demands of Affluence. Oxford: Oxford University Press.
de Rivera, Joseph, and Harry A. Carson. 2015. "Cultivating a Global Identity." Journal of Social and Political Psychology 3 (2): 310–330.
Deaton, Angus. 2013. The Great Escape: Health, Wealth, and the Origins of Inequality. Princeton: Princeton University Press.
Delanty, Gerard. 2014. "Not All Is Lost in Translation: World Varieties of Cosmopolitanism." Cultural Sociology 8 (4): 374–391.
Delmas, Candice. 2018. A Duty to Resist. When Disobedience Should be Uncivil. Oxford/New York: Oxford University Press.
Dewey, John. 1888. The Ethics of Democracy (The Early Works vol. 1, edited by Jo Ann Boydston). Carbondale: Southern Illinois University Press.
Dewey, John. 1922. Human Nature and Conduct (The Middle Works vol. 14, edited by Jo Ann Boydston). Carbondale: Southern Illinois University Press 2008.
Dewey, John. 1925. Experience and Nature (The Later Works vol. 1, edited by Jo Ann Boydston). Carbondale: Southern Illinois University Press 1981.
Dewey, John. 1927. The Public and its Problems (The Later Works vol. 2, edited by Jo Ann Boydston). Carbondale: Southern Illinois University Press.
Dewey, John. 1930. "Three Independent Factors in Morals." In The Essential Dewey, vol. 2. Ethics, Logic, Psychology, ed. by Larry A. Hickman and Thomas M. Alexander, 315–320. Bloomington: Indiana University Press.
Dewey, John. 1938. Logic. The Theory of Inquiry (The Later Works vol. 12, edited by Jo Ann Boydston). Carbondale: Southern Illinois University Press 1986.
Dewey, John. 1939. Creative Democracy: The Task Before Us (The Later Works vol. 14, edited by Jo Ann Boydston). Carbondale: Southern Illinois University Press.
Dewey, John, and James Tufts. 1932. Ethics (revised version from 1908) (The Later Works vol. 7, edited by Jo Ann Boydston). Carbondale: Southern Illinois University Press 1985.
Dieleman, Susan, David Rondel, and Christopher J. Voparil. 2017. "Introduction: Perspectives on Pragmatism and Justice." In Pragmatism and Justice, edited by Susan Dieleman, David Rondel and Christopher J. Voparil. Oxford/New York: Oxford University Press, 1–17.
Dotson, Kristie. 2012. "How is This Paper Philosophy?" Comparative Philosophy 3 (1): 3–29.
Dworkin, Ronald. 1977. Taking Rights Seriously. Cambridge: Harvard University Press.
Dworkin, Ronald. 2000. Sovereign Virtue: The Theory and Practice of Equality. Cambridge: Harvard University Press.
Dwyer, James. 2013. "On Flying to Ethics Conferences: Climate Change and Moral Responsiveness." International Journal of Feminist Approaches to Bioethics 6 (1): 1–18.
Elster, Jon. 1983. Sour Grapes. Sudies in the Subversion of Rationality. Cambridge: Cambridge University Press.

Elster, Jon. 1991. "Rationality and Social Norms." European Journal of Sociology/Archives Européennes de Sociologie/Europäisches Archiv für Soziologie 32 (1): 109–129.
Elster, Jon. 1997. Free Markets and Social Justice. Oxford/New York: Oxford University Press.
Ferguson, Ann, and Mechthild Nagel. 2009. Dancing with Iris: The Philosophy of Iris Marion Young. Oxford/New York: Oxford University Press.
Fick, Carolyn E. 2007. "The Haitian Revolution and the Limits of Freedom: Defining Citizenship in the Revolutionary Era." Social History 32 (4): 394–414.
Fine, Robert, and Robin Cohen. 2002. "Four Cosmopolitan Moments." In Conceiving Cosmopolitanism: Theory, Context, and Practice, edited by Steven Vertovec and Robin Cohen. Oxford/New York: Oxford University Press, 137–162.
Finnis, John. 1980. Natural law and natural rights. Oxford/New York: Oxford University Press.
Fleurbaey, Marc. 2005. "Freedom with Forgiveness." Politics, Philosophy & Economics 4: 29–67.
Forman-Barzilei, Fonna. 2009. Adam Smith and the Circles of Sympathy: Cosmopolitanism and Moral Theory. Cambridge: Cambridge University Press.
Forst, Rainer. 2007. The Right to Justification. Elements of a Constructivist Theory of Justice. New York: Columbia University Press, 3–25.
Forst, Rainer. 2014. "Justice, Democracy and the Right to Justification: Two Pictures of Justice." In Justice, Democracy and the Right to Justification: Rainer Forst in Dialogue, edited by Rainer Forst. London: Bloomsbury Academic.
Forsythe, David P., and Barbara Ann J. Rieffer-Flanagan. 2007. The International Committee of the Red Cross. New York: Routledge.
Fourie, Carina. 2012. "What is Social Equality? An Analysis of Status Equality as a Strongly Egalitarian Ideal." Res Publica 18 (2): 107–126.
Fourie, Carina. 2017. "The Sufficiency View: A Primer." In What Is Enough? Sufficiency, Justice, and Health, edited by Carina Fourie and Annette Rid, 11–29. Oxford/New York: Oxford University Press.
Frankfurt, Harry. 1987. "Equality as a Moral Ideal." Ethics 98 (1): 21–43.
Fraser, Nancy, and Axel Honneth. 2003. Redistribution or Recognition? A Political-Philosophical Exchange. London/New York: Verso.
Freeman, Samuel. 2007. Justice and the Social Contract: Essays on Rawlsian Political Philosophy. Oxford/New York: Oxford University Press.
Fried, Charles. 1970. An Anatomy of Values. Cambridge: Harvard University Press.
Gabriel, Iason. 2017. "Effective Altruism and its Critics." Journal of Applied Philosophy 34 (4): 457–473.
Ganguli-Mitra, Agomoni. 2013. "Off-Shoring Clinical Research: Exploitation and the Reciprocity Constraint." Developing World Bioethics 13 (3): 111–118.
Ganten, Detlev, Volker Gerhardt, Jan-Christoph Heilinger, and Julian Nida-Rümelin, eds. 2008. Was ist der Mensch? Berlin/New York: de Gruyter.
Gerhardt, Volker. 1995. Immanuel Kants Entwurf "Zum Ewigen Frieden". Eine Theorie der Politik. Darmstadt: Wissenschaftliche Buchgesellschaft.
Gheaus, Anca. 2013. "The Feasibility Constraint on The Concept of Justice." The Philosophical Quarterly 63 (252): 445–464.
Gheaus, Anca. 2016. "Hikers in Flip-Flops: Luck Egalitarianism, Democratic Equality and the Distribuenda of Justice." Journal of Applied Philosophy 35 (1): 54–69.

Giri, Ananta Kumar. 2006. "Cosmopolitanism and Beyond: Towards a Multiverse of Transformations." Development and Change 37 (6): 1277–1292.
Godwin, William. 1793 [1926]. Enquiry Concerning Political Justice and its Influence on General Virtue and Happiness. Edited by Raymond Preston. New York: Alfred A. Knopf.
Golombok, Susan. 2015. Modern Families: Parents and Children in New Family Forms. Oxford/New York: Oxford University Press.
Goodin, Robert E. 2007. "Demandingness as a Virtue." The Journal of Ethics 13 (1): 1–13.
Goodman, Ryan, Derek Jinks, and Andrew K. Woods, eds. 2012. Understanding Social Action, Promoting Human Rights. Oxford/New York: Oxford University Press.
Gosepath, Stefan. 2001. "The Global Scope of Justice." Metaphilosophy 32 (1/2): 135–159.
Gowans, Christopher W. 1994. Innocence Lost: An Examination of Inescapable Moral Wrongdoing. Oxford/New York: Oxford University Press.
Grahle, André. 2019. "Why Volunteers Should be Activists: Towards an Ethics of Ground Relationships." In Responsibility for Refugee and Migrant Integration, edited by S. Karly Kehoe, Eva Alisic and Jan-Christoph Heilinger. Berlin/Boston: de Gruyter, 149–164.
Green, Judith M. 2011. "Cultivating Pragmatist Cosmopolitanism—Democratic Local-and-Global Community Amidst Diversity." In Pragmatism and Diversity. Dewey in the Context of Late Twentieth Century Debates, edited by Judith M. Green, Stefan Neubert and Kersten Reich, 55–83. Basingstoke: Palgrave.
Greenspan, Patricia S. 1995. Practical Guilt. Moral Dilemmas, Emotions, and Social Norms. Oxford: Oxford University Press.
Griffin, James. 2008. On Human Rights. Oxford: Oxford University Press.
Grimm, Herwig. 2010. Das moralphilosophische Experiment. John Deweys Methode empirischer Untersuchungen als Modell der problem- und anwendungsorientierten Tierethik. Tübingen: Mohr Siebeck.
Habermas, Jürgen. 1995. "Kants Idee vom Ewigen Frieden—aus dem historischen Abstand von 200 Jahren." Kritische Justiz 28: 293–319.
Hahn, Henning. 2017. Politischer Kosmopolitismus: Praktikabilität, Verantwortung, Menschenrechte. Berlin/Boston: de Gruyter.
Haji, Ishtiyaque. 2002. Deontic Morality and Control. Cambridge: Cambridge University Press.
Hare, Richard. 1981. Moral Thinking. Oxford: Oxford University Press.
Harris, Hugh. 1927. "The Greek Origins of the Idea of Cosmopolitanism." International Journal of Ethics 38 (1): 1–10.
Hart, H. L. A. 2008. Punishment and Responsibility. Essays in the Philosophy of Law. 2nd Edition. New York: Oxford University Press.
Heilinger, Jan-Christoph. 2010. Anthropologie und Ethik des Enhancements. Berlin/New York: de Gruyter.
Heilinger, Jan-Christoph. 2012. "The Moral Demandingness of Socioeconomic Human Rights." In The Philosophy of Human Rights. Contemporary Controversies, edited by Gerhard Ernst and Jan-Christoph Heilinger. Berlin/Boston: de Gruyter, 185–208.
Heilinger, Jan-Christoph. 2015. "Contemporary Cosmopolitanism and Elements of its History." In Problematizing Cosmopolitanism, edited by Aron Telegdi-Csetri. Cluj-Napoca: Argonaut, 53–81.
Heilinger, Jan-Christoph. 2016a. "Konflikte in der Ethik. Anmerkungen aus pragmatistischer Perspektive." In Moral, Wissenschaft und Wahrheit, edited by Julian Nida-Rümelin and Jan-Christoph Heilinger. Berlin/Boston: de Gruyter, 145–159.

Heilinger, Jan-Christoph. 2016b. "Zwei Ideale globaler Gleichheit." Deutsche Zeitschrift für Philosophie 64 (5): 757–767.
Heilinger, Jan-Christoph. 2019. "Newcomer Integration, Individual Agency, and Responsibility." In Responsibility for Refugee and Migrant Integration, edited by S. Karly Kehoe, Eva Alisic and Jan-Christoph Heilinger. Berlin/Boston: de Gruyter, 131–147.
Heilinger, Jan-Christoph, and Thomas Pogge. 2015. "Globale Gerechtigkeit." In Handbuch Philosophie und Ethik, edited by Julian Nida-Rümelin, Irina Spiegel and Christian Tiedemann. Paderborn: utb, 304–312.
Heller, Charles, Lorenzo Pezzani, Itamar Mann, Violeta Moreno-Lax, and Eya Weizman. 2018. "'It's an Act of Murder': How Europe Outsources Suffering as Migrants Drown." The New York Times https://nyti.ms/2Rfadvk.
Henning, Christoph. 2006. "Narrative der Globalisierung. Zur Marxrenaissance in Globalismus und Globalisierungskritik." Gesprächskreis Politik und Geschichte im Karl-Marx-Haus (Friedrich-Ebert-Stiftung) 5.
Herzog, Lisa. 2012. "Ideal and Non-ideal Theory and the Problem of Knowledge." Journal of Applied Philosophy 29 (4): 271–288.
Hickman, Larry A. 2010. "John Dewey's Naturalism as a Model for Global Ethics." Synthesis Philosophica 49 (1), 9–18.
Hildebrand, David. 2008. Dewey. Oxford: Oneworld.
Honoré, A.M. (Tony). 2010. "Causation in the Law." The Stanford Encyclopedia of Philosophy (Winter 2010 Edition).
Horton, Keith. 2014. "Global Ethics: Increasing our Positive Impact." Journal of Global Ethics 10 (3): 304–311.
Hutchings, Kimberly. 2018. Global Ethics. An Introduction. Cambridge: Polity.
Ip, Kevin K. W. 2016. Egalitarianism and Global Justice From a Relational Perspective. New York: Basingstoke.
IPCC. 2018, in press. Global warming of 1.5 °C. An IPCC Special Report on the Impacts of Global Warming of 1.5 °C Above Pre-Industrial Levels and Related Global Greenhouse Gas Emission Pathways, in the Context of Strengthening the Global Response to the Threat of Climate Change, Sustainable Development, and Efforts to Eradicate Poverty. (Summary for Policymakers.).
IPCC, K. R. Smith, A. Woodward, D. Campbell-Lendrum, D. D. Chadee, Y. Honda, Q. Liu, J. M. Olwoch, B. Revich, and R. Sauerborn. 2014. "Human Health: Impacts, Adaptation, and Co-Benefits." In Climate Change 2014: Impacts, Adaptation, and Vulnerability. Part A: Global and Sectoral Aspects. Contribution of Working Group II to the Fifth Assessment Report of the Intergovernmental Panel of Climate Change, edited by C. B. Field, V. R. Barros, D. J. Dokken, K. J. Mach, M. D. Mastrandrea, T. E. Bilir, M. Chatterjee, K. L. Ebi, Y. O. Estrada, R. C. Genova, B. Girma, E. S. Kissel, A. N. Levy, S. MacCracken, P. R. Mastrandrea and L. L. White, 709–754. Cambridge, United Kingdom and New York, NY, USA: Cambridge University Press.
James, C.L.R. 2001 [1938]. The Black Jacobins. London: Penguin.
James, William. 1909. The Meaning of Truth, a Sequel to "Pragmatism". New York/London: Longmans, Green & Co.
Jamieson, Dale. 1991. "Method and Moral Theory." In A Companion to Ethics, edited by Peter Singer. Oxford: Blackwell, 476–487.
Jamieson, Dale, ed. 1999. Singer and his Critics. Oxford: Blackwell.

Jamieson, Dale. 2005. "When Utilitarians Should be Virtue Theorists." Utilitas 19 (2): 160–183.
Jugov, Tamara, and Lea L. Ypi. 2019. "Structural Injustice, Epistemic Opacity, and the Responsibilities of the Oppressed." Journal of Social Philosophy 50 (1): 7–27.
Jung, Matthias. 2014. Gewöhnliche Erfahrung. Tübingen: Mohr Siebeck.
Kagan, Shelly. 1989. The Limits of Morality. Oxford/New York: Oxford University Press.
Kagan, Shelly. 2011. "Do I Make a Difference." Philosophy and Public Affairs 39 (2): 105–141.
Kahn, Elizabeth. 2016. "Poverty, Injustice and Obligations to Take Political Action." In Ethical Issues in Poverty Alleviation, edited by Helmut P. Gaisbauer, Gottfried Schweiger and Clemens Sedmak. Cham: Springer, 209–224.
Kant, Immanuel. 1795. "Zum Ewigen Frieden." In Akademie-Ausgabe Band 8, edited by Königlich Preußische Akademie der Wissenschaften. Berlin 1923, 343–386.
Kant, Immanuel. 1797. "Metaphysik der Sitten." In Akademie-Ausgabe Band 6, edited by Königlich Preußische Akademie der Wissenschaften. Berlin 1914, 205–493.
Kehoe, Karly, Eva Alisic, and Jan-Christoph Heilinger, eds. 2019. Responsibility for Refugee and Migrant Integration. Berlin/Boston: de Gruyter.
Keller, Simon. 2013. Partiality. Princeton: Princeton University Press.
Kitcher, Philip. 2011. The Ethical Project. Cambridge: Harvard University Press.
Kitcher, Philip. 2012. "Précis of The Ethical Project." Analyse & Kritik 34: 1–19.
Kitcher, Philip. 2016. "Über den Fortschritt." Deutsche Zeitschrift für Philosophie 64 (2): 165–192.
Kleingeld, Pauline. 1998. "Kant's Cosmopolitan Law: World Citizenship for a Global Order." Kantian Review 2: 72–90.
Kleingeld, Pauline. 2012. Kant and Cosmopolitanism. The Philosophical Ideal of World Citizenship. Cambridge: Cambridge University Press.
Kleingeld, Pauline. 2013. "Cosmopolitanism." The Stanford Encyclopedia of Philosophy (Summer 2013 Edition).
Knight, Franklin W. 2000. "The Haitian Revolution." The American Historical Review 105 (1): 103–115.
Koggel, Christine M. 2002. "Equality Analysis in a Global Context: A Relational Approach." Canadian Journal of Philosophy 32 (suppl. 1): 247–272.
Kramer, Matthew H. 2005. "Moral Rights and the Limits of the Ought-Implies-Can Principle: Why Impeccable Precautions are no Excuse." Inquiry 48 (4): 307–355.
Kühler, Michael. 2013. Sollen ohne Können? Über Sinn und Geltung nicht erfüllbarer Sollensansprüche. Münster: mentis.
Kuper, Andrew. 2002. "More Than Charity: Cosmopolitan Alternatives to the "Singer Solution"." Ethics & International Affairs 16 (2): 107–120.
Kymlicka, Will. 2002. Contemporary Political Philosophy. An Introduction. Oxford/New York: Oxford University Press.
Laërtius, Diogenes. 1925. Lives and Opinions of Eminent Philosophers. Tr. by Robert D. Hicks. Cambridge: Harvard University Press.
LaFollette, Hugh. 2000. "Pragmatic Ethics." In The Blackwell Guide to Ethical Theory, edited by Hugh LaFollette, 400–419. Oxford: Blackwell.
Lessenich, Stephan. 2016. Neben uns die Sintflut: Die Externalisierungsgesellschaft und ihr Preis. Berlin: Hanser.

Lippert-Rasmussen, Kasper. 2012. "Democratic Egalitarianism versus Luck Egalitarianism: What is at Stake?" Philosophical Topics 40: 117–133.

Lippert-Rasmussen, Kasper. 2015. "Luck Egalitarians versus Relational Egalitarians: On the Prospects of a Pluralist Account of Egalitarian Justice." Canadian Journal of Philosophy 45: 220–241.

Lippert-Rasmussen, Kasper. 2018. Relational Egalitarianism. Cambridge: Cambridge University Press.

Long, Anthony A., and David N. Sedley, eds. 1987. The Hellenistic Philosophers, vol. 1. Translations of the Principal Sources, with Philosophical Commentary. Cambridge: Cambridge University Press.

Long, Graham. 2009. "Moral and Sentimental Cosmopolitanism." Journal of Social Philosophy 40 (3): 317–342.

Luban, David. 1980. "Just War and Human Rights." Philosophy & Public Affairs 9 (2): 160–181.

MacAskill, William. 2015. Doing Good Better: Effective Altruism and a Radical New Way to Make a Difference. London: Faber.

MacFarquhar, Larissa. 2015. Strangers Drowning: Grappling with Impossible Idealism, Drastic Choices, and the Overpowering Urge to Help. New York: Penguin.

Mackenzie, Catriona, and Natalie Stoljar, eds. 2000. Relational Autonomy. Feminist Perspectives on Autonomy, Agency, and the Social Self. Oxford/New York: Oxford University Press.

Mackie, J.L. 1974. The Cement of the Universe. A Study of Causation. Oxford/New York: Oxford University Press.

Mallock, David. 1967. "Moral Dilemmas and Moral Failure." Australasian Journal of Philosophy 45: 159–178.

Martin, Jay. 2002. The Education of John Dewey. A Biography. New York: Columbia University Press.

Martin, Wayne. 2009. "Ought but Cannot." Proceedings of the Aristotelian Society CIX: 103–127.

Mayr, Erasmus. 2012. "The Political and Moral Conceptions of Human Rights—a Mixed Account." In The Philosophy of Human Rights. Contemporary Controversies, edited by Gerhard Ernst and Jan-Christoph Heilinger. Berlin/Boston: de Gruyter, 73–104.

McElwee, Brian. 2016. "Demandingness Objections in Ethics." The Philosophical Quarterly 67 (266): 84–105.

McKeown, Maeve. 2017. "Sweatshop Labour as Global Structural Exploitation." In Exploitation. From Practice to Theory, edited by Monique Deveaux and Vida Panitch. London/New York: Rowman & Littlefield, 35–58.

Milanovic, Branko. 2011. The Haves and the Have-Nots. A Brief and Idiosyncratic History of Global Inequality. New York: Basic Books.

Milanovic, Branko. 2015. "Global Equality of Opportunity: How Much of Our Income is Determined by Where We Live?" The Review of Economics and Statistics 97 (2): 452–460.

Milanovic, Branko. 2016. Global Inequality. A New Approach for the Age of Globalization. Cambridge/London: Harvard University Press.

Miller, David. 1988. "The Ethical Significance of Nationality." Ethics 98 (4): 647–662.

Miller, David. 2002. "Cosmopolitanism: A Critique." Critical Review of International Social and Political Philosophy 5 (3): 80–85.
Miller, David. 2005. "Reasonable Partiality Towards Compatriots." Ethical Theory and Moral Practice 8: 63–81.
Miller, David. 2007. National Responsibility and Global Justice. Oxford/New York: Oxford University Press.
Miller, David. 2016. Strangers in Our Midst: The Political Philosophy of Immigration. Cambridge: Harvard University Press.
Miller, Seumas. 2014. "Social Institutions." The Stanford Encyclopedia of Philosophy (Winter 2014 Edition).
Misak, Cheryl. 2013. The American Pragmatists. Oxford/New York: Oxford University Press.
Moody-Adams, Michele M. 1999. "The Idea of Moral Progress." Metaphilosophy 30 (3): 168–185.
Müller, Armin. 1976. "Kynismus, kynisch." In Historisches Wörterbuch der Philosophie, Band 4, edited by Joachim Ritter, 1469–1470. Basel: Schwabe.
Munthe, Christian. 2011. The Price of Precaution and the Ethics of Risk. Dordrecht: Springer.
Murphy, Liam. 1993. "The Demands of Beneficence." Philosophy & Public Affairs 22 (4): 267–292.
Murphy, Liam. 2000. Moral Demands in Non-Ideal Theory. Oxford/New York: Oxford University Press.
Nagel, Thomas. 1986. The View From Nowhere. Oxford/New York: Oxford University Press.
Nagel, Thomas. 1991. Equality and Partiality. Oxford/New York: Oxford University Press.
Nagel, Thomas. 2005. "The Problem of Global Justice." Philosophy & Public Affairs 33 (2): 113–147.
Nath, Rekha. 2011. "Equal Standing in the Global Community." The Monist 94 (4): 593–614.
Nath, Rekha. 2015. "On the Scope and Grounds of Social Equality." In Social Equality. On What it Means to be Equals, edited by Carina Fourie, Fabian Schuppert and Ivo Wallimann-Helmer. Oxford/New York: Oxford University Press, 186–208.
Neuhäuser, Christian. 2014. "Structural Injustice and the Distribution of Forward-Looking Responsibility." Midwest Studies In Philosophy 38 (1): 232–251.
Neuhäuser, Christian. 2018. "Being Realistic About International Trade Justice." Moral Philosophy and Politics 5 (2): 181–204.
Nida-Rümelin, Julian. 2006. "Zur Philosophie des Kosmopolitismus." Zeitschrift für Internationale Beziehungen 13 (2): 227–234.
Nozick, Robert. 1974. Anarchy, State, and Utopia. New York: Basic Books.
Nussbaum, Martha. 1994. The Nature of Desire: Theory and Practice in Hellenistic Ethics. Princeton: Princeton University Press.
Nussbaum, Martha. 1997a. "Capabilities and Human Rights." Fordham Law Review 66: 117–149.
Nussbaum, Martha. 1997b. "Kant and Stoic Cosmopolitanism." The Journal of Political Philosophy 5 (1): 1–25.
Nussbaum, Martha. 2002. "Patriotism and Cosmopolitanism." In For Love of Country? Debating the Limits of Patriotism, edited by Joshua Cohen. Boston: Beacon Press, 1–17.
Nussbaum, Martha. 2006. Frontiers of Justice. Disability, Nationality, Species Membership. Cambridge: Harvard University Press.

Nussbaum, Martha. 2011a. Creating Capabilities. The Human Development Approach. Cambridge: Harvard University Press.

Nussbaum, Martha. 2011b. "Foreword." In Responsibility for Justice, by Iris Marion Young, ix-xxv. Oxford/New York: Oxford University Press.

O'Neill, Martin. 2008. "What Should Egalitarians Believe?" Philosophy & Public Affairs 36 (2): 119–156.

O'Neill, Onora. 2009. "Demandingness and Rules." In The Problem of Moral Demandingness, edited by Timothy Chappell. Basingstoke: Palgrave Macmillan, 59–69.

Ottmann, Henning. 2001. Geschichte des politischen Denkens. Die Griechen. Von Platon bis zum Hellenismus (1/2). Stuttgart: Metzler.

Pappas, Gregory. 1998. "Dewey's Ethics. Morality as Experience." In Reading Dewey. Interpretations for a Postmodern Generation, edited by Larry A. Hickman. Bloomington: Indiana University Press, 100–123.

Parekh, Serena. 2017. "Feminism, Injustice, and Responsibility." In The Routledge Companion to Feminist Philosophy, edited by Ann Garry, Serene J. Khader and Alison Stone. New York/London: Routledge, 620–630.

Parfit, Derek. 1984. Reasons and Persons. Oxford: Oxford University Press.

Parfit, Derek. 1997. "Equality and Priority." Ratio 10 (3): 202–221.

Parisi, Eva. 2019 (unpubl. ms.). Taking Equality Seriously—Why Relational Egalitarians Should Endorse Distributive Equality.

Peeters, Wouter, Andries De Smet, Lisa Diependaele, and Sigrid Sterckx. 2015. Climate Change and Individual Responsibility: Agency, Moral Disengagement and the Motivational Gap. Basingstoke: Palgrave Macmillan.

Pettit, Philip. 1997. Republicanism. A Theory of Freedom and Government. Oxford/New York: Oxford University Press.

Phipps, Alison. 2019. "Bearing Witness: The Burden of Individual Responsibility and the Rule of Law." In Responsibility for Refugee and Migrant Integration, edited by Karly Kehoe, Eva Alisic and Jan-Christoph Heilinger. Berlin/Boston: de Gruyter, 9–24.

Pinker, Steven. 2011. The Better Angels of Our Nature: Why Violence Has Declined. New York: Viking.

Pinkert, Felix. 2015. "What if I Cannot Make a Difference (and Know it)." Ethics 125 (4): 971–998.

Pogge, Thomas. 1989. Realizing Rawls. Ithaca: Cornell University Press.

Pogge, Thomas. 1992. "Cosmopolitanism and Sovereignty." Ethics 103 (1): 48–75.

Pogge, Thomas. 2007. "Cosmopolitanism." In A Companion to Contemporary Political Philosophy, edited by Robert E. Goodin, Philip Pettit and Thomas Pogge, 312–331. Oxford: Blackwell.

Pogge, Thomas. 2008. World Poverty and Human Rights. 2nd Edition. Cambridge: Polity.

Portmore, Douglas W. 2007. "Consequentializing Moral Theories." Pacific Philosophical Quarterly 88 (1): 39–73.

Prentice, Deborah A. 2012. "The Psychology of Social Norms and the Promotion of Human Rights." In Understanding Social Action, Promoting Human Rights, edited by Ryan Goodman, Derek Jinks and Andrew K. Woods. Oxford/New York: Oxford University Press, 23–46.

Rawls, John. 1971. A Theory of Justice. Cambrigde: Harvard University Press.

Rawls, John. 1996. Political Liberalism. New York: Columbia University Press.

Rawls, John. 1999a. The Law of Peoples. Cambridge: Harvard University Press.
Rawls, John. 1999b. A Theory of Justice. Revised Edition. Cambridge: Harvard University Press.
Rawls, John. 2001. Justice as Fairness. A Restatement. Cambridge: Harvard University Press.
Raz, Joseph. 1986. The Morality of Freedom. Oxford/New York: Oxford University Press.
Reiss, Hans Siegbert, ed. 1991. Immanuel Kant: Political Writings. 2nd Edition. Cambridge: Cambridge University Press.
Renton, Dave, ed. 2002. Marx on Globalisation. London: Lawrence & Wishart.
Risse, Mathias. 2012. On Global Justice. Princeton: Princeton University Press.
Roberts, J. Timmons. 2001. "Global Inequality and Climate Change." Society & Natural Resources 14 (6): 501–509.
Rondel, David. 2018. Pragmatist Egalitarianism. Oxford/New York: Oxford University Press.
Rorty, Richard. 1998. "Human Rights, Rationality, and Sentimentality." In Truth and Progress. Philosophical Papers vol. III, edited by Richard Rorty. Cambridge: Cambridge University Press, 167–185.
Ross, W.D. 1930. The Right and the Good. Oxford: Oxford University Press.
Roy, Arundhati. 2014. The Doctor and the Saint. In: Ambedkar, Babasaheb. Annihilation of Caste. The Annotated Critical Edition. Edited by Sudhir Anand. London/New York: Verso, 15–179.
Sachs, Jeffrey. 2005. The End of Poverty: Economic Possibilities for Our Time. New York: Penguin.
Satz, Debra. 2003. "Child Labor: A Normative Perspective." The World Bank Economic Review 17 (2): 297–309.
Satz, Debra. 2007. "Equality, Adequacy, and Education for Citizenship." Ethics 117: 623–648.
Schaler, Jeffrey A., ed. 2009. Peter Singer Under Fire: The Moral Iconoclast Faces His Critics. Chicago/LaSalle: Open Court.
Scheffler, Samuel. 1992. Human Morality. Oxford: Oxford University Press.
Scheffler, Samuel. 1993. "What is Egalitarianism?" Philosophy & Public Affairs 31 (1): 5–39.
Scheffler, Samuel. 2001. Boundaries and Allegiances. Oxford/New York: Oxford University Press.
Scheffler, Samuel. 2003. "What is Egalitarianism?" Philosophy & Public Affairs 31 (1): 5–39.
Scheffler, Samuel. 2005. "The Division of Moral Labor." Proceedings of the Aristotelian Society, Supplementary vol. 79: 229–253.
Scheffler, Samuel. 2010. Equality & Tradition. Questions of Value in Moral and Political Theory. Oxford/New York: Oxford University Press.
Scheffler, Samuel. 2015. "The Practice of Equality." In Social Equality: Essays on What it Means to be Equals, edited by Carina Fourie, Fabian Schuppert and Ivo Wallimann-Helmer. Oxford/New York: Oxford University Press, 21–44.
Schemmel, Christian. 2007. "On The Usefulness Of Luck Egalitarian Arguments For Global Justice." Global Justice: Theory Practice Rhetoric 1: 54–67.
Schlereth, Thomas. 1977. The Cosmopolitan Ideal in Enlightenment Thought: Its Form and Function in the Ideas of Franklin, Hume and Voltaire, 1694–1790. Notre Dame/London: University of Notre Damen Press.
Segall, Shlomi. 2010. Health, Luck, and Justice. Princeton: Princeton University Press.
Seidel, Christian. 2013. "Two Problems with the Socio-Relational Critique of Distributive Egalitarianism." In Was dürfen wir glauben? Was sollen wir tun? Sektionsbeiträge des

achten Internationalen Kongresses der Gesellschaft für Analytische Philosophie, edited by Miguel Hoeltje, Thomas Spitzley and Wolfgang Spohn. Duisburg-Essen: DuEPublico, 525–535.

Sen, Amartya. 1980. "Equality of What?" In The Tanner Lectures on Human Values, edited by S. M. McMurrin. Salt Lake City and Cambridge: University of Utah Press and Cambridge University Press, 197–220.

Sen, Amartya. 1992. "Functionings and Capability." In Inequality Reexamined, by Amartya Sen. Oxford/New York: Oxford University Press, 39–55.

Sen, Amartya. 2004. "Elements of a Theory of Human Rights." Philosophy & Public Affairs 32 (4): 315–356.

Sen, Amartya. 2009. The Idea of Justice. London: Penguin.

Seneca. 1920. Epistles. Translated by Richard M. Gummere. Cambridge: Harvard University Press.

Serra, Juan Pablo. 2009. "What is and What Should Pragmatic Ethics be? Some Remarks on Recent Scholarship." European Journal of Pragmatism and American Philosophy 2 (2): 100–114.

Sezgin, Hilal. 2017. Nichtstun ist keine Lösung. Politische Verantwortung in Zeiten des Umbruchs. Köln: Dumont.

Shachar, Ayelet. 2009. The Birthright Lottery. Citizenship and Global Inequality. Cambridge: Harvard University Press.

Shields, Liam. 2016. Just Enough: Sufficiency as a Demand of Justice. Edinburgh: Edinburgh University Press.

Shklar, Judith. 1990. The Faces of Injustice. New Haven: Yale University Press.

Shue, Henry. 1993. "Subsistence Emissions and Luxury Emission." Law & Policy 15 (1): 39–59.

Simmons, A. John. 2010. "Ideal and Nonideal Theory." Philosophy & Public Affairs 38 (1): 5–36.

Singer, Peter. 1972. "Famine, Affluence, and Morality." Philosophy & Public Affairs 1 (3): 229–243.

Singer, Peter. 1981. The Expanding Circle. Ethics, Evolution, and Moral Progress. Princeton: Princeton University Press.

Singer, Peter. 2009. The Life You Can Save. New York: Random House.

Singer, Peter. 2015. The Most Good You Can Do: How Effective Altruism is Changing Ideas About Living Ethically. New Haven: Yale University Press.

Srinivasan, Amia. 2015. "Stop the Robot Apocalypse." The London Review of Books 37 (18): 3–6.

Steinhoff, Uwe. 2013. "Against Pogge's 'Cosmopolitanism'." Ratio 26, 329–341.

Steinhoff, Uwe, ed. 2015. Do All Persons Have Equal Moral Worth? On "Basic Equality" and Equal Respect and Concern. Oxford/New York: Oxford University Press.

Stemplowska, Zofia. 2011. "Responsibility and Respect: Reconciling Two Egalitarian Visions." In Responsibility and Distributive Justice, edited by Carl Knight and Zofia Stemplowska. Oxford/New York: Oxford University Press, 115–135.

Stocker, Michael. 1971. "'Ought' and 'Can'." Australasian Journal of Philosophy 49 (3): 303–316.

Strawson, Peter. 1962. "Freedom and Resentment." Proceedings of the British Academy 48: 1–25.

Talisse, Robert. 2017. "Pragmatism, Democracy, and the Need for a Theory of Justice." In Pragmatism and Justice, edited by Susan Dieleman, David Rondel and Christopher J. Voparil. Oxford/New York: Oxford University Press, 281–294.
Tan, Kok-Chor. 2004. Justice Without Borders. Cosmopolitanism, Nationalism, and Patriotism. Cambridge: Cambridge University Press.
Tan, Kok-Chor. 2011. "Luck, Institutions, and Global Distributive Justice: A Defence of Global Luck Egalitarianism." European Journal of Political Theory 10 (3): 394–421.
Tasioulas, John. 2012. "On the Nature of Human Rights." In The Philosophy of Human Rights. Contemporary Controversies., edited by Gerhard Ernst and Jan-Christoph Heilinger. Berlin/Boston: de Gruyter, 17–59.
Temkin, Larry. 1993. Inequality. Oxford/New York: Oxford University Press.
Temkin, Larry. 2000. "Equality, Priority, and the Levelling-Down Objection." In The Ideal of Equality, edited by Matthew Clayton and Andrew Williams, 126–161. London: Macmillan.
Temkin, Larry. 2003. "Egalitarianism Defended." Ethics 113 (4): 764–782.
Tessman, Lisa. 2015. Moral Failure. On the Impossible Demands of Morality. Oxford/New York: Oxford University Press.
UNESCO. 2015. Global Citizenship Education. Topics and Learning Objectives. Paris: UNESCO.
United Nations. 2015. The Millennium Development Goals Report 2015. New York: The United Nations.
Urmson, James O. 1958. "Saints and Heroes." In Essays in Moral Philosophy, edited by Abraham I. Melden. Seattle: University of Washington Press, 198–216.
Valentini, Laura. 2011. Justice in a Globalised World. Oxford/New York: Oxford University Press.
Valentini, Laura. 2012. "Ideal vs. Non-ideal Theory: A Conceptual Map." Philosophy Compass 7 (9): 654–664.
Van Parijs, Philippe. 2007. "International Distributive Justice." In A Companion to Contemporary Political Philosophy, edited by Robert E. Goodin, Philip Pettit and Thomas Pogge. Oxford: Blackwell, 638–652.
Voigt, Kristin. 2007. The Harshness Objection: Is Luck Egalitarianism Too Harsh on the Victims of Option Luck? Ethical Theory and Moral Practice 10 (4): 389–407.
Waks, Leonard J. 2009. "Inquiry, Agency, and Art: John Dewey's Contribution to Pragmatic Cosmopolitanism." Education and Culture 25 (2): 115–125.
Waldron, Jeremy. 2000. "What is Cosmopolitan?" Journal of Political Philosophy 8 (2): 227–243.
Walzer, Michael. 1983. Spheres of Justice. New York: Basic Books.
Warburton, Nigel. 2013. "Cosmopolitans." Aeon Magazine 4 March 2013.
Welchman, Jennifer. 1995. Dewey's Ethical Thought. Ithaca/London: Cornell University Press.
Wenar, Leif. 2016. Blood Oil. Tyrants, Violence, and the Rules That Run the World. Oxford/New York: Oxford University Press.
Widdows, Heather. 2011. Global Ethics. An Introduction. Durham: Acumen.
Wikler, Daniel. 2004. "Personal and Social Responsibility for Health." In Public Health, Ethics, and Equity, edited by Sudhir Anand, Fabienne Peter and Amartya Sen, 109–134. Oxford/New York: Oxford University Press.
Wild, Verina, and Jan-Christoph Heilinger. 2013. "Cosmopolitanism Within Borders: A Normative Foundation for Health Care for Asylum Seekers?" American Journal of Bioethics 13 (7): 17–19.

Williams, Bernard. 1973a. "A Critique of Utilitarianism." In Utilitarianism: For and Against, edited by John J.C. Smart and Bernard Williams. Cambridge: Cambridge University Press, 77–149.
Williams, Bernard. 1973b. Problems of the Self. Cambridge: Cambridge University Press.
Williams, Bernard. 1981. Moral Luck. Cambridge: Cambridge University Press.
Williams, Howard. 2007. "Kantian Cosmopolitan Right." Politics and Ethics Review 3 (1): 57–72.
Wittgenstein, Ludwig. 1953. "Philosophische Untersuchungen." In Werkausgabe Band I, edited by Ludwig Wittgenstein. Frankfurt: Suhrkamp.
Wolf, Susan. 1992. "Morality and Partiality." Ethics 6: 243–259.
Wolff, Jonathan. 1998. "Fairness, Respect, and the Egalitarian Ethos." Philosophy & Public Affairs 27 (2): 97–122.
Wollner, Gabriel. 2019. "Anonymous Exploitation: Non-Individual, Non-Agential and Structural." Review of Social Economy 77 (2): 143–162.
Woods, Kerri. 2012. "Whither Sentiment? Compassion, Solidarity, and Disgust in Cosmopolitan Thought." Journal of Social Philosophy 43 (1): 33–49.
Wright, Richard W. 1985. "Causation in Tort Law." California Law Review 73 (6): 1737–1828.
Young, Iris Marion. 1990. Justice and the Politics of Difference. Princeton: Princeton University Press.
Young, Iris Marion. 1997. "Asymmetrical Reciprocity: On Moral Respect, Wonder, and Enlarged Thought." In Intersecting Voices: Dilemmas of Gender, Political Philosophy, and Policy, by Iris Marion Young. Princeton: Princeton University Press, 38–59.
Young, Iris Marion. 2000. Inclusion and Democracy. Oxford/New York: Oxford University Press.
Young, Iris Marion. 2003. "From Guilt to Solidarity. Sweatshops and Political Responsibility." Dissent Spring: 39–45.
Young, Iris Marion. 2006a. "Education in the Context of Structural Injustice: A Symposion Response." In Citizenship, Inclusion and Democracy. A Symposion on Iris Marion Young, edited by Mitja Sardoc. Malden: Blackwell, 91–101.
Young, Iris Marion. 2006b. "Responsibility and Global Justice: A Social Connection Model." Social Philosophy and Policy 23: 102–130.
Young, Iris Marion. 2011. Responsibility for Justice. Oxford/New York: Oxford University Press.
Ypi, Lea L. 2017. "Structural Injustice and the Place of Attachment." Journal of Practical Ethics 5 (1): 1–21.
Ypi, Lea L., and Katrin Flikschuh, eds. 2014. Kant and Colonialism: Historical and Critical Perspectives. Oxford/New York: Oxford University Press.
Zimmerman, Michael J. 1996. The Concept of Moral Obligation. Cambridge: Cambridge University Press.
Zwolinski, Matt. 2007. "Sweatshops, Choice, and Exploitation." Business Ethics Quarterly 17 (4): 689–727.

Index

ability 56, 115, 139, 155, 157–159, 230
– collective ability 157 f.
Abizadeh, A. 101, 105
adequacy 50, 54, 96, 179, 181 f.
aggregation 5, 55, 138 f., 142–144
aid 42, 50, 76–78, 84, 96, 214
Ambedkar, B.R. 83
Anderson, E. 5, 33, 49 f., 52, 54, 66, 68, 72 f., 76–78, 83–87, 89, 92, 95, 108, 111 f., 119, 122
Appiah, A. 24, 42
Aristotle 127
Arneson, R. 49, 51, 53, 68, 70 f., 148, 205
attachment 22, 171
attitudes 2, 10, 12, 60, 77, 123, 170, 216–218, 220 f., 225, 227
– reactive attitudes 195, 216, 218
autarchy 29 f.
authority 82, 104, 171, 212

Beitz, C. 25, 45, 95
blame 77, 153, 156, 201, 216–218, 224, 228
borders 1, 9, 21, 29, 35, 37, 41 f., 45, 48, 98–100, 105, 183, 186, 188
Brighouse, H. 173, 175–181, 183
Brock, G. 49, 92, 185, 227

Caney, S. 28, 94 f., 112, 139 f., 231
capabilities 49, 51–53, 60, 68, 80, 82, 84, 102, 202
Carens, J. 22, 94, 188
character 12, 105, 123, 128, 157, 165, 167–170, 185 f., 223, 226
chicken 145 f.
children 26, 31, 81, 100, 102, 149, 162 f., 168, 172–183, 188, 197, 201, 232
Cicero 29, 31
circle of concern 3, 31, 214, 230
citizenship 13, 21 f., 29, 86, 94, 106, 188
– global citizenship 8, 15, 21, 23, 28–30, 36, 42, 58, 64, 118, 134, 161, 193, 221, 231, 234 f.

climate change 5 f., 11, 24, 55, 57, 114, 137–139, 145–147, 152, 157, 159, 206, 232–234
Cochran, M. 119, 127
coercion 39 f., 63, 98, 101, 104 f., 107, 113, 123
Cohen, G.A. 10, 42, 62 f., 68, 81, 89, 91, 116, 184, 205 f., 215, 226
colonialism 35, 37 f., 97, 110
communication 5 f., 24, 33, 84, 98 f., 170, 226 f.
compensation 66, 70, 73 f., 76, 84, 91, 93
conflict 6, 66, 82, 85, 125 f., 129, 161, 165, 173, 199–201
consequentialism 125, 137, 144–149, 196, 212, 224
consumption 1, 145, 217
corridor-argument 67, 88, 109, 166, 168, 182 f.
cosmopolitanism
– circumstances of cosmopolitanism 3, 5–8, 23, 25, 98, 108, 121, 196, 234
– moral cosmopolitanism 2 f., 23, 27, 46, 64, 123, 197, 210 f., 220, 229
– political cosmopolitanism 41, 46
Cottingham, J. 164–167, 172, 183
culture 5, 23 f., 27 f., 42, 46, 79 f., 82 f., 96, 107, 110, 140, 186, 189, 221

demandingness objection, see over-demandingness
democracy 3, 9, 12, 43, 54, 83–86, 95, 108 f., 111–113, 122 f., 186
deontology 125, 198 f., 210, 224
desert 15, 53, 69, 73, 91, 132, 161, 217, 220, 225
Dewey, J. 5, 7, 11 f., 59 f., 119–131
dilemma 169, 200, 210, 214
Diogenes of Sinope 28
disability 50, 69, 77
disrespect 72 f., 77 f., 97, 100, 115, 169, 206
distributive objection 177 f., 189

division of labour   13, 62, 64, 79, 86, 102f., 108, 189
Dworkin, R.   26, 49–51, 53, 68f., 71, 78, 91, 116

egalitarianism
– global relational egalitarianism   9, 13f., 65–67, 92f., 97, 100f., 107, 109–112, 114–117, 206
– luck egalitarianism   52, 66–74, 76–78, 83, 85–93, 95–97, 106, 109f., 112, 115–117
– relational egalitarianism   65–68, 78–80, 83–90, 92, 97f., 101, 106, 109, 111, 116
– telic egalitarianism   75, 87f.
enlightenment   21, 28, 33–35, 41f.
equality
– distributive equality   66–68, 71, 76, 79, 86, 88, 96f., 110, 117
– fair equality of opportunity   44, 49, 68, 175f., 178–180
– footing of equality   66–68, 83, 100f., 106, 109, 116, 174, 179
– relational equality   15, 65–67, 79f., 84, 88f., 97f., 107–112, 115, 117f., 159, 166, 179, 221f., 231, 234
ethics
– global political ethics   2, 4, 9f., 12f., 43, 120, 235
– pragmatic ethics   12, 119, 125–130, 133
– virtue ethics   123, 196
ethnicity   23, 26
ethos   2, 4, 8, 10, 13f., 16, 21, 60, 62–65, 67, 79, 117, 119f., 123, 133, 194, 207, 212, 218f., 221f., 226–235
European Union   6, 21, 40, 99, 104f., 110
exclusion   1, 13, 66, 68, 72, 84, 133, 188f.
excuse   32, 58, 114, 153, 203, 214f.
– pre-emptive excuse   203, 215
existential choice   220, 234
expanding the circle   3, 31
exploitation   1, 13, 25, 41, 54, 57f., 68, 80f., 101, 107, 141

family   10, 26f., 31f., 47, 59, 69, 79, 81, 94, 115, 143, 161f., 172–183, 189, 191, 230
Fishbone, A.   73, 85

flourishing life   33, 105, 161, 222
food   5, 37, 73, 102, 131, 148, 150, 182
Forst, R.   83, 206
Fourie, C.   54, 79
Frankfurt, H.   54
fraternity   29f.
French Revolution   35
friendship   10, 27, 31, 47, 98, 149, 161f., 168, 171, 185, 187f., 191, 193

gamble   69, 95, 147
Ganguli-Mitra, A.   103
gender   23, 26, 34, 43, 69, 82
Gerhardt, V.   36f., 40
Gheaus, A.   89, 218
Global Citizenship Education   226
Global North   1–3, 55, 155, 221, 228, 231, 234
Global South   100, 114, 155
global warming   24, 55, 57, 137–139, 145, 150
goods
– basic goods   50, 165
– familial relationship goods   173, 175–177, 179–182
– non-relational goods   66, 72, 79, 87–89, 93, 96
Griffin, J.   56
guilt   7

Habermas, J.   39
habits   5, 10–13, 59, 118–120, 123, 125, 127–129, 133f., 198, 211, 227, 233, 235
Haiti   9f., 35, 100, 106
Hare, R.   200
harshness objection   73
hierarchy   54, 106f., 210
hospitality   29, 37–39
hunger   140, 150, 165, 206

impartiality   14f., 26–28, 46, 132, 150, 161–164, 172, 175, 193
imperceptible harm   142, 145
imperialism   82f.
impossible demands   193f., 201
inclusion   72f., 84, 144, 188

income 1, 3, 44, 50, 56f., 88, 94, 103, 109, 127, 149
inevitable moral failure 194f., 201, 211–218
inferior 72f., 76–78, 82, 84, 100, 108, 114, 178
injustice
– global structural injustice 12, 15f., 21, 54–57, 128, 150f., 157, 193–195, 220f., 232–234
– passive injustice 58, 230
innocence 12, 15, 143, 173, 194f., 215, 218–220
institution
– intrapersonal institution 60, 226f.
– political institution 46, 131, 152
– social institution 9, 45, 77, 102, 108, 131
integrity 52, 168, 170f., 183, 201
interaction
– absence of interaction 114
– frameworks of interaction 79, 111f., 152, 163
interference 85, 104, 113
interpersonal justification test 15, 89, 204–207
INUS condition 144
ius cosmopoliticum 36

James, W. 35, 120, 132
Jamieson, D. 123, 149, 232
Jung, M. 125f.
justice 27, 49, 70, 106, 111, 173
– global justice 4, 9f., 21, 38, 43, 45, 49, 57f., 60, 64, 92, 112, 121, 133, 185, 188, 233
– institutional justice 3, 10, 90, 218
– metrics of justice 49, 75f., 173
– scope of justice 9, 13, 21, 43, 48, 81, 101
justice and ethics 9–11, 57–62

Kafka, F. 59
Kagan, S. 144–146, 155, 196, 200, 212f.
Kant, I. 21, 26, 28, 32, 34–41, 169, 200
Kitcher, P. 12, 23, 32, 119, 121, 123, 126f., 130, 132, 142
Kleingeld, P. 36–41
Kymlicka, W. 80, 92

LaFollette, H. 119, 123f.
law
– natural law 25, 30, 32–34, 110
– universal law 30, 34, 36
levelling-down 74f.
liability model 152–156
liberal 9, 43, 45, 80f., 90, 184, 231
liberty 44, 50, 81f., 104
Lippert-Rasmussen, K. 66, 87, 115
Locke, J. 26, 34
luck
– brute luck 32, 69, 71–77, 81, 93, 174
– option luck 69f., 72f., 76f., 95
– luck egalitarianism, see egalitarianism
luxury 66, 147, 149, 182, 189

marginalisation 9, 13, 80–82, 107, 114
market 5, 41, 55, 81, 103, 141, 163, 180
Marxism 41, 80f.
meaning 22, 102, 122, 133, 138, 162f., 190f., 212
membership 21, 23, 26, 33f., 47, 108, 183–186, 188, 190
method of inquiry 125, 129f.
midwifery 132
migration 81, 99f., 114, 184, 188, 231
Milanovic, B. 25, 94
Miller, D. 4, 47f., 59, 92, 112–114, 184–189
Moody-Adams, M. 131
motivation 51, 171, 173, 176, 179, 201–203, 211f., 218, 223, 226, 230
Murphy, L. 170, 204f.

Nagel, T. 3, 7, 23, 26, 48, 94, 104, 112, 130, 152, 157, 161, 163, 191, 206, 211
nationalism 1, 45, 163, 184, 234
nationality 15, 23, 26, 28, 36, 42, 47, 94, 107, 185f., 188
NESS condition 144
normative individualism 26, 46f.
Nozick, R. 75
Nussbaum, M. 24, 28, 32f., 39, 52, 54, 60, 68, 157

Obama, B. 82
O'Neill, O. 196

oppression   1, 13, 37, 53, 66, 72f., 79–84, 86, 97, 101, 107, 126, 178, 184
– five faces of oppression   80, 83, 107
ought-implies-can   211
over-demandingness   1, 14f., 71, 85, 87f., 182, 193–197, 199, 201–205, 208, 215–217, 220

Parfit, D.   53, 69, 74f., 142–145, 155, 170
partiality   15, 48, 162–164, 168, 171–173, 175f., 178, 180–185, 188
particularism   45–49
perfection   16, 35, 165–167, 194, 210, 213, 215, 219f., 229, 231f.
pity   73f., 76f., 84
Pogge, T.   26f., 43, 47, 55, 103
polis   21f., 28–31
pragmatism   2, 5, 11, 13–15, 119–121, 123, 125, 130, 132–134, 189, 191, 222, 225
preferential treatment   14–16, 47, 163f., 168, 170–172, 183–192, 206, 229
prioritarianism   15, 29, 45, 49f., 53, 59f., 71, 115, 152, 157, 165, 196, 220, 224
privacy   77, 81f.
psychology   218f., 227

Rawls, J.   9f., 39f., 43–45, 48–50, 53, 58, 61–64, 68f., 78, 86, 88, 90f., 96, 101f., 104f., 130, 175
Raz, J.   104
reasons   75, 125, 163, 169, 171, 182, 188, 192, 200, 208f., 213
– membership-dependent reasons   15, 183f., 190
– relationship-dependent reasons   14, 183, 190
recognition   73, 82, 86, 217f.
refugee   37f., 81f., 99, 114, 231
regret   155, 186, 201, 213–216, 218
relational inequality   72f., 76–83, 88, 99–107
religion   23, 26f., 32, 34, 43, 72, 82, 148, 176, 183, 219
requirement
– necessarily non-effective requirement   210–216

– non-negotiable requirement   15, 205–212, 220
residual feelings   201, 205
respect   32, 50, 67, 72f., 76–89, 99, 104, 108, 122, 161, 179, 190, 206, 211, 222f.
responsibility
– backward-looking responsibility   97, 154, 156
– collective responsibility   85, 156
– forward-looking responsibility   57, 97, 154, 156, 224
– Responsibility model (Young)   152, 156
– responsible choice   70, 72, 88, 96, 116
rights
– basic rights   1, 15, 81, 102, 141, 189, 203, 205, 208–210, 215, 220, 222
– human rights   35, 39, 42, 56, 65, 79, 140, 153f., 162, 166, 185, 194, 197, 206, 208
Risse, M.   38
Ross, D.   200

Satz, D.   54, 94
Scheffler, S.   5, 61, 63, 68, 83f., 89, 92, 100, 107, 142, 162, 177, 183, 197
Sen, A.   51f., 56, 68, 87, 130
Seneca   28f., 31
Shklar, J.   4, 58, 230
Shue, H.   139
sincerity   214–217, 220, 231
Singer, P.   8, 32, 147–150, 175, 196
slavery   30, 32, 34f., 51, 71, 96, 228
social connection   14, 56, 137, 151, 154–156, 159, 208
society of equals   84f., 117, 122
Sophie's choice   201
statism   45, 184
Stoicism   30, 32f.
sufficiency   24f., 50, 53–57, 66f., 76, 84, 88, 96, 108f., 165–168, 178f., 182f., 188, 194, 209, 220, 222, 228
Sustainable Development Goals   6, 140, 226
Swift, A.   173, 175–181, 183

talent   44, 50f., 69, 71, 76f., 165, 175
Tan, K.   95, 111f.
Tasioulas, J.   42
taxation   176, 187, 205

Temkin, L.   75
Tessman, L.   114, 196, 209, 211, 213
Thomas Aquinas   34
tragic   169, 201
TRIPS   103
Trump, D.   234
TTIP   103

United Nations   6, 36, 40 f., 100, 140, 226, 234
Universal Declaration of Human Rights   6, 42, 140
utilitarianism   26, 51, 68, 124, 169 f.

Valentini, L.   45, 62
violence   80, 82 f., 104, 107, 231
virtue   9, 29, 45, 49, 56, 147, 167, 224, 232
Voigt, C.   73 f.
Voltaire   34
vulnerability   56, 77, 114, 139, 222

Walzer, M.   185 f.
wealth   1, 28, 50, 57, 75 f., 88, 93 f., 102, 108 f., 117, 228, 230
welfare   49, 51 f., 54, 68, 70 f., 75–78, 81 f., 87, 90 f., 94, 185
– equal opportunity for welfare   51, 53, 68, 70 f.
Wenar, L.   8
Widdows, H.   5
Wild, V.   35
Williams, B.   36, 168–171, 183, 201 f., 214
Wolf, S.   161
Wolff, J.   63, 72, 77, 226
worst-off   44, 49, 53

Young, I.M.   3–7, 9 f., 14, 54–56, 63, 73, 79–83, 91, 100, 107, 122, 137, 141, 151–159, 162, 178, 210 f., 218

www.ingramcontent.com/pod-product-compliance
Lightning Source LLC
Chambersburg PA
CBHW031805220426
43662CB00007B/536